Starting

ONL
BUS

KIM BENJAMIN

Starting Your Own

ONLINE

BUSINESS

KIM BENJAMIN

crimson

This edition first published in Great Britain 2009 by
Crimson Publishing, a division of Crimson Business Ltd
Westminster House
Kew Road
Richmond
Surrey
TW9 2ND

A catalogue record for this book is available from the British Library.

ISBN 978 1 85458 478 6

Printed and bound by MPG Books Ltd, Bodmin, Cornwall

Contents

Introduction

If you've decided you want to start an online business, you're in good company. The internet has created a whole new generation of millionaires and quite a few billionaires in the last decade, offering entrepreneurs a completely new route to market.

The likes of industry behemoths Amazon, Google and eBay quickly spring to mind when mentioning the words 'online business'. While the scale of these companies today defies imagination, it was a very different story when they started. Jeff Bezos, the man behind Amazon, began the business in his garage, eBay first traded from founder Pierre Omidyar's spare bedroom, and Google was conceived as a research project by two Stanford University undergraduates, Larry Page and Sergey Brin. It too used garage space in the early days.

Their success is proof that starting an online business can be as simple as setting up a basic shop on eBay to sell a few wholesale items, or coming up with a completely new online concept and a novel way of monetising it. There are no conventional opening hours to stick to nor is there a specific location as a base. An online business appeals in equal measure to ambitious entrepreneurs in search of the next big thing as it does to the one-man band looking for a flexible business that can be run from home, offering a good work/life balance.

While the first commercial use of the internet was in the 1990s, there's no escaping the fact that dot coms boast a colourful history, one that can easily rival those of more established businesses. The online business boom of the late 1990s and the turn of the Millennium – when anyone and everyone was setting up businesses online – saw the normal rules of business being rewritten, with vast amounts of capital raised on the back of business plans scrawled on cigarette packets. In the wake of the dot com bubble bursting, which saw the demise of businesses such as Boo.com, Webvan, Beenz and Pets.com, the online sector learnt more than a lesson or two. In recent years the prospects for internet shopping or e-commerce propositions in particular, where goods and services are traded over the internet, have remained healthy.

The web continues to revolutionise retail – shoppers from all over the world on eBay alone can click onto 100 million items in 50,000 categories, hunting for the best prices and bargains. The internet allows price comparison like never before and globalisation and international trade have opened the door to whole continents of suppliers providing products and services, and at prices that offer the true entrepreneur mouth-watering mark-up opportunities.

What's more, internet shopping is also growing at its fastest rate in six years, defying the current gloom on the high street, with the number of internet shoppers hitting an all-time high at a rate almost 10 times that of the overall UK market, according to Verdict Research. And with the array of software available, pretty much anyone can set up an e-commerce proposition.

Online businesses, however, aren't just confined to the e-commerce model – there are opportunities and money to be made from web-based subscriptions and services, and more and more companies are recognising the potential of advertising on the web. Whatever your motivation for starting your own online business, whether it be to simply achieve a better work-life balance or taking the first step towards rivalling the likes of Amazon and eBay, we've packed this book with practical hands-on advice for you to not just read, but act on. The book is structured to take you through the journey of starting an online business from concept to planning, from launching your website, raising finance, to finding suppliers and generating interest for your brand.

Case studies

These experts have been there and done it, and turned their online businesses into a sensation. Larry Page and Sergey Brin began Google in 1998, and it is now recognised as the world's largest search engine. Nick Robertson launched AsSeenOnScreen in 2000 (renamed ASOS in 2003), in an attempt to cash in on the public's desire for clothes and accessories worn by celebrities. Price comparison website moneysupermarket.com, founded in 1999 by Simon Nixon, has established itself as a leading online service enabling consumers to compare a wide range of products. Read about their experiences here, and benefit from their expert advice throughout the book.

These businesses may not be national phenomena, but they are certainly well positioned to give their advice on starting an online business. Most have launched in the past five years, and are now well established within their communities. These are companies you should aspire to be like within a year of opening, and they've got some great advice to help you on the way.

Larry Page and Sergey Brin, Google

Type: Search engine
Start year: 1998

In the spring of 1995, Larry Page and Sergey Brin met at Stanford University, where they were both studying computer science. More than 10 years later, and they are known in most quarters as the founders of Google, widely recognised as the world's largest search engine. Sergey and Larry had both grown up surrounded by science and technology and they were convinced there was a better way of approaching search. Sergey was quoted in an earlier interview as saying: 'I loved computer science and math in general and bringing applications to end users, creating something that people appreciate'.

At the time, several rudimentary search tools existed, but a search on one of them would generally yield thousands of results that were not ranked in any order of relevance. According to Larry, the perfect search engine would understand exactly what you mean and give back exactly what you want. 'At Google, we had one simple idea which now seems obvious – the fact that the ranking in search does matter', says Sergey. 'That was not a high priority in web research at the time. We sort of stumbled upon a way of doing the ranking'.

As Sergey recalls, the pair originally developed page rank by playing around with links on the web. After careful research, Larry and Sergey concluded that the number of links pointing to a site was a measure of its popularity and they also decided that links could be weighted.

'We came up with the notion that not all web pages are created equal and we developed analysis on this', said Sergey. 'When we were studying this, we were sure we wanted to have search as a big application. At the time we weren't thinking of how hundreds of millions of people could use this, we were thinking of how a single person would use it. Given the resources we had, we wanted to see how we could create a really good search engine for a small number of people'.

Both Larry and Sergey had not set out to build a business, being more interested in the research and how they could take this further. They developed a prototype of their search engine later called Google to represent the vast amounts of data on the web. The site's popularity soared from word-of-mouth on the university campus, as users quickly discovered how much faster and more relevant its results were compared to other sites.

The founders attempted to sell the technology to Alta Vista, the market leader at the time as well as other companies such as Yahoo! and Excite, but no one was willing to take up the offer; at the time, search did not present any obvious revenue-generating opportunities. Furthermore, Google's goal to produce results in a split second did not make it an ideal medium for advertisers. The next step for Larry and Sergey was to market Google themselves.

'At the time there were around five major search engines and they had decided that search was not that important after all', recalled Sergey. 'We thought we'd give it a try – there are relatively few downsides to trying.'

The pair received funding from Andy Bechtolsheim, a co-founder of Sun Microsystems and from friends and family to kickstart the business. Growing investment in IT meant they needed to seek out more funds, this time at the height of the dot com boom of the late nineties. In 1999, Google closed a deal with two venture capitalists, each backing the business with £7.5m. At this stage, the firm's business model was to earn income by licensing their search technology to other partners, but this was not bringing in enough revenue so Larry and Sergey began to look at other ways of boosting the business.

They came up with the idea that whenever someone searched for a topic, they would display small text adverts relevant to the subject of the search alongside the more prominent natural search results. This model evolved into what is known now as pay-per-click advertising. By 2004, in addition to the core search engine, the business offered Google Images, a huge library of searchable images and Google News, a service that aggregated stories on any particular subject from around the world. It had also introduced Gmail, a web-based email service. In that same year, the founders listed the search engine on the Nasdaq stock exchange, where its shares rose to $100 by the end of the first day of trading, valuing the company at $23.1bn (£11.5 bn).

Google may be the only company in the world whose stated goal is to have users leave its website as quickly as possible and the business continues to innovate. Part of its phenomenal growth has come from its AdSense offering, which enables other websites to install a Google search box on their site; when users click on the contextual ads that Google supplies alongside the result, the partner website earns some of the fee that advertisers pay to Google.

And what keeps Sergey awake at night? In a previous interview he said: 'You should not be spending most of your time thinking about the competition. At Google, it's valuable to spend time thinking that we have the ability to analyse data and that great products come out of it. There are many things we can apply – technologies and creating new things are the exciting things to lose sleep over.'

Nick Robertson, ASOS

Type: Online fashion
Start year: 2000

Fashion and advertising are often viewed as two of the most glamorous industries to be involved in and Nick Robertson has had the fortune to have worked in both. He began his career in the advertising industry, before moving on to the position of associate director for media planning business Carat UK in 1991.

In 2000, Nick co-founded Entertainment Marketing, which provided product placement within television and film for clients including Samsung, Honda, Sky+ and Tropicana. A natural progression emerged to bring celebrity lifestyle to the consumer and the idea for ASOS (formerly known by AsSeenOnScreen) was hatched in June that year. The original business plan was based on selling products and brands online (everything but clothes) enabling consumers to purchase products endorsed by celebrities.

Robertson raised just over £2m from friends and family, with the condition that the business would float on AIM (the stock market for smaller, growing companies) in the near future. 'Our business plan was written on the back of a cigarette packet but the exit strategy for our investors was a little more defined', says Nick. 'Everybody does something for something, so when we raised the money, we ensured we had an exit plan for investors in place.'

He believes that two areas were significant to the business' growth. Uptake of broadband was on the increase and soon after launch, Robertson hired Lorri Penn, a fashion buyer who had worked at leading high street fashion retailer Topshop and who had an eye for spotting the latest celebrity trends. Penn approached suppliers to source clothes similar to those seen on celebrities, and according to Nick, this helped to move the business firmly into fashion, prompting the name change to ASOS. The site began to sell clothes that allowed consumers to emulate the style of celebrities like Victoria Beckham and Jennifer Aniston, but for a fraction of the cost.

'The key to our business plan was to be flexible and understanding – don't get into a market unless you understand it thoroughly', says Nick. 'This was particularly true when we launched the business as the internet was evolving so quickly – we were changing our business model on a day-by-day, week-by-week basis.'

Getting the technology right was crucial too. 'We launched back in the days when technology could very often let you down. We spent a lot of money on the website and it took a long time for sales to catch up. I wasn't tech-savvy but I was fortunate enough to employ people who were.'

By 2003, the business had gone from strength to strength and broken even, with a turnover nudging £8m. Demand for the site's products continued to soar. But in December 2005, an explosion at the fuel depot next door to ASOS's warehouse dealt the business a serious blow, as the warehouse went up in flames, crippling the business over the crucial Christmas period. Nearly £4m worth of stock was destroyed and 19,000 orders had to be cancelled as they could not be fulfilled.

'Having our warehouse next to a fuel depot was probably not the smartest move. We closed the business for six weeks and had a holding page in place of the website, announcing a clearance sale', recalls Nick. 'Having insurance and our customers' details was crucial – we emailed all our customers who were affected and gave them refunds – it's important to be transparent and keep in touch with customers when anything affects the business'.

The clearance sale attracted hordes of shoppers and ASOS has doubled its revenues every year since the fire. Nick believes the success of ASOS has been down to focusing on the brand and its products, as well as keeping issues such as logistics top of the agenda.

'Logistics is such as important part of an internet business – you simply can't fail in this area', he says. 'If you know an order is not going to make it, you have to let the customer know. There is no point in driving traffic to a website if you are going to disappoint your customers'.

Surprisingly for an online brand, ASOS invests heavily in offline advertising, with press ads in women's weeklies targeted at its core market. This has certainly paid off as in October 2008, the site had 1.88 million registered users and 0.95 million active customers (those who have shopped in the last six months). In 2006, ASOS launched a monthly women's magazine, which now boasts a circulation of nearly 430,000. The business now offers more than 19,400 branded and own label product lines across womenswear, menswear, footwear, accessories, jewellery and beauty, with around 1,150 new product lines being introduced every week.

'When it comes to managing the growth of an online retailer, fundamentally we have not done anything different to how traditional retailers would approach it', believes Nick. 'The internet is still evolving and the key to a successful online business is to keep moving forward. Customers are fickle – if you evolve, customers will go with you. If you stagnate, they will go elsewhere'.

FROM THE EXPERTS:

Simon Nixon, moneysupermarket.com

Type: Price comparison
Start year: 1999

Simon Nixon might not have enjoyed studying figures – he dropped out of an accounting and finance course at Nottingham University after just one year – but he certainly knows how to use them to create a business opportunity. His idea for moneysupermarket.com, an online price comparison service for financial products ranging from mortgages to insurance, to savings and loans, launched in 1999 at the height of the dot com boom and grew out of two other businesses based on financial services.

After taking the decision to leave university, Simon had the option of selling pensions and life insurance, but was not inspired by this prospect. Instead, he decided to specialise in mortgages and came up with the idea of teaming up with a local sales office, in order to get sales representatives to contact him directly to set up mortgages for their clients. While working on mortgage enquiries, he spotted a gap in the market – there was no easy way for mortgage brokers to compare deals that were available. He subsequently launched a fortnightly trade magazine, *Brokers Update*, in 1990, listing the best deals and products for reference. The magazine turned out to be a success, and a few months later, Simon was making more money from magazine subscriptions than from arranging mortgages. He decided to devote himself full-time to the business, but within two years, subscriptions had started to dwindle as mortgage brokers were increasingly turning to technology as a source of finance information – it provided more immediate data than that contained in the magazine.

Quick to spot the next opportunity, Simon used funds generated by the magazine to write a software program that was updated daily over the internet, allowing brokers to enter criteria and find the most competitive mortgage. Software programmer and business partner Duncan Cameron came on board and the pair launched Mortgage 2000 in 1994.

Towards the end of the 90s, internet access was increasing and broadband too was achieving higher levels of penetration. This led Simon to believe that the real money lay in offering the same kind of service to people who actually wanted mortgages rather than those selling them. moneysupermarket.com was launched in 1999, and makes its money every time a consumer clicks on a link to a financial services provider. The business has never needed any external funding, as it grew from Simon's existing ventures, so many of the administrative and legal structures were already in place.

'The business evolved from the start, from small, to medium to big and we've never bitten off more than we can chew,' says Simon. 'It's been an evolution rather than a revolution and we've never sought external funding. If we'd had a big injection of cash, it would have meant taking a bigger risk. I never liked the idea of taking on venture capital as it would mean less control over the business.'

As the business grew, Simon took on researchers who specialised in personal finance to boost content and recruited internet developers to manage the technical side of the business. In the early years, moneysupermarket.com did not invest in any advertising, relying instead on press coverage, which Simon says was crucial to business growth. 'It's critical to have media coverage and PR. It can be a cost-effective way to drive traffic to your site as well as helping you with issues such as branding,' he says.

Technology also played an important part in business growth. In 2002, moneysupermarket.com developed technology that made the site faster and more efficient. When a consumer keyed in their details, the technology used enabled hundreds of sites to be searched, with the results being shown on one page. By 2003, the business had expanded into new markets, with Insuresupermarket.com offering consumers the ability to compare insurance quotes in real time using technology that was also developed in-house. Travelsupermarket.com followed a year later, enabling consumers to search for and compare online flights and related travel products.

'Diversification has been critical to the business's growth and success,' believes Simon. 'We wanted to become the number one price comparison site, not just for money but for other areas too. We launched insurance first as it was related to money, followed by travel, home services and most recently shopping.'

Moneysupermarket.com floated on the stock market in 2007 at 170p a share, valuing the group at £843 million and making Simon £102 million in the process. Most recently, the site has been making use of web 2.0 technologies, such as blogs and forums. 'We invite comments from our customers and encourage them to visit forums,' says Simon.

The onset of the credit crunch in the last year, however, has seen the company experience some tough times, and it has suffered a drop in share price as well as increased competition from the likes of Tesco. In a trading statement released at the end of 2008, the business said that its insurance and travel businesses would help to compensate for the 'inevitable weakness' of its money site which it said was being impacted by the credit crunch.

In February this year, Simon stepped down as chief executive of the business, to take on the role of executive deputy chairman. He retains 54% of the business and works one day a week at moneysupermarket.com, focusing on strategic innovation and development.

Jamie Murray Wells, Glasses Direct

Type: Online prescriptions glasses retailer

Start year: 2004

Glasses Direct was conceived with the aim of providing cut-price prescription glasses over the internet, allowing people to afford several pairs. The idea came to its founder, Jamie Murray Wells, while he was at university, when he found he needed a pair of reading glasses and was shocked at the price he would have to pay – £150. 'I chose a market that was getting to grips with the web,' says Jamie. 'The optical industry was one of the few sectors that had not yet made the move online, there was the precedent to build on this and do something different.'

His idea was simple. Instead of walking into a high street opticians and paying through the nose, simply enter your prescription on the internet, choose your frames, and Glasses Direct will supply you with your glasses, within a week, for just £19. 'I chose an online business model as it was the quickest way to reach as wide an audience as possible,' says Jamie. While the idea came to him fairly quickly, doing the research was another matter altogether. Jamie was met with a wall of silence from everyone across the optical industry when he tried to research the actual cost of making glasses. Each laboratory he called would not disclose any information on prices or supply.

On the brink of giving up on the idea, he called one more laboratory and got the information he needed. But that was just the start. Suppliers were equally reticent, and even when one was secured it withdrew its services only a matter of weeks after he launched Glasses Direct. This could have driven the company into the ground, but Jamie recognized that the industry opposition was based entirely on its price protectionism, and he was spurred to take them on.

The business was launched in the front room of his parents' house in 2004 and has gone from strength to strength, securing angel funding and a multi-million investment deal through venture capitalists in 2007. The business has recognised the importance of putting customers first and has strived to make the web experience as interactive as possible. 'We had a customer oriented-approach right from the beginning, which is important as the web can be quite anonymous,' says Jamie. 'We needed to make it more transparent and we're always looking at ways of making the website increasingly interactive.' An example of this includes a virtual mirror, which enables customer to upload photos and try glasses remotely.

Today Glasses Direct is the largest direct-seller of glasses in the world, selling a pair every three minutes around the clock and has achieved a multi million pound turnover.

Simon Wadsworth, The Retail Factory

Type: Retail and office supplies
Start year: 2006

In the late 1980s and early 1990s, Simon Wadsworth worked for the European Commission, exploring how advanced technology and telecommunications could bring economic advantages to rural parts of Europe. Wadsworth was an early adopter of the internet, having set up his own web design agency, Brand New Media, back in 1994. It began with four staff in Yorkshire but through a combination of hard work and a policy of not taking no for an answer, Wadsworth built up an impressive blue chip client list, including companies such as Procter & Gamble and Tesco.

Such diligence paid off when the business was sold in 2000 for just over £5m. Ever the entrepreneur, Simon set up a digital marketing agency called Swamp in 2002, working with clients such as Heinz, The Football Association and Sharp. Just over two years ago, Wadsworth decided to put his internet knowledge to good use by founding his own online business, The Retail Factory, which has since grown into one of the leading suppliers of retail and office supplies in the UK. Its products include office furniture, computer supplies and safety and security tools.

The business was funded through Simon's own money, and the Small Firms Loan Guarantee Scheme, with a factoring service helping with cash flow. 'Having built and run several digital agencies, it was time to put into practice what we have been telling our clients for years,' says Simon. 'The part I am most proud of is our digital offering – we have a built a very large e-commerce site that is fully integrated with our customer relationship management system.'

As an e-tailer, one of the biggest challenges Simon has faced is co-ordinating the number of suppliers (the business currently has more than 100) and the sheer volume of products the site sells. These number well over 30,000 and are sourced from all over the UK and Europe.

While Simon has had a wealth of experience in all things online, setting up The Retail Factory has been a learning curve, particularly where timescales are concerned. Certain aspects of the business have taken longer to take effect than at first anticipated. 'Be realistic about timescales – you won't get to number one in Google overnight and in some competitive markets, it could take years and deep pockets,' says Simon. 'It takes a lot longer than you think to do all the things that are necessary for a great e-commerce site.'

Simon is now in the process of ensuring that The Retail Factory becomes the dominant one-stop-shop for all retail supplies in the UK and Europe, as well as being a key spokesperson for the new media industry.

Glenys Berd, LoveThoseShoes.com

Type: Shoe retailer
Start year: 2003

When Glenys Berd decided to set up an online shoe business, many people told her that the idea would not work, as customers would need to try the shoes before committing to a sale. Despite this feedback, she persevered with her idea and founded LoveThoseShoes.com in 2003, a site offering innovative footwear that looks both practical and stylish and which offers health and beauty benefits.

Glenys had already built up a background in internet retailing, having previously launched an online womenswear business in 1997. The idea for the new venture sprang from her need for a pair of trainers and having done some research, she came across MBT (Masai Barefoot Technology) shoes. 'I wanted some new trainers and was bored of just leather and laces. Whilst researching on the web, I came across a new brand just being developed, trainers that did you good', she says.

Glenys launched her website and started importing MBT trainers. Not one to rest on her laurels, having sold thousands of pairs, she went in search of new products. While browsing the internet, she uncovered a mass of people searching for EarthShoes, which help alleviate back pain and which are manufactured in the US. After a small amount of correspondence and negotiation with the US, Glenys secured an exclusive deal to become the distributor of EarthShoes for the UK.

'I had a couple of businesses already running, spotted a gap in the market and filled it', says Glenys. 'When we started the business the internet was still very new and none of the facilities that exist now were available. There was also nobody to teach us what to do so we had to learn through trial and error.'

Glenys ploughed her own savings into LoveThoseShoes.com, bringing the Earth brand to the UK while continuing to search for new and innovative products. In 2005, the company signed an exclusive five-year deal worth £30m to become the official distributor for Earth in every country outside North America.

According to the company, LoveThoseShoes.com has grown into the number one website selling shoes with positive health benefits, with customers buying around 5,000 pairs of shoes every month. Word of mouth from customers has played a big part in promoting the business.

Mark Leather,
Country Products

Type: Health food store
Start year: 1983

In the early 1970s, Mark Leather saw a niche in the market for high-quality, ready-packed goods for the health food, delicatessen and grocery trade. At the time these foods, such as pulses and seeds, were sold loose, but Mark saw the opportunity to package the food for the customer, and therefore increase impulse sales, and solve problems of cross contamination and stock rotation in one fell swoop. He initially funded the business with only £50, buying stock, selling it on, and repeating this process. The business grew organically, serving a wide variety of customers – from health food shops and pharmacies, to offices and cinemas.

The company had a web presence from 1994, when they set up a simple website, but in 2004, they launched the e-commerce side of the site and the business took the leap online. Mark remembers he took a while to be convinced an online business would work: 'I couldn't believe that customers would purchase say a kilo of brown rice online instead of at the local health store – boy was I wrong!' He was eventually convinced by his web designer, who pointed out they had the stock, an invoicing system in place, order pickers and a delivery system set up – so the transition to online retailing could be achieved for a very small additional outlay.

It hasn't necessarily been from the volume of online sales that Country Products has seen the impact, but from the amount of wholesale customers that see the online shop and then choose to buy from it, and establish a relationship. Mark sees the business' online presence as an essential 'shop window', and says that 'an online business is one of the easiest most economic ways of expanding your business'. He believes that it's now imperative for businesses to have an online presence.

With little technical knowledge pre-launch, Mark believes a 'common sense approach and sensible business practice are all that is required'. He advises others moving online to use local, small firms that you can build a relationship with, and to use 'someone who doesn't talk too much jargon, someone you can meet and speak with face to face'.

Mark believes one of their best business moves ever was moving payment providers to Sage Pay (formerly Protx), which were recommended to them by their web designer. The system provided a simpler, easier and speedier process, which benefits themselves and their customers. They have also benefited from lower costs and charges, an important factor in the current climate.

Mark's advice to anyone starting a business online is first and foremost to listen to advice from others who have been there, done it, and made the mistakes so you don't have to.

1

Idea to reality

Idea to reality

I f you're determined to make your dream of starting an online business come true, in this chapter we take you through the first steps to turning your idea into reality. From getting the right experience and finding out the best support networks, to the different types of online business available, to targeting the right customers and evaluating a website, we'll cover the essential steps. We'll also examine the current market conditions and why it could be the perfect time for you to start an online business. After this chapter, you should have a pretty good idea of your concept and the steps you can take to make it work.

In this chapter we'll cover:

- Is an online business right for you?
- The experience you need
- Support networks
- Market conditions – is now a good time?
- Your idea and USPs

- The different types of online business
- Identifying your target market
- Standing out from the competition
- Evaluating a website

➡ IS AN ONLINE BUSINESS RIGHT FOR YOU?

The beauty of an online business is that it's suited to just about anyone. You don't need to have a particular set of qualifications or industry experience. You don't need an MBA from a business school and nor do you need to be based in a specific location. You can operate an online business from anywhere, as long as you've got access to an internet connection and a bit of business know-how. Ask yourself why people buy products and services on the internet. The answer is quite simple: they do so because it's easy, efficient and they can instantly see what is available.

There are reams of studies, reports and research dissecting the DNA of successful business people. The significance of nationality, ethnicity, gender, age, education, class, experience, wealth, socio-political demographics, access to support and finance, and every other remotely explorable contributing factor have been analysed to death.

What conclusions have ever been drawn? None worth listening to, other than, in theory at least, there's no reason anyone, from any background and any walk of life, can't successfully start and run their own business. So be assured, whatever your concerns and anxieties: you can do it.

'Doing it' is actually far more representative of the average entrepreneur's make-up than any of the numerous factors detailed above. People who start their own business are the ones who stop talking about their dreams and plans and actually make them happen.

IN MY EXPERIENCE:
Glenys Berd, LoveThoseShoes.com

The internet gives you a progressive and reactive arena to work in, and means that, with the right team around you, you can turn an idea into a business overnight.

Motivation

What exactly is it that prompts people to set up an online business? For surprisingly few, money is the main motivation and as the dot com boom and bust at the turn of the Millennium proved, online millionaires are not made overnight. For others, being their own boss is the decision maker. For most it's to realise a dream, idea or desire to live a life that's more fulfilling, whether that be working closer to their family, in an environment they're more comfortable with or simply the challenge of earning their own income.

This is the most common reason people decide to start an online business. It's one of the most popular businesses you can start from home so it's ideal for those couples and families looking to spend more time together, and one of the most flexible businesses to set up and run. The web lets you test out business models cheaply. You can start small, see what works and build on that.

FROM THE EXPERTS:
Sergey Brin, Google

It's important to do what you love. I loved computer science and math in general, loved being part of the technology curve that has resulted in some great applications and creating something that people appreciate. I pursued what I loved – I played with computers when I was very young and my dad is a mathematician.

Others, such as those who have been made redundant or those who, for whatever reason, struggle to find employment, turn to running their own businesses because they feel there's little alternative to get ahead. But they still 'do it' instead of giving up. People start their own business for individual and deeply personal reasons and as such what's perceived as 'success' is almost always related to personal challenges.

What it takes

Enthusiasm and motivation aren't all it takes of course, as proved by the number of super-keen people who put every last drop of energy into starting online businesses only to see them fail within the first year. It's important not to be put off by statistics. Yes, people fail but many succeed as well, and remember, it's a personal measure. Lots of first-time business people don't succeed in others' eyes but use the experience positively to either start another business or return to employment with a greater sense of fulfilment.

But you also have to consider risk – business is all about balancing risk and reward and unless you are fully aware of the implications of running a business and what impact this will have on your life and relationships, then you are increasing your risk.

IN MY EXPERIENCE:

Glenys Berd, LoveThoseShoes.com

Start it small and don't invest too much at the beginning until you understand what you are doing.

Becoming your own boss and setting up a small business is one of the most rewarding, exciting and fulfilling things you can do in life, but it's also one of the most stressful, testing and demanding experiences. It's often said getting married and moving house are the two most stressful events most people take on in life and starting a business could arguably be the third.

If you think you're escaping the '9 to 5' or 'the rat race' as often referred to in other business books, think again. Forget the idyllic movie representations of business people enjoying long lunches, days on the golf course or at the beauty spa. Unless you happen to strike it rich and come up with the next Amazon, that vision is nothing more than fictitious.

For at least the first two to three years, put the holidays on hold and expect to work longer and harder than you are now. Expect to make sacrifices with family and friends who, no matter how much you explain, won't understand why you've turned into an obsessed bore who ruins dinner parties and nights out with the latest trends in search engine optimisation and how to play Google at its own game. You'll need the emotional resilience to cope with feeling isolated from your usual support networks and will need to find the time to find new ones.

For online business owners, the longer hours and isolation can make it hard to meet new contacts. You effectively have a sales outlet that is open 24 hours a day, 365 days of the year and a global customer base. Sure you'll be mixing with the public, but the fact that you can operate your business at all hours of the day means your opportunity to get out and meet other business owners will need to be carefully

✦ TIP

If you have read all this and are undaunted by the prospect of setting up your own online business, then you probably relish a challenge and are ready to take the plunge and start now.

planned. The stereotypical image of entrepreneurs working all hours of the week and at weekends can fast become a reality. This means that taking the odd holiday can become a contentious issue. The beauty of the web is the ability to access it from anywhere but consequently, you could find yourself working when you are meant to be relaxing, and this could have a negative impact on personal relationships and your well-being.

Analysing your skills

While passion and determination are vital assets for any entrepreneur, in excess they can be dangerous. Critical skills are important and none more so than when looking at yourself – and that starts now.

There are skills an online business can't survive without. At its most naked your business needs you to have a basic understanding of technology; an ability or inclination to sell; confidence in negotiating with suppliers; an understanding of digital marketing techniques; decisiveness; leadership; initiative by the bucket load and, especially for running an online retail business, a firm understanding of the customer experience and how to enhance this.

Here are a few skills you need to start an online business:

- An aptitude for selling
- Negotiation skills
- A basic understanding of technology
- Decisiveness
- Initiative
- The ability to multi-task
- Experience of customer service
- Leadership

IN MY EXPERIENCE:
Glenys Berd, LoveThoseShoes.com

To start and run an online business, all the normal skills you would expect from running a company are needed, but you also need an understanding of how the internet works and what tools you can utilise to make your site successful. Oh, and a psychology degree – just kidding, but it does help when you're dealing with 'virtual customers'!

This is by no means an exhaustive list but there are hundreds of multi-million pound industries, making decisions that affect hundreds of thousands of people, who will happily admit that their skills don't encompass the range outlined above. They are able to compensate for this though, as they are surrounded by consultants, advisors and experts in particular fields.

⚲ TIP

You don't need to be tech-savvy to start an online business, but making the wrong IT decisions can cost you extra money and time as your business grows. So it's a good idea to keep up to date with the latest internet technology trends, think about what functions you want your website to perform and then explore the technology options.

The reality is somewhat different in a small business, where the enormity of the task in hand starts to bite: you're highly unlikely to have the luxury of being able to call on other people from day one – maybe even from day 356 or 752. Running a small business is a demanding, jack-of-all-trades challenge where you, and only you, will be at the centre of all activity. Sure, you can hire an accountant and a sales person but you'll need the critical nous to analyse the progress of your business in a blink and that takes certain abilities and a rounded perspective.

FROM THE EXPERTS:
Simon Nixon, moneysupermarket.com

To succeed in an online environment today, an idea is only 20% of what is required. You also need marketing skills, both on and offline, and experience on the IT side too. Three people setting up a business in a bedroom sounds simple, but in reality there's more to an online business than that.

It's these abilities that dictate who can run a business and who can't. The upside is that you can teach and equip yourself with the basics. If you want to succeed badly enough, you won't be embarrassed about admitting where you need to go back to school, ask questions and get help. You'll make mistakes, learn from them and move on. Remember, each time you do that and pick up something new the risk of failure decreases and the chances of success grow.

Ultimately, if you have the desire, are realistic about what you're letting yourself in for, and are willing to learn and get your hands dirty, there's certainly no reason why you can't succeed in running an online business. Not everyone does, of course, but being in business is all about balancing risk and reward.

Experience needed

As mentioned previously, anyone can start up an online business. There's no reason you can't succeed without having any prior experience of the online environment. There are no compulsory courses or exams to take and many of today's most successful online businesses are run by people who had a good idea, who offer great customer service and who have the ability to distinguish themselves from the competition.

 IN MY EXPERIENCE:
Jamie Murray Wells, Glasses Direct

I chose a market that was getting to grips with the web – the optical industry was one of the few sectors that had not yet made the move online. There was the precedent to build on this and do something different, to bring a new take to the industry.

Statistically, there's no evidence that people are more likely to succeed if they've been in business before and the increasing numbers of 'teenpreneurs' making their fortunes fresh out of school proves a lack of experience certainly shouldn't be a barrier.

It's also true you'll learn most from the mistakes you'll inevitably make. Just as you really learn how to drive only after you've passed your test, no amount of experience will prepare you for the many unexpected hazards and pitfalls you'll have to learn once you're in the driver's seat. This is particularly true of business in an online environment, where trends and technology are constantly evolving, providing a myriad of opportunities to learn and mistakes to make.

It'd be foolish to discard the value of experience, however. Regardless of what anyone tells you, banks and investors operate on a purely risk against reward policy and the fact that they'd prefer a proven track record in business or industry over almost any other factor in an investment proposition should tell you everything you need to know about the importance of experience.

IN MY EXPERIENCE:
Mark Leather, Country Products

A common sense approach and sensible business practice are all that is required – I see an online business as an easy way to 'dip your toes' into business – you can run it in the evening or weekends until it's up and running.

It might not be backed up statistically, but it's instinctive to trust someone with the experience to do something well more than someone just starting out. If you visit the dentist do you place your trust in the senior member of the practice or the latest recruit fresh out of college? There's no reason why the junior wouldn't have a wider knowledge of the latest practices and be the more skilled operator of course, but he or she would have it all to prove and that's the position you'll find yourself in if you go into the online business sector without any experience.

It's also a fair assumption that the more experience you have, the better informed your decisions are. The more of the pitfalls you know about, the earlier you'll see them and the easier it'll be to avoid them. Founder of easyJet and the numerous easyGroup brands, Sir Stelios Haji-Ioannou, is known as a risk taker, and while a supporter of young entrepreneurs, he believes 28 is a better age to start a business than straight from school or university because by then you'll have had time to understand how companies operate and, crucially, have made mistakes at someone else's expense.

In essence, this is fairly obvious. However, by the very fact you feel it necessary to pick up this book, you may have never previously started and run your own online business; or if you have, you are looking for further advice.

IN MY EXPERIENCE:
Glenys Berd, LoveThoseShoes.com

When we started the business the internet was still very new and none of the facilities that exist now were available. There was also nobody to teach us what to do so we had to learn through trial and error.

Relevant experience

Possibly you've worked in retail. If you've worked in retail even at a shop floor level, you'll be feeling fairly confident you understand the everyday operations of selling stock. If you've management level experience of ordering and maintaining stock, negotiating with suppliers, excelling at customer service and dealing with remote orders, then all the better.

Having experience related to the type of online business you are planning is not always necessary. It might be that you've got skills honed in other businesses. Maybe you've run a different business in the past or come from a technology background so feel comfortable setting up an internet business or it could be you're a champion sales or marketing person who thinks you're capable of reinventing the wheel.

FROM THE EXPERTS:
Nick Robertson, ASOS

One of the benefits in starting ASOS was not having a retail background. I approached the business with a clean sheet of paper, without any baggage.

You may be an expert user of the internet or an online shopping addict, but just because you've had experience of this environment does not mean you will have an idea how to run a business in this area. For instance, when you purchased products online, it's doubtful you were thinking about how much stock was available, whether the business had one or 10 members of staff, how much they earned and whether people running the site had done the design themselves or used a professional web designer.

It's always different on the other side of the screen – all you see is the finished product, with little appreciation of the blood, sweat and tears that have gone into the back end of the site. No matter how much you think you already know, there will be more, and still more to learn. Entrepreneur Nick Porter's first company, a design agency called Two Men and a Mouse, collapsed in 1997 and he decided to return to regular employment to learn new ideas that would help him to overcome mistakes in the future. He put lessons learned to good use and in 2004, set up events company Fresh, which reached sales of £2m in its first year of trading.

A site specialising in fashion items differs greatly to one that sells widgets – the fashion site will concentrate on imagery and presentation and will need to be constantly updated to reflect industry trends, while a site selling widgets is likely to be less focused on the look and feel, containing essential product information and enabling users to find products quickly and easily.

Online travel sites need to offer some form of customer contact outside of normal office hours to cater for those people who experience problems travelling at weekends or in the evening, for example, and therefore are more staff intensive than other types of online business. Some online businesses can be remotely maintained and therefore need minimum staff levels, while others by their very nature appeal to technically minded people.

So it can make sense to try and get experience in an environment that is similar to the one you are looking to start in. Online businesses differ according to whether they are retail or whether they offer services, for example, and so too do their revenue models. Social networking and dating sites use ad placements and affiliate programmes to create revenues, retail sites make money from product sales and subscriptions and business-to-business sites rely on a mixture of sales, services fees and contracts to generate cash.

Therefore it's important to have experienced diverse practices so you're able to apply a broader range of thinking to your strategic decisions, especially when looking to carve a niche or innovate in areas that are crying out for a new approach.

You shouldn't necessarily be put off from starting an online business if you've never worked in an online environment before. No matter what it says in the business manuals, if you've set your heart on starting-up and got as far as buying this book, you're highly unlikely now to put your grand plans on hold for a year or two while you sign up for some online training courses. Likewise you might have worked in retail all your life so how on earth do you go and land a job that teaches you how the business side of an operation works?

The reason a lot of people decide to plough on without the necessary experience, contrary to those disapproving business advisors who seem to get more satisfaction from tutting and saying 'we told you so' when businesses go wrong, is more down to a lack of time or money than arrogance or naivety.

✦ TIP

If you are looking to break into an industry you are not familiar with, consider getting experience to see if it is an area you are interested in pursuing further. Your friends and family may already be involved in that industry, so see if you can shadow them for a day to get a flavour of what lies ahead.

So where can you get experience from?

Most people looking to start their own business know they should probably get some experience but aren't sure where to fit it in or even how to get the experience. If you are in the online game, though, different rules apply. You can do the necessary research in the evenings at home so you can fit around family commitments – all you need is an internet connection to explore the world wide web. You can even tinker with basic website design, by designing some mock-ups of what you envisage the site should look like.

There's no one answer that'll work for everyone. For some people, working on their site in the evening and at weekends while serving out their notice of employment is the obvious solution; for others it's a case of dedicating a period of your pre-start-up or 'research' time to getting some inside information.

You could consider contacting established online businesses and ask if you can shadow someone for the day. You might get nowhere, but you'd be surprised how many owner-managers will understand your situation – they've all been there before and they are likely to welcome the help of someone who is keen to learn, especially if you are able to offer your services for free or in return for advice.

If you're really unable to commit a set period of time to gain experience, contact your local Business Link or Chamber of Commerce to see if there are any guest speaker events focusing on online business. Listening to someone's warts and all tale of how they very nearly didn't make it and what lessons they learnt can be invaluable and will give you at the very least a taster of what to expect.

Making these initial contacts might feel awkward and scary, especially if you're not accustomed to the world of business networking, but just remember, all the people you approach were once in your position. If you get a no – polite or otherwise – just brush it off and move on to someone else.

Support networks

The first support network you'll need are your family and friends, regardless of whether they are involved in the business or not. It doesn't matter how much you attempt to separate your business from your personal life – in the early days of starting up, your business will impact on your family so it's vital that both you and they are prepared for what lies ahead. If your family (spouse, partner, children, parents) aren't on board with you 100%, at some point, you, your business and/or your family will bear the consequences.

IN MY EXPERIENCE:

Glenys Berd, LoveThoseShoes.com

When starting a business, so much time and mental energy goes into it, so it's important those around you don't add to the pressure but support what you feel you need to do to succeed.

New businesses require a tremendous amount of time and nurturing to develop and become successful; time that is taken from elsewhere, often from the family. Unless you're starting a 'family' business where all members are participants, someone will inevitably feel left out, or neglected. Our family members don't always share the same dreams we have. Their priorities may be something far from business success.

This is particularly important in the world of online businesses – the majority of them are started from home and remain there for quite some time until you decide to source premises. Your family are likely to be immersed in the business from day one but from an observer's point of view – while they can see what is going on, they may not always understand why it's happening.

To make sure your family doesn't suffer due to your own ambitions, before you pursue your dream business, sit down with them and discuss the following:

- Will the business venture take away from quality time spent with family members? If so, how much is acceptable to all involved?
- Will the new business be initially funded or supported using family monies? If so, will this put a financial strain on the family?
- Do all family members agree this is a potentially successful business idea?
- Do all family members realise that most new businesses do not succeed?
- If the business is not showing signs of becoming successful, what operational time period will the family tolerate before the business is considered a failure and should be sold or closed down?
- If the new business fails, what is the alternative plan for income?

Some of the questions listed may not have obvious answers until the business has started up and operated for some period of time. Since circumstances may vary regularly with new business, plan to review this list with the family about every six months to see what situations may have changed.

Your family needs to be in total support of your new business idea, or somewhere and at some point, somebody will suffer. Consider whether your 'big idea' is worth the possibility of distancing yourself from your loved ones, enduring a breakdown in relationships or even the finality of a divorce. Business owners with complete family support stand a much greater chance of success. Talk to your family and trust in their opinion.

IN MY EXPERIENCE:

Simon Wadsworth, The Retail Factory

It's vital to have support – people mainly focus on business support networks but the most important starting point is having it in your personal life, such as child care.

How other entrepreneurs can help you

The reason we asked some of the leading names in online business to contribute to this book is that there's simply no better place to get advice than from those that have, as the saying goes, 'been there, done it and got the t-shirt'. Entrepreneurs trust other entrepreneurs more than anyone else and naturally form support networks that might at first appear cliquey but are almost always actually born simply out of a shared understanding of each other's fairly unique lives.

Like all relationships you'll find that with support networks you'll get out what you put in. Networking comes naturally to some people; it fills others with dread. If you're the first sort of person, you're probably already aware of the value of getting out and meeting others. In business you can't know too many people (although admittedly there are networking addicts who spend so long swapping business cards, they forget there's an actual business to be run) or enough 'friends' to call on to get you out of a mess.

If you're the second type of person, you're going to have to be brave and bite the bullet. Get yourself to a business networking event, have a glass of wine and simply chat to people about what you're doing. It can be daunting, but once you've taken the plunge at one event, chances are you'll be raring to go to others and will wonder what you were scared of in the first place. After all, many of the people at these events are in or have been in the same boat as you and the reason they are there is to talk and make contacts so make the most of such opportunities.

⋆ TIP

You might even be able to gain some valuable leads that you could convert into customers. Chey Garland set up call centre business Garlands in 1997 and to attract her first clients, she asked her local business networking club if she could speak at one of its monthly meetings about the company.

The online world is certainly an industry where it pays to have contacts – the environment develops at a faster pace than other sectors so advice from peers can be invaluable. A website is anonymous so it's useful to know who is on the other side of the screen. Furthermore, you are not restricted by geographical boundaries so you could literally build up contacts all over the world in a very short space of time.

Networking is also a great way of picking up recommendations. Most people recommend people they use – whether good or bad – so don't swallow their advice blindly, but knowing an accountant or lawyer who's experienced in your sector or knowledgeable of the area is a far more valuable lead than your standard Google search.

Don't confine your networking to physical events, either – and starting an online business means you have little excuse for not using the internet to build contacts. Social networking is growing beyond the fun and games of Facebook and MySpace into a serious business tool and with sites such as LinkedIn, BT Tradespace and Startups.co.uk you can interact with other entrepreneurs and business advisors. While it lacks the face-to-face personal touch it's far less scary and you won't have to spend time travelling.

You can also see what business bodies and lobby groups are available both for small business and online ventures. The Federation of Small Businesses, Forum of Private Businesses, British Chambers of Commerce and Business Network International are all recognised lobby and small business groups which aim to represent, champion and advise small businesses, while you should also contact organisations such as e-commerce trade body Interactive Media in Retail Group.

As well as Startups.co.uk, the government's official support service Business Link can provide you with practical advice, and it's worth reading up as much as you can about the various aspects of starting a business you're most concerned about. There's a wealth of information out there so take advantage of it.

IN MY EXPERIENCE:

Mark Leather, Country Products

Listen to recommendations, never be afraid to take advice – let other people make the hard or costly mistakes. After all 'not everyone has to invent the wheel'.

Business mentoring

Finally, think about getting a mentor – this could be someone you know or you could contact several companies who provide matching services.

You don't have to follow this route, though. You also don't need a high profile celebrity entrepreneur mentor. Someone who's done what you wish to do should be your number one criterion. An experienced entrepreneur who you can turn to once every month or so to test out ideas on and gauge advice from will prove just as, if not more, valuable.

FROM THE EXPERTS:

Simon Nixon, moneysupermarket.com

I never had a business mentor but I was inspired by Richard Branson and read many business books about him. If you can find a mentor for yourself and your business, it's definitely a good idea.

Don't be scared to approach someone you don't know. Many entrepreneurs feel a responsibility to encourage and help others and will be only too willing to help. If they're not it'll almost certainly be because they're simply too busy (either running their own businesses still or possibly helping someone else). If that's the case, ask someone else. You'll soon get used to moving on quickly and without a grudge when met with the word 'no'!

The more support you actively surround yourself with, the less likely you'll feel like you're in this on your own. For all the highs running your own online business will bring, there will be down times too and understanding from your family and friends, and knowledgeable contacts to seek advice from will be worth their weight in gold.

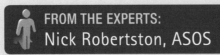

FROM THE EXPERTS:
Nick Robertston, ASOS

Finding support networks was quite hard as not many people had done online retail before, there was no one there! But the principles of high-street retail still applied to the online world and I've met people over the years who have given me some advice.

List of support organisations

The Federation of Small Businesses: www.fsb.org.uk

Forum of Private Businesses: www.fpb.org

British Chambers of Commerce: www.britishchambers.org.uk

Business Network International: www.bni-europe.com/uk

Business Link: www.businesslink.gov.uk

Startups: www.startups.co.uk

➡ GOING INTO BUSINESS WITH PARTNERS / FRIENDS

Online businesses are one of the most popular couple-run businesses or ventures run by friends; as many can be started from someone's home, it's an ideal way to combine work with family commitments and in terms of hours worked, online businesses are much more flexible than bricks-and-mortar firms. Indeed, they can be great businesses to run with other people. Who better to trust sharing such an enormous emotional challenge with than your closest friends and family?

It's easy to see why, idealistically at least, it appeals. When you consider how much of our waking lives we spend earning money to enjoy in comparatively small spaces of time with the people that mean most to us, combining the two to get the best of both worlds is a compelling argument.

What's more, it can work brilliantly. The attributes for a healthy relationship – trust, honesty, the ability to listen, understanding, the unity of or tolerance of shared or different interests – translate well into business. Google was started by two university undergraduates who went on to study computer science, and they shared a common skill – they both just happened to be geniuses with computers.

Shared understanding is the key to making a business started with friends or family work. It's essential to be sure that, aside from your personal relationships, there's a business case for working together. Ideally your skill sets should complement each other so the business benefits from supporting two people – if it's unlikely you'd otherwise recruit this person alarm bells should be ringing.

If your decision to work together does make business sense, there's no reason you shouldn't continue: just be aware of the consequences. If the business doesn't work out then relationships could turn sour and the trauma of losing a business could be doubled by also losing an otherwise lifelong friend or partner. Is the sharing of your finances and knowledge (which you could get elsewhere) worth the sacrifice? Ultimately it's your call, but be wary of rushing into something you could regret and agree how you'll communicate inevitable frustrations with each other to keep the relationship healthy.

FROM THE EXPERTS:
Simon Nixon, moneysupermarket.com

I brought in friends and contacts that I respected and admired when I started moneysupermarket.com and it worked very well. But be very wary of who you pick and it's critical that you retain a majority shareholding so everyone knows who has the most power and who calls the shots. If everyone has an equal shareholding that is when fallouts can occur.

If your business partner is more of an associate than a friend, you need to be clear in your mind that you trust and like this person sufficiently to share such an epic journey with them. It's likely you'll be working intensively with them for a number of years so you'll clearly need to get on. Indeed, if you're not friends with them, you probably want to consider why if it's anything other than not knowing them intimately enough – and if that's the case, perhaps you need to know them better.

Aside from having the skills you don't have and vice versa, look for a partner with whom you have a natural business chemistry; someone who can enthuse you and whom you can inspire. Good partnerships, from business to sport and even entertainment, combine characters who together can create a greater sum total than their individual efforts and that's what you should aspire to build.

You'll need to balance reward, responsibility and risk. Make sure you're clear what your goals are for the business on a shared and personal level, what you want in the short, medium and long term and what your respective roles are. Ensure you're each staking the same degree of risk. And, simple as it sounds, make sure you're happy and comfortable and have clear lines of communication for it to stay that way.

However, with all partnerships, expect the unexpected. Two in five marriages ending in divorce shouldn't dissuade you from getting hitched, but it should be enough of a warning to get legally binding shareholder agreements drawn up. This should cover what happens to the business and shares if any combination of unthinkable outcomes occur including, as morbid as it might seem, either of your deaths.

➡ MARKET CONDITIONS: IS NOW A GOOD TIME?

It's likely that the current economic downturn has made you think twice about whether now is a good time to start your own online business. You may have felt the impact on your mortgage repayments, shopping bills or at the petrol station. There's no denying that economically it's a difficult time and unlike previous dips in the economy, a quick resolution doesn't appear forthcoming and the forecasts are pessimistic.

Banks have cut lending options and it's certainly a tougher climate in which to raise funds for a business than, say, two years ago. This, of course, also impacts on what consumers have to spend and as a consequence, high street retailers have also been hit hard.

FROM THE EXPERTS:
Simon Nixon, moneysupermarket.com

An online business has lower overheads than other forms of business and can offer you national reach. If you are aspiring to be a national player, online is the most cost-effective route to choose. In current market conditions, online opportunities are probably 20%–30% lower than they were 12 months ago, but there are always opportunities when you can find a niche.

If there is one positive sign that online businesses should take from the current environment, particularly those specialising in retail, it should be that internet retail is still growing (albeit at a much slower pace than in recent years) even while other retail is stagnant and shrinking. The reason for this could be explained by the fact that online shopping tends to be more cost-effective but industry figures show that on average people are still spending a lot more online. Furthermore, online businesses require virtually no overheads and offer you the ability to work at any time you like from virtually any location, so there is flexibility as well as potential cost savings to be made.

What the internet does well is support those savvy consumers who are prepared to search out a bargain. Online retailers have traditionally offered competitive pricing and focusing on areas such as reliable delivery and customer service could mean that your business meets the emotional needs of customers in a recession.

IN MY EXPERIENCE:
Glenys Berd, LoveThoseShoes.com

In the current market conditions, make sure you understand who your target market is. Don't try to compete directly with the big-boys – find a product/site idea where you can be unique even if it is a niche market. You can always have several niche sites rather than one general site.

With a bit of work, a website can be a powerful and cost effective advertising tool in a tough market. A presence on the web enables small businesses to compete with larger companies that have bigger marketing budgets. Providing your website is always available your reach can be as big as you want it to be.

Starting in a downturn can also be a positive. As hardnosed as it sounds, other businesses failing frees up retail units, keeps rents low and floods the recruitment market with talented staff you otherwise mightn't be able to afford or attract.

IN MY EXPERIENCE:
Mark Leather, Country Products

Our biggest benefit to our business comes not from the revenue received online but the volume of wholesale customers that see our online shop and want to purchase from us. After all who picks up a telephone directory these days? If you want something you look on the internet so get your 'Shop window' out there.

If you can establish yourself on limited resources and build a loyal customer base when times are tight, you'll flourish in more affluent climates. There's never a bad time to start a good business, so don't let market conditions put you off: just make sure you plan even harder to get your offering spot on.

 TIP

If you are looking to set up an online retail business, there's no doubting it's a difficult time for retail but every company that fails presents a new opportunity and there's no bad time to start a good business. And if you can establish your model during a downturn, chances are it'll flourish when the economic climate improves.

➡ YOUR BIG IDEA: USPs

You've got an idea. Do some research, check out a few websites that seem similar to what you want to achieve and analyse them. Ask yourself these questions: what do you like about their approach and how does it relate to what you are trying to do? Are there any functions missing from these websites that you think yours could benefit from?

 IN MY EXPERIENCE:

Jamie Murray Wells, Glasses Direct

Glasses Direct was third time lucky, I'd already looked at two other ideas, gambling online and property online. Regulations were too heavy for gambling and property was not as disruptive as we wanted. We wanted to shake up an industry.

Types of online business

You'll probably already know what type of online business you'd like to start and run. Indeed, when you first stumbled upon the idea of an internet venture, you were almost certainly thinking of running a certain type of business.

For many of you it'll be as simple as wanting to run the type of business you've always enjoyed visiting on the web and probably purchased products from. For others among you, an online business will represent an opportunity to spend your working day embracing a passion or hobby, such as fashion or music. The more opportunistic and entrepreneurial among you will have spotted a trend, gap in the market or need for a certain type of online business.

FROM THE EXPERTS:
Sergey Brin, Google

At the time we launched there were five major search engines, but what we found, almost by accident, was that through the structure of the web, we could create a search engine that was better. We thought we'd give it a try – there are relatively little downsides to trying.

Even those of you who initially wanted to just run any online business are unlikely to have stopped your imagination skipping ahead of itself, dreaming about what type of business would suit you best. Essentially then, however unpolished, you'll have an idea of the type of online business you want to run; ie what products or services it will offer.

Picking a type of online business is only half the challenge, though. Next you'll need to explore the specifics of that type of business to start sculpting exactly what your offering to the market will be.

TIP

Start by making a list of what will make your online venture unique. Your USPs will define how your business is different from the competition and will slowly build its identity and brand. Your USPs will be your sales story to convince people they should buy from your company instead of elsewhere.

Having established the idea for your business and decided what makes it stand out from the competition, there are three basic online business models you can follow:

E-commerce: the most closely aligned to the traditional business model of selling. With an e-commerce site you sell a product or service. Customers buy directly from your site, and the products are then either delivered to them or downloaded. Examples of e-commerce sites include Amazon, eBay, Play.com and lastminute.com

Advertising: with this type of site, the aim is to get as many visitors as possible, increasing the number of customers your advertisers reach. Content on this kind of site is usually completely free for the site user, providing them with either information or entertainment. Examples of such sites include social networking operations such as Facebook, Bebo and MySpace.

Subscription: similar to the advertising model, subscription sites generally provide information or entertainment, but the difference is the user pays to access all or part of that content. This type of site is particularly common in the business-to-business world.

You can of course base your site around a combination of one, two or all of these internet models.

The good news is, as a small business, you've far more flexibility and opportunity to find unique routes to appeal to customers. Carve out a niche or focus on a specialist category and gauge demand. In online retail, you'll be competing with the likes of Tesco as well as smaller players, so selling something that is niche and desirable will get you noticed. Offer incentives to build up a customer base, such as giving discounts to customers who refer a friend.

Your USP could be that you offer substantial savings over high street prices. This is the model that spurred Jamie Murray Wells to launch online glasses retailer Glasses Direct. Not only did Murray Wells take on much larger corporate giants, but he has also helped the UK public to save more than £15 million on their glasses, while still generating healthy sales.

When drawing up your USPs, consider the following suggestions to differentiate your offering:

- Superior customer service
- A wider or more focused selection of products
- Premium services
- Budget offering
- Faster, more flexible delivery
- Ethically sourced
- Better after sales support

WHO ARE YOUR CUSTOMERS?

Once you've a clear idea of what your online business is and what its USPs are, you need to define who your customers will be. Without doing this you won't be able to properly plot the viability of your business in a business plan.

To assess if your business could work you'll need to prove there is enough demand for the product or services you're selling for the price you're charging.

IN MY EXPERIENCE:
Glenys Berd, LoveThoseShoes.com

Research your market and be passionate about your ability to succeed as a business, rather than falling in love with your 'product'. The internet is reactive so what's hot now, might not be soon and if you're objective about your product then you'll foresee the changes you need to make before the market does.

For some online businesses reliant on seasonal peaks and troughs this can be a complicated process and will involve investing in areas such as search engine optimisation and web design, in order to build interest well before these seasonal peaks occur to maximise sales.

Don't fall for the mistake of convincing yourself that just because you love the idea, then others will. Too many people skip the process believing 'if you build it, they will come'. It's a saying built in Hollywood not the real world, where the reality is people can't come if they don't exist. . . or they can't afford your prices. . . or there's already a website offering what you do and more. Unfortunately there are plenty of great-sounding 'ideas' that simply aren't viable. Banks will expect to see evidence of an existing customer base and so should you if you're using your own money or, quite simply, you want the business to have a chance of working.

Identifying who your customers are

Before you can explore if your customers exist in sufficient numbers you need to establish exactly who you're looking for. There are standard demographic outlines of consumers you should use.

Social grade	Social status	Occupation	Annual earnings estimate
A	upper middle class	higher managerial, administrative or professional	£50k +
B	middle class	intermediate managerial, administrative or professional	£35-£50k
C1	lower middle class	supervisory or clerical, junior managerial, administrative or professional	£25-£35k
C2	skilled working class	skilled manual workers	£15-£25k
D	working class	semi and unskilled manual workers	£7-£15k
E	those at lowest level of subsistence	state pensioners or widows (no other earner), casual or lowest grade workers	£5-£7k

You essentially want to know what the profile of your target customer is: are they male or female? How old are they? What's their disposable income? What other brands do they also consume? How much would they spend with you and how frequently?

Research the market

Now you know what type of online business you want to start and who you'd ideally like your prime customers to be, you need to know if those people actually exist and whether they can find your business online.

Researching the market isn't a guessing game. Check out online statistics and demographics, particularly those that refer to your target audience. Too many people invest in all the right internet marketing strategies, only to find out that they don't really know who their market is. Those people that are increasing their search activities, for example are likely to appeal to younger and faster adopters of technology. If your target audience is likely to be older, you'll need to think of ways to draw them to your site. The point is to pay attention to internet marketing data that is relevant to your target audience.

Homemade surveys

Carry out your own research with the public as well. Take to the streets and carry out surveys and questionnaires exploring anything that can prove your case that a market for your online business exists. Ask respondents how much they'd spend a month on the products you're planning to sell and ask them to tick if your USPs would make them choose you over a competitor site.

Asking personal questions such as people's income or age is likely to put them off taking part, so instead ask them to tick ranges which will fit with the demographic research you've unearthed and have identified as your target customer. The more people you interview within these ranges, the more powerful your research will be.

DIY market research

Questions to ask members of the public

- How often do you go online?
  Hardly ever, once or twice a month, once or twice a week, more than twice a week
- How old are you?
  Under 18, 18–24, 25–34, 35–50, 50+
- What's your wage bracket?
  £5–£7k, £7k–£15k, £15k–£25k, £25–£35k, £35k–£50k, £50k+
- Would you welcome an online shop selling [enter your products here?

Research companies

There are professional research companies that you can hire to carry out feasibility studies. For most of you their services will be out of your price range, and be wary of companies who claim to do this for comparatively low rates as it's likely they'll merely accumulate information already in the public domain that you could do yourself.

TIP

Try the Research Buyers Guide when looking for reputable sources for market research. www.rbg.org.uk has a fully searchable directory of market research providers.

Well carried out professional research can prove worth the investment however, especially if you're seeking substantial finance. If you pursue this route, be clear exactly what you're looking to achieve and perhaps even research investors first to find out how you can meet their expectations. And be careful what you spend. While some investors will be impressed by professional research, others will question your business acumen if you've spent a considerable slice of your start-up capital just proving that market exists.

➡ COMPETITION AND DIFFERENTIATION

Competition tends to come in two forms: directly from other sites selling the same or similar products, and indirectly from other ways those customers can spend money they'd otherwise spend with you.

Direct competition is relatively simple to research and observe, but indirect competition is subject to constant change, market forces and trends. For instance, mobile phones have changed the spending priorities of teenage girls. Where once, their pocket money would be spent on cosmetics and clothing, a significant percentage now goes on top-up cards.

DVD rental shops don't just compete with other shops selling DVDs but also cinemas and online film websites, as another example. So it's not just rival online businesses and bricks-and-mortar shops you need to consider when looking at competition, but anything competing for a slice of your target customer's disposable income.

Competition isn't always a negative however, and is increasingly seen as collaborative. In the online environment, affiliate marketing uses one website to drive to another, and while the websites aren't in direct competition, they offer similar sorts of items, target similar audiences or offer related products.

Researching and learning from competitors

That said, no matter how much you've set your heart on running a certain type of business in cyberspace and are convinced you'd do it better than the incumbents, it rarely makes sense to launch an online business in a saturated market. Too many 'me-too' businesses have come and gone to the dot com graveyard. Remember, you're proving the market as much as your online business.

As frustrating as it might seem, people don't always surf the internet with their heads and even if you present a better product for a superior price, some shoppers simply won't break habit or misplaced loyalty, so it's unlikely you'd ever take 100% of another business' customer base.

You should cross reference the number of competitors in your area and their USPs with your demographics in order to establish if there's room for another business. It could be that on reflection you identify a new USP that would give you a better chance of securing market share – and that's perfectly healthy. This process is all about proving the business viable so don't be scared to tweak the concept where sensible.

> **FROM THE EXPERTS:**
> **Simon Nixon, moneysupermarket.com**
>
> It's critical to check out the competition and see how they compare against your potential products.

Competitors should also provide a way of benchmarking your proposition and pricing. Visit their site, take in the customer experience, where possible speak to customers to get a feel for their reputation and try to identify as many places as possible where you can score an advantage.

➡ HOW TO EVALUATE YOUR WEBSITE

Take every opportunity you can to test your concept. It's likely you'll still be tweaking it a year from launch, but by then you'll have overheads, time constraints and running responsibilities to deal with, so take every chance you get while researching and starting-up to test, test and then test again. It's true that websites can be changed relatively easily, but it's expensive to do this so it's important to get the main part of the design fixed and then add features if necessary at a later stage.

Get your friends, family and business contacts to visit your site (if you have a basic version up and running) or explain the concept to them and ask them to give feedback. Website design has an important effect on how people interact with your site, which then has a bearing on sales and levels of 'stickiness' and we'll be covering more of this later on (see p.121). If you don't have a basic version of a site that people can link to (all you really need is your homepage), design a mock up that you can send out and invite comments and criticisms. Consider conducting an email survey – after all, you are launching an online business. If you intend on selling products online, give them away in exchange for honest feedback. It's important to try and sell as well. You'll quickly find out if your prices are too high, or on the flipside, if you're shifting units like hotcakes, then perhaps you're not charging enough.

Feedback

For any concept testing you do, make sure you record the results, it's all good for tweaking your model and also compelling evidence to use in your business plan and when pitching for finance; even for PR.

The founders of Innocent Drinks constantly refer to the day they tested a selection of initial smoothie recipes out on visitors to a jazz festival asking people to place their empty cups in either a 'yes' or 'no' bin under the banner 'Should we quit our jobs to make these smoothies full-time?'

The more feedback you can get, the closer you'll be to selling products people actually want once you're open and hopefully you'll be building customer and brand awareness along the way.

Things to remember:

- It's too much hard work to start an online business if you're not fully committed to seeing it through. Know what you're getting into before you start.

- If you don't have enough experience, get some before you launch.

- Talk it through with friends and family. They may still offer support even if they're not convinced by the idea.

- If you can't do it alone, think long and hard about the type of person you want as a partner.

- Identify a USP from the very beginning.

- Do your research, and make it thorough.

- Know your competition inside out.

- The online world moves at a rapid pace, so keep up to date with the latest developments.

STRATEGY

DEVELOP

S

IN

2

Business planning and finance

How to write a business plan

A business plan is a must-have for any serious start-up. It aims to capture your company's financial aim, its operations and its present and future direction. Without a business plan, you can wave goodbye to raising any finance, as it's the first thing any potential backer, be they friends, family, bank or private investor, will want to see. You won't be able to actually write it yet, though. For that, you'll need to compile all the data that the rest of this section covers.

In this chapter we'll cover

- How to write a business plan
- The different types of business plan and the many uses you can put yours to

- Budgeting for the year
- Forecasts
- Trading projections
- Deciding your prices

WHY YOU NEED A BUSINESS PLAN

Don't be overly daunted by writing a business plan – it's not difficult and if you do it, it probably won't be tedious either – in fact, if anything, it will help to reaffirm why you are doing what you are doing by giving the reasons for the business being established, including your goals, aspirations, prospects for future growth and what features will set it apart from the competition.

Tim Waterstone, founder of bookseller Waterstone's, did not have the most auspicious of starts when it came to writing a business plan. He visited his local bank, where the bank manager asked for 16 copies. Tim later found out that the plan was used on an internal training course to illustrate the type of business no self-respecting bank should invest in. But the rest, as they say, is history.

Certainly, there's no avoiding writing a business plan; and the more you embrace it the more you're likely to actually find it a meaningful and useful process than merely a way of appeasing the bank. A good business plan will give you something to constantly refer back to when making tough decisions and strategy calls, and should be a working document you update as the business progresses.

IN MY EXPERIENCE:

Glenys Berd, LoveThoseShoes.com

If you can't get the fundamentals of your business plan onto one side of A4 then more pages aren't going to make things any better. Remember, build your business to make money at very low volumes as it will always take twice as long for things to happen than you think. Halve the revenue and double the costs and if it still flies, then go for it.

Doing a business plan isn't as hard as you might think. You don't have to write a doctoral thesis or a novel. And the good news is that there are plenty of business plan templates available that you can research to guide you in the process – you can download them from the internet or even consider asking your bank what sort of document it expects to see. You can also carry out a SWOT analysis, a method for describing your business proposition in terms of these factors that have the most impact. Essentially you nominate the strengths and weaknesses, and then identify threats and opportunities. (see p.332 for an example).

Don't worry too much about the design and layout of a business plan at this stage, though. Much like CVs, people often obsess unnecessarily about the supposed best format, structure, length and lay-out when what's far more important is that the document contains all the necessary information and is easy to understand. In the heady days of the dot com boom, many entrepreneurs' business plans were scrawled on the back of cigarette packets, but these days you'll need to come up with something more substantial.

FROM THE EXPERTS:
Nick Robertson, ASOS.com

Our business plan was written on the back of a cigarette packet but the exit strategy for our investors was a little more defined.

➡ WHAT TO INCLUDE

Ask yourself the following questions. How are you going to develop your business? What timescales are you looking at? Who is going to be involved, and in what capacity? How are you intending to manage the money?

A standard business plan outlines the following:

- What your business and your website will do
- Who your customers will be
- Why people will buy your products
- Evidence this market exists and its potential
- Evidence of why your business will survive when others don't; that is, an analysis of the competition
- Who you are and why you're going into business
- Why you believe you've got the skills and expertise to run an online business; your qualifications and experience
- Details of any other directors or key management
- How you will fund the setting up of the business
- How you will repay any money you borrow
- What your ongoing costs and overheads will be

- Sales and revenue forecasts for the first 12 months of business
- Details of suppliers and contracts
- Your goals for the first 12 months and then beyond that

That might sound fairly exhaustive, but it should be. Your business plan should present a watertight argument as to why and how your online business will work. If it doesn't, then you should be asking yourself if the business is still such a great idea.

➡ HOW TO GET STARTED

However unique your business idea, there will be companies elsewhere doing something similar, and undertaking some market research on these will help you understand your target market a little better. Companies have been classified into various categories by the UK government under the Standard Industrial Classification (SIC) system; start by identifying your particular class and identifying your SIC code. This will then help you search for data on your competitors and other industry participants. Then, seek some data from sources such as Cobweb (www.cobwebinfo.com), which produces various business profiles. This will enable you to obtain an external perspective on the characteristics of similar firms in your field.

Assess demand levels

One of the most difficult things to predict is the level of demand for your products or services. The general rule is to use conservative estimates on likely demand and to use proxies where data is hard to come by. One should also use proxies to help even when the idea is innovative or unique, rather than plucking figures from the air, or claiming there are no comparative figures available.

What to avoid

Cash not profits

How often have you heard small business owners saying they simply haven't got time to plan? The reality is, probably all too often, that many businesses draw up a business plan only when they need it for a specific reason, such as to raise finance. But the busier you are, the more you need to plan.

Most people think in terms of profits instead of cash. When you imagine a new business, you think of what it would cost to make the product, what you could sell it for, and what the profits per unit might be. We are trained to think of business as sales minus costs and expenses, which equal profits. Unfortunately, we don't spend the profits in a business. We spend cash. So understanding cash flow is critical. If you have only one table in your business plan, make it the cash flow table (see p 336).

Inflating your ideas

Don't overestimate the importance of the idea. You don't need a great idea to start a business; you need time, money, perseverance, and common sense. Few successful businesses are based entirely on new ideas. A new idea is harder to sell than an existing one, because people don't understand a new idea and they are often unsure if it will work. Plans don't sell new business ideas to investors, people do. Investors invest in people, not ideas. The plan, though necessary, is only a way to present information.

IN MY EXPERIENCE:

Glenys Berd, LoveThoseShoes.com

Any business anywhere needs to be well run – so it's necessary to have the skills, knowledge and probably most importantly, good staff and cash flow management. An open mind is also important, so you learn from your mistakes as you go along and don't keep repeating them. The technology, idea and person behind the business are just the things that gets it off the ground in the first place.

Leave out the vague and the meaningless babble of business phrases (such as 'being the best') because they are simply hype. Remember that the objective of a plan is to secure results, and for results, you need tracking and follow up. You need specific dates, management responsibilities, budgets, and milestones. Then you can follow up. No matter how well thought out or brilliantly presented, it means nothing unless it produces results.

Sales projections

Sales grow slowly at first, but then shoot up boldly with huge growth rates, as soon as 'something' happens. Have projections that are conservative so you can defend them. When in doubt, be less optimistic. Consequently, be honest. Don't exaggerate revenues and underplay overheads in order to make the plan work. Bank managers will have seen thousands of applications in their time and will see straight through it – and, of course, you'll be kidding yourself and invalidating your business plan as a useful document, as well as wasting your time. If anything, veer on the side of caution.

Many entrepreneurs say that, with the benefit of hindsight, when planning a business you should halve the income you anticipate and double the expenses you expect to pay – any discrepancy in your favour will be a bonus. Others insist they would never have secured the funding they needed without a few white lies and that whatever you ask for the bank will give you 20% less. Ultimately it's your call, but remember, your business plan should plot your progress and skewing it for any purpose limits how much it can help you.

> ### ✦ TIP
> Your business plan should plot your progress so be realistic about anticipated levels of profit – you need to strike a balance between what you know you can achieve and what will sway investors in your favour.

Using your business plan

Tailor your plan to its real business purpose. Business plans can be different things: they are often just sales documents to sell an idea for a new business. They can also be detailed action plans, financial plans, marketing plans, and even personnel plans. They can be used to start a business, or just run a business better. In all these different varieties of business plan, the plan matches your specific situation. For example, if you're developing a plan for internal use only, not for sending out to banks or investors, you may not need to include all the background details that you already know. Description of the management team is very important for investors, while financial history is most important for banks.

Your business plan should cover several areas in detail, but you'll need to strike the right balance between being concise and being overly verbose – the latter will irritate more than it impresses. Potential investors will be far more concerned with being

> ### ✦ TIP
> Use your business plan to prove to yourself that your business can survive and prosper, not just as a tool to accessing finance.

able to access key information than with whether you have flair with words. Where appropriate use bullet points and break up the text; bite size chunks of information are far easier to absorb. Don't leave anything out but keep it brief; people can always contact you if they need to know more.

> FROM THE EXPERTS:
> Nick Robertston, ASOS.com
>
> The key to our business plan was to be flexible and understanding – don't get into a market unless you understand it thoroughly. This was particularly true when we launched the business as the internet was evolving so quickly – we were changing our business model on a day-by-day, week-by-week basis.

➡ DIFFERENT TYPES OF BUSINESS PLAN

Start-up plan

The most standard business plan is a **start-up plan**, which defines the steps for a new business. It covers standard topics including the company, product or service, market, forecasts, strategy, implementation milestones, management team, and financial analysis. The financial analysis includes projected sales, profit and loss, balance sheet, cash flow, and probably a few other tables. The plan starts with an executive summary and ends with appendices showing monthly projections for the first year.

Internal plans

These are not intended for outside investors, banks, or other third parties. They might not include detailed description of company or management team. They may or may not include detailed financial projections that become forecasts and budgets. They may cover main points as bullet points in slides (such as PowerPoint slides) rather than detailed texts.

Operations plan

An **operations** plan is normally an internal plan, and it might also be called an internal plan or an annual plan. It would normally be more detailed on specific implementation milestones, dates, deadlines, and responsibilities of teams and managers.

Strategic plan

A **strategic** plan is usually also an internal plan, but it focuses more on high-level options and setting main priorities than on the detailed dates and specific responsibilities. Like most internal plans, it wouldn't include descriptions of the company or the management team. It might also leave out some of the detailed financial projections. It might be more bullet points and slides than text.

Growth and expansion plans

A **growth** plan or **expansion** plan, or new product plan will sometimes focus on a specific area of business, or a subset of the business. These plans could be internal plans or not, depending on whether or not they are being linked to loan applications or new investment. For example, an expansion plan requiring new investment would include full company descriptions and background on the management team, as much as a start-up plan for investors. Loan applications will require this much detail as well. However, an internal plan, used to set the steps for growth or expansion funded internally, might skip these descriptions. It might not include detailed financial projections for the whole company, but it should at least include detailed forecasts of sales and expenses for the company.

Feasibility plan

A **feasibility** plan is a very simple start-up plan that includes a summary, mission statement, keys to success, basic market analysis, and preliminary analysis of costs, pricing, and probable expenses. This kind of plan is good for deciding whether or not to proceed with a plan, to tell if there is a business worth pursuing.

➡ BUDGETING FOR THE YEAR

Predicting figures for the first year of your business when you are just off the starting blocks might seem a little premature but when you're working out your costs, it's essential that you plan for the first 12 months – not just your start-up costs but overheads too. To make this more manageable, break these down into one month, six months and then first year budgets.

This will help you to plan your business finances, assessing areas such as how much money you have and how much revenue you need to generate your target profit. Budgeting will also be a good measure of whether your business plan is along the right path, or whether it needs adjusting.

For a full budget and to see how viable your business is you'll need to balance revenue forecasts against costs. It's just as crucial to work out and keep track of how much you're spending, not just the sales you hope to get through the site. Without expenses any forecasts or even sales prove very little as regards how profitable your online business can be. The good news is that it's far easier to work out reliable costings than revenues, especially if you veer on the side of caution.

Begin by looking at all your **initial start-up costs**. All the costs of getting your online business up and running go into the start-up expenses category. These expenses may include:

- domain name and hosting fees
- initial stock
- computer equipment
- online credit card sales
- website design costs

This is just a sample list and you probably won't have trouble adding to it once you start listing your costs.

Your **operating costs** are those expenses that your business will incur on an ongoing basis; essentially what you'll need to pay out each month. They may include:

- your salary
- staff salaries

- telecommunications
- website maintenance
- utilities
- stock
- storage
- distribution
- promotion
- loan payments
- office supplies
- maintenance
- professional services (ie accountancy fees)

Again, this isn't a complete list and outgoings will vary from month to month. However, once you've completed your own lists you should have a fairly good idea, even if they're ballpark figures, of what revenues and/or funding you're going to need to support your business over

TIP

As well as estimating sales figures, it's essential to work out and keep track of how much you are spending, in order to build up a full picture of your budget.

a month, six month and yearly basis. These figures should go into a financial budget plan towards the end of your business plan which also takes into account, of course, how much money you can realistically make.

➡ MAKING REVENUE FORECASTS

Sales forecasting is notoriously difficult and the point where many business plans fall down. This is because either the business owner is hopelessly optimistic or the plan only succeeds in proving the business isn't viable because of the number of sales needed to generate a profit. Similarly, the cost that goods would need to be priced at is unrealistic or the cost of sustaining the business until it breaks even is unsustainable.

The biggest challenge is that you don't have any previous sales history to guide you. This is hopefully where your market research can help with examples of sales figures for online businesses operating in a similar market. Also consider what stage your search engine optimisation (see Part 5 for more information on this) is at – how easy will it be and how long will it take for people to find your site online?

However, this isn't entirely adequate as it's highly unlikely you'll perform at a similar level to your competitors for perhaps up to a year.

The simplest forecast is to start by working out what you hope to be selling within six months. Work this out per unit per day so you have a gross sales figure and multiply that by the number of 'opening' days in a month. Technically speaking, an online business is open 24 hours, 365 days of the year. Next, look to scale proportionately from month one, where you're unlikely to have many sales, upwards to month six. You can then extrapolate that scale over 12 months for an annual sales forecast.

In addition to that one forecast, carry out the process three times with a pessimistic, optimistic, and realistic outlook. Next try and put a real-time calendar next to your 'month one', 'month two' etc taking into account the peaks and troughs in trade you anticipate and are suggested from your research. Many online businesses see huge variations season-by-season, with many taking over half their annual profits during the build-up to Christmas.

Once you've worked out your financial outgoings (both initial start-up and ongoing costs) you can put the two together to produce a clearer analysis of the viability of your business on paper and when your business will break even.

Begin by compiling month by month expenses and sales forecasts. In the same way you accounted for peaks and troughs in sales, look at months where you expect expenses to be higher than others. For instance, if you cater for the Christmas rush you may buy far more stock in September, October and November than other months of the year.

 TIP

Ensure you take seasoned peaks and troughs of your business into account.

Again, ensure you prepare three income/outgoings projections: pessimistic, optimistic, and realistic. Also try and account for the fact that the price you can purchase stock for will hopefully decrease as your sales levels increase. However, that's a calculation you probably want to reserve for your optimistic forecast unless you've already got such an agreement in place with your suppliers.

While your calculation will inevitably alter from month to month (something you'll need to be wary of when managing cash flow) the point where your sales equal your expenses is where you 'break even' and hopefully go on to generate profit.

There are some formulae used to demonstrate this:

Break-Even Point (£) = Fixed Costs ÷ Gross Margin Percentage
For example: An online business buys portable fans for £10 each, marks them up and sells them for £20. Their monthly expenses (fixed costs) are £12,000. This means the break-even point would be £24,000 or 667 units.

£12,000 ÷ (10/20) = £24,000

This level of information should give you a much more powerful overview of not just how viable your business is, but what funding is required and when. It also enables you to pre-empt when you may need assistance with cash flow or credit.

Having this at your fingertips won't just impress investors and the banks but should also give you a much firmer grasp on your buying decisions when it comes to actually sourcing stock, for example.

➡ DECIDING YOUR PRICES

If you are planning an online retail business, before you make any forecasts, plot any projections or arrive at a principal sum you'll need to borrow to start your online business, you need to think about roughly how much money you can make from the products or services you intend to sell. As it's difficult to tell exactly how much you'll sell, it's safer to start by looking at how much profit you can make per item sold, often referred to as 'per unit'. To do this, you'll need to start setting prices.

Exactly how much you intend to sell individual items for might seem like minutiae that can wait until later when you have 'big vision' considerations such as securing a bank loan, finding premises and creating a brand. However, it's actually a much bigger factor in deciding whether your business will work than any of those, and as such needs to be at the forefront of your planning. You can't possibly know how feasible a business is without being clear about the fundamentals of any operation involving sales: ie how much money you make per transaction.

The two key elements of deciding your prices will be:

1. The costs of goods
2. Your operational expenses

The cost of goods should include any associated cost in the development or acquiring process such as packaging and delivery etc. Operational expense incorporates all your overheads such as staff wages, marketing and technology.

The sum of the two costs subtracted from the price you set will, in theory, be the profit you generate – although, of course, there are many outside influences that have the potential to impact on your bottom line.

You'll need to begin by ensuring you know exactly how much your product costs to the point it goes through the virtual till. You'll also need to establish the running costs of your business. You probably don't know all of them at the moment so make estimates and keep tweaking and adjusting the calculation when you know more.

If you don't have a thorough grasp of your figures, you'll be exposing your business to risk. For your online business to succeed, you'll need to know at all points what any item you sell costs you to buy and how much you make when you sell it.

At the end of the day, you need to make money from the business. It is profit that will pay your salaries and your mortgage and what the bank manager or investor needs to be confident about if they are to lend you money.

Developing a pricing strategy

Knowing what a product costs you and the percentage profit you'd like to make is rarely all it takes to make your online business proposition viable, unfortunately. The missing key consideration in this equation is, of course, a customer base that wants to buy at the figure you've set.

For some products such as official sports merchandise or branded items like iPods the manufacturer will have a suggested or minimum pricing policy to avoid price wars or heavy discounting which, while making things easier, will limit ability to make the profits you've factored for.

Think carefully about setting up an e-commerce business selling such goods as it's likely you'll be competing against large retailers who have the advantage of buying in bulk and multi-million pound marketing budgets. If price was one of your USPs it's unlikely you'll compete here.

Check out the competitors

Do some research and find out what your competitors are charging – if you decide to undercut them, you'll need to work on keeping your overheads at a minimum. For example, if you decide to undercut a shop selling premium home electronics, you'll need to negotiate a superior supply rate with the manufacturer, which is highly unlikely. So you'll need to find another way of reducing your overheads, perhaps by offering a 'no frills' website design that requires little maintenance and which you can update yourself.

While budget or no frills online shops make some of the most profitable e-commerce operations, it's a strategy not without risk. Squeezing profits means there's little margin for error and you'll feel the impact of a drop in sales far quicker. Larger chains will know this and if they see you as a threat, could match your prices (even if it meant they'd be selling at cost value or even a loss) to force you out of business.

In the current economic climate, consumers are likely to be steered more by price than by anything else. On the plus side, the main resource many will be heading straight for will be internet comparison sites and providing you've invested in search engine optimisation (we'll cover more of this later in Part 5), your site has a good chance of being indexed and therefore noticed.

While people expect to find deals and bargains on the internet, being the cheapest isn't necessarily the best strategy to pursue. Many small internet businesses have managed to steal a march on the competition by providing value that is not price-based, and focusing on qualities such as luxury and service.

Other pricing strategies

Business manuals will talk about a few other strategies for pricing:

Keystone pricing

This refers to the practice of simply doubling the cost price of a product, but it's fairly academic now as there are few products which offer the chance to make such a mark up.

Multiple pricing

This is an increasingly popular strategy and a clever way to incentivise shoppers into buying more than they originally intended, or to shift poor selling stock. It involves offering multiple products grouped together for one superior price. For instance, buying two pairs of jeans selling individually for £30 for £50, or one pair of the jeans and a £20 t-shirt for £40. It presents the illusive feeling of value for the shopper and if you've ensured you're still making your desired profit, can be a very effective pricing model. Buy one get one free food menus are another prime example, where the profit made on the cost of drinks for two people almost always generates enough to compensate for any profit sacrificed to entice people through the door.

Round down pricing

There's also a school of thought that shoppers round down a price instead of rounding it up, so it's better to price goods at £9.99 not £10. That's increasingly dismissed now though and some shops actually play on the notion of transparency and honesty of a rounded £10 price tag. In reality, other than all those missing pennies, it's unlikely to make a massive difference. If you're able to drop prices to, say, £9.49, than perhaps the argument becomes relevant again.

Discount pricing, sales and price reductions

These are also a crucial part of pricing strategy and certainly shouldn't be confined to traditional sales periods such as January. Neither should it be viewed as a way of shifting dead stock.

Loss leaders

The most effective and common discount pricing method in retail, and the one that causes the biggest challenge for online businesses competing with large chains and supermarkets, are loss leaders. The idea is that by pricing one in-demand item at cost price (or even below), you'll entice customers who will buy more than just that item. You'll have noticed supermarkets frequently competing for the lowest price for staple goods.

Cost-plus pricing or mark-up pricing

These are the terms commonly given to deciding your own profit amount or percentage to be added to its cost; it is likely to be where you'll start but it shouldn't be your only consideration. Most successful pricing strategies will include several of the pricing policies and almost always at the same time. This can be confusing, but always revert to the basic principle of knowing what you're paying and what you're making at the price you're selling at. Stick to that and you can't go wrong.

➡ PITCHING YOUR PLAN

If you have a great business idea and the figures work on paper you're half way there. However, you'll never realise that potential of a great business plan unless it's presented in the correct way.

Before presenting your business plan double check to make sure that the document looks professional. No typing, grammar or spelling mistakes. Use graphs and charts where appropriate and titles and subtitles to divide different subject matters. While the aim is to make it look good, you should avoid expensive documentation, as this might suggest unnecessary waste and extravagance.

The length of a business plan depends on individual circumstances. It should be long enough to cover the subject adequately and short enough to maintain interest.

Practise your presentation in front of the mirror, family and friends and get them to critique you.

IN MY EXPERIENCE:

Simon Wadsworth, The Retail Factory

Imagine having to stand in front of a group of potential investors or a bank, and persuading them to part with their cash – the business plan is really a sales pitch.

Things to remember:

- Don't just write your business plan for your investors, use it as your main guide for the direction of the business.

- Include all the necessary detail but don't overload it. A good plan is thorough but succinct.

- Be realistic with your sales forecasts. It's better to underestimate than overestimate.

- Have three different trading forecasts – pessimistic, optimistic and realistic.

- It makes sense to work on your budgeting, revenue forecasts and pricing strategies at this point to ensure that your business plan is as accurate as possible.

2.2
Raising finance

J ust under a decade ago, raising finance for a dot com business seemed almost like a no-brainer. When the bull run ended for hundreds of companies that used the internet to deliver products, goods and services, only a handful of dot coms emerged resilient. Today, raising funds for an online business is a very different story.

While the beauty of an online business means that the overheads are relatively low (you won't for example, need to invest in premises, at least in the early stages), expect your business plan to be scrutinised much like any other one when you are looking to raise finance.

If you have a couple of thousand to spend and don't want to borrow anything, then an online model is perfectly do-able. But you'll still need funds to build your website and to invest in its growth, as well as meeting marketing costs and these can mount up. Financing a website, for example, can cost as little as £500 for the most basic offering or as much as £20,000 for one with the potential to dominate a market.

So if you're serious about having an online business for the long-term, you might need to take on outside investors at a later stage, and perhaps sooner than you think. Jamie Murray Wells, for example, founded internet business Glasses Direct in 2004 and decided to take on outside investors towards the end of that year, at the same time as expanding the business from his home to offices.

In this chapter we'll cover:

- Finance options
- Friends and family loans
- Equity finance
- Banks
- Applying for a loan
- Pitching for finance
- Paying yourself

FINANCE OPTIONS

It's likely you'll have three funding options for setting up an online business. The first is to fund it yourself, the second is to use a bank and the third is to seek equity investment from private investors. The route you choose may, to some extent, depend on the business model you have adopted. It may be nearly a decade since the dot com boom and bust, but some online business models still tend to be regarded with a certain degree of caution when it comes to raising finance, and the current economic climate is not making the search for funding any easier.

IN MY EXPERIENCE:
Jamie Murray Wells, Glasses Direct

The low-risk way to go about raising initial finance is to do it in chunks over a couple of years. You need to allow six months to raise each stage of finance.

There are also various grants specifically set aside for people looking to start an e-commerce or online venture. Of course, the current economic conditions mean that raising finance is a tougher proposition than ever before so it's even more important that you prepare cash flow projections in your business plan that adequately reflect what you need to borrow.

FROM THE EXPERTS:
Simon Nixon, moneysupermarket.com

If you're looking to raise finance in the current economic climate, you've got to have a very compelling idea, a strong business case and a proven track record in the industry you are targeting.

Funding it yourself

Funding it yourself should be a fairly simple decision: either you can or you can't. There really is no such thing as free money so for pure efficiency nothing makes better financial sense than resisting borrowing altogether. On the downside, it's an option few are blessed with.

FROM THE EXPERTS:
Simon Nixon, moneysupermarket.com

As a business, we never had to raise external funding – we grew organically. We never bit off more than we could chew so the business evolved with gradual costs that we were in control of.

It's also an area some are distinctly uncomfortable with. Ask yourself if you really want to invest your life savings in a venture when it's possible to borrow from a bank. Possibly not. If that's the case, the first question to ask is: if you're not convinced why should any other investor be? The second is: how much can you comfortably put in? Banks are likely to expect you to match whatever they lend you and you'll do well to find an individual who'll give you their cash to play with while you keep your own in the bank.

TIP
It can actually be sensible to fund start-up costs with a loan and save a slice of your own cash for running costs and future investment; borrowing for a loan will be less expensive than an overdraft or credit cards. There could also be tax advantages to structuring how much you invest yourself and borrow. This is the point where you should get an accountant on board who'll advise you on the best way to proceed.

Friends and family

'Fools' is often jokingly tagged onto the end of this duo and not just for its alliterative appeal. Start-up businesses are risky investments, even when they're backed by the canniest of high yielding, wealthy business veterans. Yet strangely, people seem willing to part with princely sums for decisions based on little more than emotion, love and the conviction someone they believe in will look after their money. There is no shortage of successful internet businesses that started off with funding from friends and family. ASOS is one and Steve Pankhurst and Jason Porter, founders of the phenomenally popular website, Friends Reunited, raised £50,000 from friends who received shares in the company in return.

As you're the one looking for the money, not blindly pumping it in, this might not concern you. Indeed, it's easy to turn the situation on its ear and let your determination to get your dream online business up and running convince you that you're actually doing them a favour by letting them share in your success. If all goes well, this could be true.

It's what happens if it doesn't that you need to consider. Many friendships and relationships have gone out of the window as the bailiffs have walked through the door, so think long and hard about raising funds from friends and family. Explain the risks, get any investment tied up in a legally binding contract that secures the rights of all those who have invested and ensure that those investing are aware that there is no guarantee that the business will succeed. Funding from friends and family, when it works, will leave you the freedom to save bank financing for a later stage when you're looking to expand and grow.

FROM THE EXPERTS:
Nick Robertson, ASOS.com

We raised just over £2m from friends and family, with the condition that the business would float on AIM (the stock market for smaller, growing companies) in the near future. Everybody does something for something, so when we raised the money, we ensured we had an exit plan for investors that was defined.

Equity finance

Equity finance involves giving away a percentage of your business in exchange for the money you require to start or grow your business.

Equity finance usually comes from one or more wealthy individuals commonly known as business angels who are often experienced entrepreneurs with money to invest in other up and coming companies. While the reality is far removed from the drama of the TV show, these are the kind of deals struck on the BBC hit series *Dragons' Den*.

TIP

Equity finance is where you give away a percentage of your business in exchange for the money you require to start or grow.

It's also possible to raise equity finance through organised public or private funds which are usually run by either experienced entrepreneurs or investment companies. Private equity deals usually fill the gap between standard bank loans and venture capital deals, but can vary from anything from £10,000 to £250,000.

Venture capital (VC) works on the same principle but is run by large organisations and deals are usually in excess of £500,000, although this is rare for start-up businesses and the VC will usually expect to place someone on the board, so you'll need to be comfortable with this arrangement.

FROM THE EXPERTS:
Simon Nixon, moneysupermarket.com

Venture capitalists are looking for a business that has already proven itself and that can be taken to the next stage. I didn't like the idea of raising venture capital, as it meant having venture capitalists on your board and less control.

Private equity is certainly more common but not easy to find. However, if you've run an online business before or have a proven track record in your planned sector it might be that you'll find an investor willing to back you from day one.

TIP
There's one thing all advisers agree on: if you can keep 100% to start with then do so. Those in the investment world will no doubt argue it's way smarter to own 50% of a company worth £1m than 100% of one worth £100,000 – and clearly that's true.

The problem is that whatever you're giving away at the start won't be worth very much, so it's almost certain you'll lose a chunky slice of what in a few years' time might seem a meagre sum. It's far better to use debt finance and then refinance once you've in a better position to bargain from and can offer a greater chance of reward for the investor's risk.

Taking on an equity partner also provides a new sense of responsibility and pressure. With the money comes a need to create a substantial return in an agreed period of time and once you commit to that the decisions you make must become more focused on generating that return than what works for you in a lifestyle scenario. That can be a very healthy motivation and it's worth it if that's the type of business you want to run.

Regional venture capital funds

The Capital Fund: www.thecapitalfund.co.uk

South East Growth Fund: www.segrowthfund.co.uk

East of England Fund: www.createpartners.com

South West Regional Venture Capital Fund: www.southwestventuresfund.co.uk

Advantage Growth Fund: www.midven.com

East Midlands Regional Venture Capital Fund: www.catapult-vm.co.uk

Yorkshire and Humber Fund: www.yfmventurefinance.co.uk

Capital North East: www.nel-capital.co.uk

North West Fund: www.nwef.co.uk

Sources of business angel funding

Advantage Business Angels: www.advantagebusinessangels.com

Beer & Partners: www.beerandpartners.com

British Business Angel Association: www.bbaa.org.uk

Envestors: www.envestors.co.uk

Equus Capital: www.equuscapital.co.uk

Great Eastern Investment Forum: www.geif.co.uk

Hotbed: www.hotbed.uk.com

London Business Angels: www.lbangels.co.uk

North West Business Angels: www.nwbusinessangels.co.uk

Pi Capital: www.picapital.co.uk

SWAIN: www.swain.org.uk

Yorkshire Association of Business Angels: www.yaba.org.uk

Xenos: www.xenos.co.uk

(NB: some sources only cover certain areas of the UK)

IN MY EXPERIENCE:
Jamie Murray Wells, Glasses Direct

I received £650,000 of angel funding and many millions of venture capital. You need to be very creative about how you raise money. We really looked at how we could leverage debt and how to talk to a lot of different investors. We thought about different finance options such as friends and family, angel networks and venture capitalists.

Grants for websites

As well as exploring the opportunities above, as an online business start-up, you may qualify for certain grants to help launch your website. Contact your local authority in the first instance as the number of grants and amounts available varies between different councils. IT and e-commerce grants are normally available up to £1,000, to help you meet the costs of designing a website, purchasing a domain name and acquiring software. To qualify for these, your business will most likely need to be based in a specific region of the UK and will need to be operating in a certain sector, such as retail.

BANK OR DEBT FINANCE

Banks lent £44.8bn to small businesses in the 12 months to September 2007 representing an increase of 10% on figures from the same period in 2006, according to the British Bankers Association (BBA). This year, the figures are likely to be much less optimistic, with doom and gloom surrounding the state of the economy playing its part. The BBA has admitted that the pace of growth has slowed compared with the previous quarter and the same period last year and the onset of the credit crunch has meant that businesses will find it harder to secure loans from banks.

On a more positive note, earlier this year, the Government unveiled details of business loan schemes designed to offer help to small businesses across the UK that are having problems accessing finance from their banks. The schemes are aimed at encouraging the banks to lend more and will help those businesses that are having cash flow difficulties and those that are looking for investment for future growth.

There are three main packages available, and although not all of them apply to start-ups, they are worth noting as they are designed to help your business as it grows.

Working capital scheme: designed to help banks increase all types of lending, such as existing and new loans. The scheme is open to companies with a turnover of up to £5m.

Enterprise finance guarantee scheme: open to businesses with a turnover of up to £25m, to enable them to secure loans of between £1,000 and £1m, repayable over 10 years.

Capital for enterprise fund: this £75m fund will enable businesses to sell debt in exchange for equity.

As banks are continuing to make finance available, they should be your first port of call when looking to finance your online business. Banks are vastly experienced in helping start-ups and should be able to offer a number of finance packages tailored to suit your needs as well as providing a fair degree of support. A good bank manager should be able to give you a clear explanation of your options and what is expected to meet any lending criteria.

Be warned though, that banks see thousands of business plans and will see through any overly optimistic forecasts, dressing up of figures or holes in your business plan, so you'll need to ensure your research is comprehensive.

Choosing a bank

It's natural that you'll probably turn to your current bank first – after all, you are already familiar with them. At least half of a successful banking relationship relies on the ability to work with the bank manager who has been assigned to your case, rather than the bank itself.

Different banks offer different incentives such as so many years' free banking to open a business bank account as well as pricing and organising their charging mechanisms differently. Some offer a greater level of service and usually offer lower interest rates or higher charges as a result, while other banks specialise in keeping basic costs low but offering little service.

Even if you're keen to stay with your main bank, do shop around and examine the start-up packages on offer, if only to check you're not missing out on something offered elsewhere. If you are, negotiate.

While there are savings it's likely you'll ultimately derive more long-term value from finding a bank you're comfortable with, which makes the effort to listen and understand your business and, ultimately, will lend you the money you need to start-up.

Even if you've decided on a bank offering make sure you meet the bank manager you'll be dealing with. The relationship with your bank manager is absolutely fundamental to your success, especially in raising finance. Managers will have a threshold of loans they can sign off and even though you'll be assessed by the bank's credit and decisions programmes, having your manager onside will make a massive difference.

TIP

Be warned: bank managers will vary within banks, not just from bank to bank and it's essential that you have a good relationship. If you like a package at one bank but don't click with the manager, ask to see another. Alternatively, check your manager is experienced within your focus area; it could make a difference.

➡ ACCOUNTS

There's no escaping from it: you need to know your numbers. At any point you should know how much money you've got in the pot, how much you owe, what you're committed to in orders, any salaries you might be paying, how much your assets (stock, website and equipment such as computers) are worth and, if anything, how much you're owed. You should know what you've taken that day (preferably that hour) and what you're going to make for the rest of the hour, day, week, month, year.

You should know it and you should understand it. Otherwise you'll have no idea how the business is performing and no solid financial base from which to make decisions.

The basics you should understand are how to read a balance sheet of your income and outgoings, called a **profit & loss sheet**. Here's an example:

Profit & Loss sheet example	£	£	£
Sales/turnover			**60,894**
Opening stock (1st of month)	3,000		
And purchases made	24,253		
		27,253	
Less closing stock (30/31st of month)		4,278	
Cost of goods sold		31,531	
Direct labour costs		7,364	
			38,895
Gross Profit			**29,363**
Overheads			
Rents and rates	3,294		
Heat, light and power	783		
Insurance	106		
Indirect wages and salaries	7,296		
Marketing costs	571		
Printing, stationery and consumables	1,951		
Computer costs	758		
Telephone	939		
Depreciation of assets	3,697		
Legal and professional fees	750		
Bank and finance charges	264		**20,409**
Net profit before tax			**8,954**

We'll cover the finances you need to know once you're up and running in Part 7 (see p.281).

To begin with you certainly don't need to know much else, though. Not everyone is great with figures and this is where accountants come in. If you pay for any outside help in setting up your online venture, an accountant with experience in the sector will almost certainly prove useful and offer the best return on investment.

If you think you'll need the services of an accountant, though, find one early in the process. Too many people wait until the end of the tax year when the annual tax return looms, to sort out their accounts. By this time they are likely to have accumulated piles of paper. An accountant can sort this out for you but leaving it that long can make it an expensive and time-consuming process. Involve them early on and they'll get your financial data straight from the start and almost certainly find ways of making you some fairly significant savings. They can also give you some invaluable business advice in the early stages of your business when you might need it the most.

➡ APPLYING FOR A BANK LOAN

Bank loans are one of the most common and preferred type of finance for start-ups, suitable for paying for assets such as computers and for start-up capital and other areas where the amount of money you need is not likely to change.

Banks however have very clear expectations of what they want to see from your business plan before they'll give you a penny and it's crucial you bear this in mind.

They'll want to see you've accounted for all eventualities, your own income and been realistic about your anticipated revenues. They will have clear criteria you'll be expected to meet for them to be convinced they'll see a return on their investment. If you're at all unsure about your forecasts or figures it's worth speaking to a bank manager before submitting any loan application to see if you're heading along the right lines or need to have a rethink. It's far better to spend time at the beginning refining your plan and application for a loan than to start the process and find there is still a considerable amount left to do.

Depending on how much you want to borrow, banks will usually expect to see that you're matching what you're borrowing with your own money and could also ask for security against your home. This is something that puts many people off and can seem understandably frightening. If you reach this point and are having second thoughts, you're possibly not ready to start a business after all. What you're about to do inevitably involves a high level of risk. However, providing it works it's also full of rewards. If you're not convinced that the balance is in your favour you have to ask why the bank should be.

If you can't offer the security the bank is asking for, you could apply for a loan through the government's Small Firms Loans Guarantee Scheme which guarantees bank loans up to £250,000. While notoriously bureaucratic and inconsistent in its outcome, it is welcomed by all the main banks and did support 2,629 loans last year, with a total value of around £207m. The average loan value was £76,950.

TIP

As a rule of thumb, banks are likely to expect to see security for all loans above £25,000.

IN MY EXPERIENCE:
Simon Wadsworth, The Retail Factory

We funded the business through a mixture of our money and The Small Firms Loans Guarantee Scheme run by the government. We also used a factoring service to help cash flow.

If you're reluctant or unable to offer security or match the bank's lending the other option is to lower the amount you want to borrow. Providing you've a decent credit rating and can offer reasonable evidence you'll be able to afford the repayments, banks will often give sanctions to personal loans up to around £15,000 which can be used for start-up costs and repaid over a period of time, ranging from 36–84 months.

Banks will also offer you credit card and overdraft facilities, but will discourage you from using them for anything other than cash flow management and short term borrowing. That's not to say you can't use them however you see fit but, especially in the current climate, be very careful about borrowing anything you couldn't afford to pay back at very short notice or you could find yourself in real trouble over a relatively small amount.

 # PITCHING FOR FINANCE

Before we get into the detail of what you should say, how you should dress, and what banks and investors expect when you pitch for finance, it's important to highlight one all significant, and too often overlooked fact about borrowing money: banks (and investors) want to lend it.

Regardless of how bad the economic climate gets, banks and investors will always lend money if they're confident they'll get a healthy return. After all, they are in the business of making money. Your challenge then isn't to beg and grovel for any scrap of money you can get your hands on, but to present a compelling opportunity for them.

It's on this premise you should base your pitch. Remember banks are investing other people's money so they need to, as closely as possible, guarantee a return. They're certainly not gamblers. You'll need to present a clear, low risk proposition that demonstrates how the money will be spent and, crucially, how it'll be repaid and when. While investors might be entailing a slightly higher degree of risk and possibly expect to, they won't entertain anything but a sensible punt.

IN MY EXPERIENCE:
Simon Wadsworth, The Retail Factory

Have sizeable up front investment secured if you intend taking an existing market online as competition will be high and established players have significant advantages.

Preparation

Make sure you're 100% prepared. If you're actually making a presentation, be clear about all your facts and figures and know them off by heart. It's likely that a bank will have already read your business plan by the time you get to pitch or talk through your proposition so you should be prepared for questions that delve beyond the facts and figures.

If you are making a presentation, view this as good news that the bank wants to talk further. However, think what else they might want to ask you. Critique your own business plan or ask others to do it for you with a view to pre-empting any questions that stand out. Practising a pitch in front of family and friends can help prepare you and offer you tips on areas for improvement.

A clear concise answer will reassure the bank you're clear about what you're doing and that this matters to you sufficiently to have put the effort in. Don't attempt to try and answer a question if you can't; this only sends a message that you'll try and fudge. All investors prefer honesty so be upfront and admit you don't know, but suggest you could certainly find out. Perhaps even flatter them by thanking them for bringing it to your attention.

Appearance

Dress smart. If you are not in the habit of wearing a suit, put on a smart shirt and trousers/skirt. The fact that how you dress not how talented you are or how great your business idea is might determine if you get a bank loan or not is a contentious issue for many people. For others, wearing a suit demonstrates a sense of professionalism and desire to be taken seriously. Whatever your personal view, it's probably best to err on the side of caution and assume that the majority of bank managers will still expect you to dress smart. Neglecting to do so is risky and can put you on the back foot from the start. If you're someone who simply couldn't bear to change their appearance then by all means dress as you see fit, but be aware one of the most important attributes of a small business owner needs to be flexibility and your reluctance to adapt could be viewed as representative of your personality.

Otherwise, if you go into the room feeling confident you've put your homework in, have belief in your idea and are looking smart there's every chance the bank will believe you're the type of individual they're looking for. There are, however, no guarantees in business.

Dealing with a No

Rejection is something you should get used to quickly. There's every chance several banks will say no before one says yes. See each rejection as a learning experience or rehearsal for the one that says yes.

Find out why they've said no, as the feedback might be useful. Don't let it dampen your spirits though, there's always more money out there. And don't argue with the decision either. Disputing a bank's decision to say no is as futile as arguing with refereeing decisions; you're never going to change their minds.

➡ PAYING YOURSELF

Your business plan should include how and what you intend to pay yourself for at least the first year – and it's essential you include this in any borrowing that you take out.

It's true that banks and investors love to see you're making massive sacrifices to see your business get off the ground. If you can afford not to take a salary for the first few months or even the first year, they'll expect you to do this. It not only ensures all profits can be reinvested back into the business, but demonstrates just how badly you want to succeed and how determined you are.

That said, it's simply impossible for many people to do this and while an online business incurs relatively low overheads compared to other types of business, it isn't just for people wealthy enough to have six months' salary in the bag. If you can't survive without taking a salary out of the business, whatever you do, don't pretend you can. Trying not to pay yourself and hoping you'll somehow muddle through almost never works and is foolish to try.

Everybody has to pay a mortgage or rent; everybody has to eat; everybody has reasonable living expenses – and lenders do understand that. Not paying yourself a wage will just mean you end up borrowing elsewhere and, conversely, lenders can actually view that as bad management. Saying you can live on £500 a month when your mortgage is £1,000 a month isn't going to look too clever.

Lenders also dislike it when they lend an initial amount of money based on forecasts they've been told are realistic only for the borrower to promptly return needing more. Again that doesn't speak much for management or your forecasting skills.

It's far better to include your wage as a cost of the business. Indeed, it actually sets your business out on a solid model from the outset. Anyone who stepped into your shoes or acquired the business would expect to either earn a wage or pay a managing director a wage and your business model needs to be able to support that. For example, a business that claims to be generating a healthy profit of £50,000 but whose owners are effectively working for free, perhaps isn't as successful as it might first appear.

✦ TIP

So what's a realistic amount to pay yourself? There are very few statistics for average earnings for online businesses, but review your personal spending habits, assess how much you need to support your lifestyle, look at this figure and be conservative.

Having said that, don't expect to pay yourself a fortune. Investors won't appreciate you pulling up at the bank asking for a loan in a Ferrari dressed head to toe in Armani. If you're coming from a corporate background to escape the pressured rat race, be realistic. You're setting up your own online business and are expected to work hard first and reap the rewards later.

Things to remember:

- Consider your finance options carefully. What's best for you, straight loans or giving away a share of the pie?

- Make sure family and friends are clear about what they're getting involved in before you accept any cash from them.

- Be prepared when pitching. You need to know your figures inside out.

- Be realistic. It's better to ask for the cash in advance than ask for help when you're in trouble.

Legalities

Trademarks, domain names and copyright

Running a business comes with a host of legal obligations and it's essential that you protect yourself, your business and your customers from any potential legal threats. The internet is well established as a business model, but many related laws are still evolving so it's equally important to keep up to date with internet legalities as well as being aware of the basics.

The other point to bear in mind is that the internet gives you an instant global customer base – people from all over the world can log on to your site and buy goods or services. As such, you'll need to be aware of rules governing global e-commerce as well as regulations that relate to trading in the country you are based in.

While other areas such as cash flow, planning and PR (public relations) make your business, failing to stay inside the law – no matter how tedious it feels – can break it. This chapter will cover the legal obligations you need to consider when starting and running an online business, covering issues such as securing a domain name, copyright and distance selling regulations. We'll also look at the kind of insurance you will need to protect your customers, your staff and your business should anything go wrong.

In this chapter we'll cover:

- Trade names and trademarks
- Securing your domain name
- Privacy policies
- Terms and conditions
- Copyright
- Legislation that affects you
- Maintaining a database of customers
- What can go wrong

➡ TRADE NAMES AND TRADEMARKS

Trademarks are signs, symbols, logos, names and colours (things that can be described in writing) that differentiate your business from that of your competitors. It's one of the ways customers will recognise your company and its products, and businesses generally spend a lot of time and effort on names. The right name for the business or a product could help you stand out from the crowd; the wrong one could place you in a legal dispute.

Trademarks are powerful and valuable assets. Protecting your trademarks should be an important consideration whenever a new business or product is being launched. Trademarks help customers and other businesses identify your products and services and also the reputation and goodwill that has been built up. All too often others may wish to copy, and attempt to share your success. This may or may not have an immediate effect on turnover, but others using your name could prevent trademark registration and the exclusivity it offers. In addition, any adverse publicity or poor reputation your rival may acquire may affect your business if customers cannot differentiate between the two names.

To register your trademark, apply to the Intellectual Property Office. Do some research to ensure that no one else has applied for the same or a similar trademark and make sure you are satisfied with your choice, as you can't alter your trademark once your application has been submitted. List all the goods and services you want your trademark to cover, as again, you can't add any later.

Your biggest challenge with trademarks is likely to be ensuring you are not infringing someone else's. It's vital that you don't do this or that you take action if you think someone is using your trademark. A quick search on the internet will help point you in the right direction, but it might not be the definitive answer as to whether a trademark has been registered or not, so if in doubt, err on the side of caution. Follow up an internet search by carrying out an exhaustive trademark search. The more unique your trademark, the more likely it is to be successfully registered.

✦ TIP

You could also check with a trademark adviser to see if the name and logo you have chosen are not infringing any existing trademarks. If you have big plans for your website, it makes sense to register your trademark from the outset.

Having a trademark, however, does not mean you can automatically use this for your domain name – someone may have already registered the domain name you want for the same, similar or different goods and services. You can take legal action if you think someone is using a domain name to pass off their goods and services as yours or if someone has taken out your trade name as a domain name in order to try and sell it back to you. Nominet.uk is the registry for .uk internet domain names, and provides a dispute resolution service for .uk domain names.

IN MY EXPERIENCE:

Glenys Berd, LoveThoseShoes.com

It's important that you choose a site name that can be trademarked; a lot of names can't as they are just common words. The best way is to use something made up and original.

 # SECURING YOUR DOMAIN NAME

Assuming that no one has beaten you to it, anyone can register a domain name. Nominet.uk, the internet registry for .uk domain names, encourages companies and individuals to register a domain via an ISP (internet service provider). This is because the majority of ISPs are Nominet.uk members. Once you have registered with an ISP, they will then submit the application to Nominet.uk, ensuring a more thorough and secure process.

However, contractual terms, charges and service levels vary dramatically, so it is worth noting that shopping around is key to finding the best deal for you. Some ISPs offer domain registration, others include free web space and email addresses or more specialist options.

Always read the small print and ask to see copies of the terms and conditions for domain name registration as well as your right to move across to another ISP if you are unhappy. If you don't register with an ISP there are around 6,000 companies who have domain registration facilities. It can often be worthwhile paying the extra to deal with an up-front reputable company that won't let you down.

> ### ✦ TIP
> Even if you are not going to use your domain name straight away, you should register it first. A list of accredited ISPs are available through the InterNIC website at www.internic.co.uk and you can carry out a search on the site to see if a domain name is available. Nominet.uk also provides a list of accredited ISPs.

There are some online packages and ISPs that will offer you a domain name for free such as Microsoft's Office Live. However, you may still wish to register the domain name independently.

Once you have decided upon the company which is going to register your name, the process is generally swift and painless.

First, you will be asked to pay a fee to secure your domain. Once this is done, the company will then send you a template of your registered domain name to the network information centre (NIC). Each country has its own NIC, which is a centre where all the details of registered domains are held.

If your registration is accepted the company you have chosen will set up a domain name system (DNS) entry. Essentially, this means assigning your name to a name server that collates and keeps all registered names so that your domain can be found on the internet. The process takes between two and three days.

Once these stages are complete you are alive and kicking on the internet and are able to use your name.

What does it cost?

There are a variety of packages on offer. Some are cheaper than others and it often depends on what other services are included (for example, registration fees and support service fees). Fees can range from free to £200 for .co.uk names – but this depends on levels of service and support.

Prices will vary, depending on what your business needs, but there is an average price you will pay for single domain name registration.

To protect your brand, it's worth registering your domain name in both .com and co.uk versions, which are the top-level domain names for businesses. If you have high hopes for your online business, it might be worth registering several variations of the name, or versions in which it might be misspelled, to ensure you catch as many potential customers as possible.

> **TIP**
>
> Domain names are normally registered through an agent known as an internet service provider (ISP). The price you pay (an annual fee) and service you receive will vary from agent to agent, but it's essential you use one that is registered.

➡ PRIVACY POLICIES

A privacy policy is information displayed on your website that lets your customers know what you do with their personal information. It's an important consideration – with the rise in identity theft, people are becoming extremely sensitive about how companies handle their personal data and are therefore cautious about exactly how much they reveal. If your customers submit details about themselves as part of a registration process or during a transaction (this could include personal and financial information or data related to their activity on the site), they will expect such data to be heavily protected. Failing to provide information on this will erode any trust you may have built up.

The policy describes what you will do with such information. For example, you may use it to help improve the customer experience on site, for your own marketing purposes or for records of transactions. A privacy policy is particularly important if you intend to run a website that collects personal data from its customers. Most websites normally include a link to their privacy policy on the bottom of the website homepage.

A privacy policy should ideally include the following:

- Any information you might collect on your customers
- How you intend to use this information
- When you might use such details to contact customers
- Whether you will be disclosing this information to anyone else
- People's choices regarding any personal details they may have submitted, such as how to update or remove these
- Cookies and how your site uses them

You can use this opportunity to inform customers that if they choose to opt in with their personal information, you may use this to send them marketing communications or to pass their details on to carefully selected third parties.

➡ TERMS AND CONDITIONS

You need to include terms and conditions to give users information about your website content and what they can and can't do with it. These usually appear on a link at the bottom of the homepage – by using your website your customers accept your terms and conditions in full. The detail of these depends very much on what type of online business you are running but they should basically contain the following information:

- An introduction to the site and who you are
- Your limitations of liability (a disclaimer)
- The fact that the website contains material which is owned or licensed to your business, and that reproducing it is not allowed unless it is in accordance with the copyright notice (see section below for more on this)
- Any rules relating to use of chat rooms or forums – for example, you will remove any malicious postings or offensive wording
- Rules related to unauthorised use of the website
- Contact details

TIP
You can download an example of different terms and conditions to use from www.businesslink.gov.uk

➡ COPYRIGHT

The growth of the internet has led to the infringement of copyright becoming more and more commonplace. Many people have fallen foul of copyright rules by inadvertently copying material without first asking for permission. As soon as a piece of work is created, copyright comes into force.

You have full rights of ownership over any content you create or have created for your website. An internet copyright notice sets out the copyright position of your website content, such as whether you will allow the material to be downloaded or distributed by visitors. An example might be:

This website and its content is copyright of 'business name' – © 'business name' 2007. All rights reserved.

Don't ever copy material from other sources to display on your website without first asking permission, although in some cases, this isn't necessary. This includes if the material is going to be used for teaching purposes, for news reporting and for reviewing, for example.

LEGISLATION THAT AFFECTS YOU

Insurance

As you're yet to open the virtual doors to your business, it's unlikely you've much enthusiasm for thinking about all the things that could go wrong. However, while it's not the sexiest element of starting-up, ensuring your business has the necessary insurance cover will protect all the hard work you're putting in elsewhere.

Some insurance cover is required by law, others make total business sense even though they seem an expensive overhead to take on when first starting out. Instead of looking at what insurance will cost you now, you should consider the implications of a disaster on your business.

Employers' Liability Insurance (ELI)

If you employ one other member of staff you are required by law to have this cover or you could face a fine. This type of insurance helps you meet the cost of compensation for staff if they are injured while working. Policies generally start at around £10m worth of cover to include legal expenses. However, ELI doesn't mean you're untouchable. You must still honour all your health and safety obligations, carry out regular risk assessments and have all the appropriate paperwork to back this up. To find out more about your health and safety obligations visit the HSE website: www.hse.gov.uk.

Product liability insurance

Although not compulsory by law, if you are selling products online, you'd be very foolish not to take out this kind of cover, as it will protect you against claims made against your business by members of the public and you need to protect yourself should anything untoward happen. However, it's still your responsibility to ensure your goods meet all the necessary requirements.

Premises insurance

You might not have premises as such that your customers visit, but as your business grows, you may consider renting or buying premises to accommodate staff and technology developments. Your online business' chances of survival will be severely compromised if the actual premises are damaged. You can take out cover against damage as a result of any number of unforeseen occurrences such as floods, fires, or malicious damage. Landlords will sometimes cover certain aspects of buildings damage. The more measures you take to limit damage, such as CCTV and metal roller shutters, the easier it'll be to keep premiums down.

Contents insurance

As premises insurance only covers the physical building, you'll need to make sure the contents of your business are also adequately insured against damage or theft. This will cover stock, technology, furniture and anything else included in the policy.

Business interruption insurance

While covering you against the costs of repair and replacement, contents and premises insurance won't necessarily help with any income you lose while your business is closed as a result of unforeseen events. This is where business interruption insurance comes in.

When the Buncefield oil explosions occurred in December 2005 several companies with warehouses in the vicinity went out of business overnight. Online fashion retailer ASOS could easily have been one. It lost £3m worth of stock in its busiest week of the year, cancelled and refunded 19,000 orders and closed the site for six weeks. Fortunately, CEO Nick Robertson had the company insured to the hilt with a firm disaster recovery plan in place. Business interruption insurance covered ASOS for the lost business and included provision for an extensive advertising campaign for relaunch. When the site began trading again in late-January 2006, it took record sales on its first day.

FROM THE EXPERTS:
Nick Robertson, ASOS

Having our warehouse next to a fuel depot was probably not the smartest move. We closed the business for six weeks and had a holding page in place of the website, announcing a clearance sale. Having insurance and customer details was crucial – we emailed all our customers who were affected and gave them refunds.

➡ REGULATIONS

As an online trader you are subject to the same laws as other retailers, such as the Consumer Protection Act, the Sale of Goods Act 1979, and the Supply of Goods and Services Act 1982, as well as a few internet specific ones.

If you're planning to sell online you will need to be familiar with the Electronic Commerce (EC Directive) Regulations 2002. Nearly all commercial websites are covered by these regulations so there's no getting away from them, and no excuse for not knowing them.

To comply, your customers must have certain information including your business' name, physical address and email address. You must also give details of any professional body with which you are registered, and display your VAT registration number if you have one.

The Companies Act 2006 also requires all UK companies to state the company registration number, place of registration, and registered office address on all of their websites. You do not have to display this information on every single web page. It is commonly placed on the 'About us' section of the site.

As well as displaying the appropriate information on your e-commerce website you must also be aware of the Distance Selling Regulations. These regulations are designed to protect the consumer when they are not actually in the presence of the vendor during a sale. The regulations cover sales made via the internet, email, phone or mail order or digital television. However, they do not apply to business-to-business transactions.

Under the regulations, the seller is required to:

- Give consumers clear information including details of the goods or services offered, delivery arrangements and payment, the supplier's details and the consumer's cancellation rights before they buy. This information must be provided in writing.

- Give the consumer a right to a cooling-off period to cancel the sale contract within seven working days.
- Give the consumer written confirmation of their order.
- Deliver the product within 30 days unless otherwise agreed.

There are however, some exceptions to rules surrounding cancellation of contracts for businesses offering accommodation, transport and catering or leisure services. This only applies where services have been agreed for a specific date or time period. Other exceptions include the sale of customised or perishable goods, sealed audio or video recordings, or opened software, as well as items or services bought via auctions.

You can find out more information on the regulations by visiting the website of the Office of Fair Trading at www.oft.gov.uk.

➡ MAINTAINING A DATABASE OF CUSTOMERS

One of a business's greatest assets is its list of customers, which is effectively a source of past sales and potential future revenue. A database can also help you identify key trends and important information such as your most and least profitable customers. With an internet business, your customer database is likely to (or hopefully will) contain thousands of email addresses.

Keeping this up to date can be time-consuming and challenging though. People's email addresses change on a regular basis and most people have more than one email address (for example a business and personal one) so it's essential to keep customer details up to date and ensure you don't duplicate. Email data decays rapidly – people can change from one email service provider to another with alarming frequency and with people changing jobs more often these days than in the past, work emails can quickly go out of date.

Getting up to date details of email addresses and other customer information that can help you with your marketing, such as age, marital status, and family situation can prove to be a challenge, though. Consumers are increasingly wary of providing any information about themselves while online, largely as a result of the rise in identity theft. There have been many instances, documented in the media, of criminals finding out people's personal details and using them to open bank accounts and get credit cards, loans, state benefits and documents such as passports and driving licences in these customers' names.

Spam is another reason people are reluctant to part with their email address. Most of us have experienced the frustration of entering our e-mail address on one website and soon after receiving volumes of spam e-mail. So what steps can you take to build and maintain a customer database, and encourage customers to part with their details?

- Be clear at all times about how you will be using customer data. Your privacy policy should cover this in detail and ensure you stick by what you say.
- Safeguarding personal information you collect goes without saying. We'll cover this in Part 4, in the security section (see p.143), but try not to use obvious names for your database files such as 'customer details', 'email list' or 'subscribers'. Spammers are skilled in scouring the net for email addresses they can harvest and naming files in an obvious way is playing right into their hands.
- Clean your database on a regular basis – as mentioned, email data decays far more rapidly than postal or telephone data. Every time you send an email newsletter or alert for example, make a list of bounced email addresses that you can clean your original list against. You might have an impressive database of 50,000 customers and their details, but it will be worth very little if only a small portion of these details are correct.

Cleaning your data

There's little doubt that email marketing campaigns are far more cost-effective to run than postal ones but if you don't ensure the email addresses you hold on your customer database are valid ones, you will be wasting time and money.

If your basic customer information is misspelt, out-of-date or inaccurate, you won't be able to gain your customers' trust. No one likes to receive an email where their name is misspelt – more often than not, it will be deleted. Clean data helps you to maintain good customer relationships by minimising the likelihood of annoying or offending your customers through data inaccuracies.

➡ WHEN THINGS GO WRONG

In Part 4 (p.143), we will cover issues your business might face, such as security threats and the risk of hackers hijacking your customers' details for identity theft purposes or harvesting their email addresses and sending unsolicited emails. Job listings website Monster.com for example, suffered a security breach in early 2009, during which time hackers obtained unauthorised access to the database and downloaded account logins, as well as the corresponding personal information. The website warned that the stolen data could be used to launch phishing attacks.

In such instances, it's imperative to react quickly to restore customer confidence. When running an online business, it can be tempting to try and sort everything out remotely. But don't just rely on email to sort things out, get on the phone if you have to and drag people out of bed if necessary – after all, this is your dream business and it could be your livelihood on the line.

When you make calls, ensure you record or take copious notes of discussions, including times that calls have been made, the content and the person you spoke to, plus their telephone extension.

Online retailer Amazon.com came under fire a few years ago when consumers said the retailer did not adequately protect customer details. Amazon responded immediately by promising that it would heighten its protection on customer data, refrain from selling its customer database to marketers and narrow the wording of its exceptions. The company also promised to provide specific examples of how data is used and what data it gathers from customers.

IN MY EXPERIENCE:

Glenys Berd, LoveThoseShoes.com

The legal side is something you simply have to get right. Check out what the big boys do, such as Amazon, to see what you need to show and do so without spending a lot of money on lawyers.

Things to remember:

- Keep up to date with new legal developments, as the internet is a fast-moving environment.

- Look after your customer data – people will not trust companies where data breaches occur.

- Ensure your privacy policy is clearly written and easy to find on your website.

- Always contact your customers as soon as something happens that may affect them.

- Clean your data regularly and consider outsourcing this if you don't have the resources in-house.

Registering your business

Naturally your energies will be focused on getting your online business launched and trading – but before you can start this you'll need to register your business. What can seem an overly-complicated and laborious process isn't actually that difficult once you've established the basics and gathered all the information you'll need to register.

You'll need to decide what legal structure your business will take, be it a sole trader, partnership or a limited company, complete the necessary paperwork and then submit your registration to Companies House, one of its licensed agents or HMRC. The legal implications and paperwork differ for each structure so make sure you pick the one that is best for your business and fulfil all the required steps to forming that type of company.

In this chapter we'll cover:

- Sole traders and partnerships
- Limited companies

- Registering as a limited company, including how to name your business and the company officers you need

➡ THE DIFFERENT LEGAL BUSINESS STRUCTURES

There are essentially three legal or accounting structures you can choose from when starting your online business. You can go it alone by being a sole trader, team up to form a partnership or operate a limited company. Choosing the right structure is important, so you'll need to give it some serious thought. It is possible to switch between different structures after you've started your business. For example, you may start out as a sole trader, and then decide to register your business as a limited company or partnership. You will save yourself a lot of work if you establish the most appropriate business structure beforehand though. Below is an explanation of the different legal structures you can choose from when starting your online business and guidance on which structure is most suitable for both you and your web venture.

Sole traders and partnerships

Registering as a sole trader, essentially just you on your own, is relatively straightforward, record-keeping is simple and you get to keep all the profits after tax. As a sole trader you are the single owner of your business and have complete control over the way it is run. However, and this is quite a crucial factor, the law makes no distinction between the business and you as the owner. This means you'll be solely responsible from your own personal wealth for any debts if the business runs into trouble. This differs to a limited company (which we'll come to) where debts, but also profits, are liable to the company not the individual.

If you choose to run your online business as a sole trader you must register as self-employed with HMRC within three months of your trading start date otherwise you could be fined and charged interest on any outstanding tax and National Insurance payments you owe.

If you're forming your business with one or more other people you need to register as a partnership. As with the sole trader model, each partner is responsible for any debts the business incurs. Each partner is also self-employed and receives a percentage of any returns from the business, which they are then taxed on. The partnership as well as the individuals within it must submit annual self-assessment returns to HMRC and keep stringent records on business income and expenses.

Starting an online business as a sole trader or partnership venture can prove the easier option initially, especially if you don't have ambitions for rapid growth. There is less paperwork involved and you will not need to register and send annual returns to Companies House. It is also much easier to withdraw funds from the business as essentially, all profits make up your own earnings. However, as well as the financial liability that lies at your feet, as a sole trader it is much more difficult to grow the business and you may find it harder when dealing with creditors and suppliers.

Limited liability companies

Registering as a limited (Ltd) company is probably the best legal structure to go with if you have any intention of growing your web venture beyond the smallest of operations. As well as offering you a degree of personal financial security should your business run into financial difficulties, it will also give you more credibility when seeking finance or credit. Registering your online business as a limited company also makes tax and succession planning a lot easier.

If you expect your online business to maintain a healthy amount of trade and return high levels of profit you will definitely want to go with the Ltd model. Profits will be subject to corporation tax, which currently stands at half the 40% income tax rate you could end up paying as a high-earning sole trader. Limited companies pay corporation tax on profits and company directors are taxed as employees in the same way as any other people you employ.

A limited company is very different from a sole trader model where there is no legal distinction between you and the business. A limited company is a separate legal entity to the people that run it. Profits and losses belong to the company, and the business can continue regardless of the death, resignation or bankruptcy of the shareholders or directors. Your personal financial risk will be restricted to how much you have invested in the company and any personal guarantees you gave when raising finance for the business. However, if the company fails and you have not carried out your duties as a company director, you could be liable for debts as well as being disqualified from acting as a director in another company.

> **TIP**
>
> If you decide to register your business as a limited company you will need to allow more time to deal with the paperwork as it is a much more administration-heavy process than running a business as a sole trader. It will also require more stringent record keeping and auditing throughout the entire life of the business.

You get help with this from an accountant, of course, and if you have aspirations of your business employing staff and making healthy profits (who hasn't?) a limited company is almost certainly the structure for you.

➡ REGISTERING AS A LIMITED COMPANY

To register your business as a limited company you must submit the appropriate paperwork to Companies House, the official UK government register of UK companies or one of its registered formation agents. What follows is a guide to the process, and documents and requirements involved in turning your business into a legal entity.

> **TIP**
>
> Download all the forms you need to fill in at www.companieshouse. gov.uk. You can fill these in online, or send them to Companies House by post (see the website for address).

Although it is possible to register a limited company yourself, unless you have done it before you are probably going to need to engage the services of a solicitor, accountant, chartered secretary or a company formation agent. Formation agents use their own software that works directly with the Companies House systems. If you want to register your company electronically (most are registered this way) you will need to have the specific Companies House electronic interface – hence the need for a formation agent. However, you can still deliver the physical documents directly to Companies House without the need of a formation agent or specific electronic interface.

It can be far easier to register using an official formation agent and that's what most people do. There are lots of these agents listed on the Companies House website and all use slight variations of the same software. Look at several and pick one that sounds the most helpful or whose online system looks the easiest to use, providing the prices are sensible.

Finally, you can buy an 'off the shelf' company. You will receive a ready-made limited company that has designated company officers listed on the paper work. You simply transfer your name, and the names of any other company directors once you receive your documentation. The process can be completed on the same day and many accountancy firms will have several ready-made limited companies that they can sell to you. This is the quickest option, and with the exception of registering the company yourself, can often be the cheapest too.

Costs

Prices for formation agents can be up to £200 depending on the level and speed of service you require. A key advantage of using a formation agent is the advice they can give you on compiling the necessary documents and the right structure for your business. Companies House does not provide this service when registering, so if you are unfamiliar with the process it is advisable to get help to avoid errors. Going through the registration process yourself can be time-consuming, especially if you make a mistake, and Companies House staff will not advise you about specific matters such as the content of the documents you are required to submit.

Alternatively, you could also get assistance from an online registration company. The standard service usually costs £30–£100 including fees, but since some documentation needs to be posted, registration usually takes three to eight days, although there are a few same-day services now coming onto the market. This option is usually cheaper than using a formation agent, although you will not receive the same level of personal service.

TIP

It's worth noting that it costs as little as £15 to register directly with Companies House so what you're paying for is the service of an agent to help you through the process or an online agent's software.

Company officers

Once you have established whether or not you need help in establishing your company you will need to decide on who the company officers will be, and what your business will be called.

Limited companies are required by law to have named company officers. Company officers are the formally named directors and company secretary as stated in the Articles of Association, one of the documents you submit to Companies House that is explained in more detail below. It is a legal requirement for company officers to be in place at all times and for their names and current addresses to be written on the registration documents. If there is a change in company officers, Companies House must be informed straight away. All private limited companies must have at least one director and a company secretary.

Company directors

Company directors are the people that manage the company's affairs in accordance with its Articles of Association and the law. Generally, anyone can be appointed company director and the post does not require any formal qualifications. However, there are a few exceptions:

You are prohibited from being a company director if:

- You are an undischarged bankrupt or disqualified by a court from holding a directorship
- You are under 16 (this only applies in Scotland)

Company directors have a responsibility to make sure certain documents reach the registrar at Companies House. These are:

- Accounts
- Annual returns
- Notice of change of directors or secretaries
- Notice of change of registered office

Directors that fail to deliver these documents on time can be prosecuted and are subject to fines of up to £5,000 for each offence. On average, 1,000 directors are prosecuted each year for failing to deliver accounts and returns on time so it is not a responsibility that can be taken lightly or ignored.

Company secretary

This person's duty is not specified by law but usually contained within an employment contract. For private limited companies, secretaries are not required to have any special qualifications.

The main duties of a company secretary are to:

- Maintain the statutory registers
- Ensure statutory forms are filed promptly
- Provide members and auditors with notice of meetings
- Send the Registrar copies of resolutions and agreements
- Supply a copy of the accounts to every member of the company
- Keep or arrange minutes of meetings

Naming your business

As well as establishing your company officers, you will also need to pick a company name to register the business with. The name of your business does not have to be the same as the name of your online venture, however. If you open three shops, all with different names, you can still run them as one limited company. You will need to establish your company name before you think about filling out your registration documents, as there are certain rules to consider.

The name you choose for your company must:

- Feature the word 'limited' or 'ltd' at the end. For Welsh companies the equivalent 'cyfyngedig' or 'cyf' can be used, but documentation must also state in English that it is a limited company.
- Not be made up of certain sensitive words or expressions (listed by Companies House) without the consent of the Secretary of State or relevant government department.
- Not imply a connection with central or local government.
- Not be offensive.
- Not be the same or similar to one that appears in the Index of Names kept by Companies House.

You can search the index of business names already registered on the Companies House website free of charge. If your chosen name is too similar to another, an objection can be lodged within 12 months following the incorporation of your company and you could be forced to change it. See more about the process of choosing a company name and the legal implications that go with it, in the *Identity* chapter on p.113.

Documents to submit

When registering a limited company there are four documents that must be provided to Companies House. These are:

Memorandum of Association

This document sets out the following:

- The company's name
- Where the company's registered office is located – England, Wales or Scotland
- What the company will do – this can be as simple as: 'to conduct business as a general commercial company'

Articles of Association

This is where you set out the rules for running your company. You must state how shares will be allocated and transferred, how the directors, the secretary and your meetings will be governed. And if you decide not to adopt the standard articles of the Companies Act in full (known as Table A) you have to submit your amended version when registering. Once your company is incorporated you can only make changes if the holders of 75% of the voting rights in your company agree, so it pays to get this right at the outset.

Form 10

This document gives details of the first director(s), company secretary and the address of the registered office. Company directors must also give their name, address, date of birth, occupation and details of other directorships held in the last five years.

Form 12

This document is the statutory declaration of compliance with all the legal requirements of the incorporation of a company. It must be signed by either one of the company directors or secretary named on Form 10, or the solicitor forming the company. The signing of the document must be witnessed by a solicitor, a commissioner for oaths, a justice of the peace or a notary public. Form 12 must not be signed and dated before all of the other documents are completed, signed and dated.

Once all that's been submitted your online business is a fully-fledged limited company, but don't forget: the legal structure you choose when you start trading isn't set in stone. You can alter your structure, or even float on the stock market should your business become successful enough. For now though, you can concentrate once again on the launch!

Things to remember:

- Assess your business structure options carefully. It may be cheaper to stay as a sole trader but are the risks to your personal finances worth it?

- When registering as a limited company make sure you've gone over your documents meticulously before submitting them. If you make a mistake you'll have to submit them again.

- Search the list of submitted business names on the Companies House website before you get your heart set on one. It may not be available.

4

Setting up

Identity

B uilding an identity for your company is one of the most enjoyable aspects of starting an online business and is probably an area you have devoted a great deal of time to. The identity, including the business name, website URL, branding, style and image of your online venture is what creates the experience for your customers and helps to make your business stand out from the competition.

Think of your website as a virtual shop window. It's the first thing customers will see and what they will base their impressions on. The identity of your website will be the first step in the realisation of your desire to start your own business so make sure it reflects what you set out to do in owning your own online business.

In this chapter we'll look at:

- Choosing a name/website URL
- Establishing your identity
- Style and design

- Branding your site, this includes your logo should you choose to have one

➡ CHOOSING A NAME/WEBSITE URL

What's in a name? Business names are funny things and their importance polarises opinion. It's easy to understand the ambiguity. Think of any successful online retailer, brand or product that you buy from and in almost every instance, the name is the very last consideration and least important factor in your conscious buying decision.

That said, business names are how we all identify and refer to those online businesses and products and it's often what we remember most. And while some names bear little significance to anything, the smartest names undoubtedly form part of the branding and identity that pulls us in.

It's safe to assume that you won't improve a poor online business with a great name, and a great one shouldn't suffer too badly from an average moniker. Let's face it, what you sell or provide, for what price and how good your service is will determine whether people like your business or not.

But that doesn't mean names aren't important.

A good name will:

- Draw attention and attract people to your site
- Communicate a clear message about your business's identity
- Lend itself well to PR and set you apart from the competition

A poor name will hinder all of the above. So they're the basic principles you should work on when planning a name.

Website names

A website name is known as the URL (uniform resource locator) or the domain name (see p.89 on how to secure your domain name). This is what your potential customers will use to find your website. It needs to be something that is memorable and ideally not too long. It also needs to be easy to spell, to eliminate the chance of customers making typos. If your business is selling baby accessories, you'll want to include the word 'baby'. A straightforward domain name for example www.leathershoes.co.uk will not only instantly signal to customers what your business is about, but will also be useful for search engine optimisation and marketing purposes. When your traffic logs show people typing your site's name into the search engines to reach you, it's a good indication that your site is developing a strong brand.

Don't make the mistake, however, of naming your company simply because it's a well-searched word or term. It's not about appearing on the most searches, just the right ones and near enough to the top. Andrew Selby had to rebrand his iPod accessories company because the original name, I-magine (a clever enough name as a shop), returned nothing but John Lennon search results.

> **TIP**
>
> When thinking about names that'll work on the internet, think search. Nine tenths of visitors to all websites arrive at your website via a search engine. For search, read Google.

Admittedly, many of the best domain names have already been taken so you'll need to exercise some creativity and do some careful research. Ideally, your business should have one name and this will be used for the domain and to name your website, becoming your brand. This will be the main way that customers will know your business. When it comes to domain names, the advantages and disadvantages of using a short or a long one have been hotly debated. There are several arguments to support both sides. A long domain name is likely to rank higher on the search engines and you'll have more room to describe your service or product offering. A short domain name however is easier to remember, faster to type into a browser and chances are it will be spelt correctly.

> **TIP**
>
> Make a note of several domain names that you like and test it out among friends and family. Ask them questions such as: do they like the sound of it, what comes to mind, is it catchy and memorable?

You can use up to 67 characters although few websites' names ever use that many, as you run the risk of people misspelling the address and being directed elsewhere, and long names tend to be less punchy and memorable. There are a variety of extensions to choose from, such as .com, .co.uk, .biz and .net. Try to choose a domain name with .com as this is still the most popular extension.

As a new online business, it's likely that your ideal name has already been 'taken' or registered by another company, but there are certain tricks of the trade that can help you get around this. Many businesses have simply added in a hyphen to names that have already been taken. While this means that search engines can distinguish your keywords better, your potential customers may not realise your website name has a hyphen and will simply type in the words, so you run the risk of sending them somewhere else entirely. You'll have to weigh up just how important that name is and whether it's worth using with a hyphen.

Choosing a website URL

- Register a domain name which has a popular keyword that is relevant to your sector
- Have several domain names in mind as your preferred choices may already be taken
- Keep it short and therefore memorable
- Ensure the URL is easy to spell

TIP

If you decide to incorporate your business you need to make sure you pick a name nobody else has. If you run your business as a sole trader this is not as much of an issue but you still need to be aware of the legal implications of choosing an offensive moniker, or one with certain banned words. Check Registering Your Business for more on the legal aspects of choosing a name.

➡ ESTABLISHING YOUR IDENTITY

When you decided to start your online business, you probably had a vision of running a virtual company, selling goods or providing services that you are passionate about.

You shouldn't lose site of that vision. It's quite possibly changed a little from the planning stage where you further identified USPs, pricing strategies and differentiators, but essentially it's still that vision, combined with these factors, that makes up your online business's identity.

IN MY EXPERIENCE:

Glenys Berd, LoveThoseShoes.com

In terms of 'identity' use your gut instinct, it will most likely give you the best identity out there.

It's certainly not just the products you sell, the prices you charge or the services you provide that will determine whether people visit your site and part with their cash. You'll need to create a site that attracts customers and encourages them to spend.

IN MY EXPERIENCE:

Jamie Murray Wells, Glasses Direct

In terms of building an online identity, the web allows you to put the customer first and you should make the most of this. Provide as much information as you can about your product and include features such as reviews.

Too many online businesses don't communicate that identity, however. For some reason they have it in their head but lose sight of it when actually building the site. That's where the discipline of being a business person as well comes in.

Don't neglect your USPs

Keep going back to those USPs: other than products it sells or services it provides, what is your online business? What will it look and feel like? If it's upmarket premium goods you're selling to a customer with a high disposable income then the identity, from logo to design, price to packaging should reflect that. In turn, if you sell eco goods or ethically sourced products you'll want that to be entwined in all that you do.

Many businesses talk about core values and many entrepreneurs like to draw up a list of values that reflect their online business's identity as a reminder to themselves and staff. It can certainly pay to constantly revisit them to ask: is this what we're about? Are we sticking to our USPs?

Once you sacrifice those USPs – start selling different products or offering new services simply because you think you can make a nice return or compromise on quality to generate sales, for example – your business stops becoming what you started out to be. This can be particularly difficult during the early days of trading and site development, but your whole sales story has been built on a unique identity and losing sight of it is a major, but commonly made, mistake.

IN MY EXPERIENCE:
Mark Leather, Country Products

The worst sites to me are those inhuman, large corporate sites, where there is never a mention of a person's name, no address, no telephone number, or sites that hide behind a nameless, faceless 'brand'.

BRANDING YOUR SITE

Branding differs from identity as it focuses more on what people think of your business and what it stands for. Whether you like it or not, people will form opinions about your site from the moment it launches. They'll have views on what it looks like, the products or services it offers, the customer service and assign it, consciously or not, among the other brands they're exposed to and buy from.

The likes of Disney, Nike, Apple and Coco-Cola have distinctive brands that are instantly recognisable and which speak for the sector they are in. Think Disney and family and entertainment spring to mind. Apple, meanwhile is linked to technology, innovation and cutting-edge products, while Nike is not just about running shoes but about the sporting industry and athleticism. Brand names also need to be catchy and memorable. eBay founder Pierre Omidyar had originally named the business Echo Bay Technology, but when he tried to register it, he found it had already been taken by a Canadian mining company. So he chose the next closest name by shortening it to eBay.

How much you care about branding is likely to be dependent on how much you intend to grow your business. If your sole ambition is to make a nice living from it, you probably don't need to think too much about building a brand, simply maintaining your reputation should suffice. If your intentions are to expand and to one day establish a heavyweight presence online, then branding needs to be at the forefront of your thinking.

Either way, return sales will be crucial so you should be thinking about how people think about your business, and that means more than having a flash site. A great internet brand comes about from creating a great user experience. It's the way you treat customers, the level of interaction you look to have post-sale and how you communicate this in your advertising or marketing. This is particularly important for online businesses – as all transactions are carried out remotely, the whole notion of customer service can seem rather anonymous, with queries dealt with via email or through a call centre, rather than face-to-face, as in the case of a physical shop. Take Amazon as an example. The online retailer has built its reputation partly on the back of its customer service, delivering goods when promised and replying promptly to customer queries.

Deciding what your brand should stand for is about considering how you want people to view you. That should come, essentially, from who your customers are and what you're looking to sell. If you've researched your customers fully you should have a clear idea of their tastes, the ways they prefer to shop, the experiences they like and in turn don't like, and that should give you a clear idea of how you should look to position your brand to them and the outside world.

Your logo

One of the key aspects of brand-building is having a logo that is simple, distinctive and which is recognised beyond the boundaries of language, using either words or images. Coca-Cola for example uses a text-based logo whereas Apple's is marked by a symbol. Consider the likes of internet brands eBay, YouTube and Google. eBay is known the world over for its colourful logo – it's instantly recognisable. Google may be the most popular search engine in the world, but its multi-coloured logo can probably lay claim to equal levels of popularity. Its logo changes with the seasons, or to mark a famous person's birthday, so much so that people are attracted to the site just to see what logo is being used on that day. Video-sharing site YouTube's distinctive red, black and white logo was designed by its founder, Chad Hurley.

As you establish your brand, the logo and colour scheme for your site should be consistent and clearly visible on every page. If you look at various other websites, you'll notice that most logos are displayed on the top left of the pages. You should scope out the identity of your business before you commit time or funds to a logo, as it should communicate identity and your USPs to your customers at all times.

Your logo is one way people will remember you and it's certainly how many customers will form their first impression of you. Images and colours are very powerful methods of communicating messages and you want to think carefully about the logo that should emblazon your website and how this will be translated offline. Your brand shouldn't just exist in cyberspace – ensure that it is reflected offline, such as on your business cards, stationery, packaging and any promotional items.

That said, don't rush out and commission a brand identity group. It's often just a case of finding a logo that simply and clearly radiates your business identity. The fuller brief you can write about what your business is, who your customers are and what your USPs are, the more a web designer will be able to produce something close to what you're looking for. It's a subjective decision of course though, so it's always an idea to give an example of logos you like and don't like. You could consider seeking the advice of a professional consultant who can carry out some market research around designs that work online and with focus groups. It won't be cheap, but you'll be getting professional advice.

Alternatively a logo created by a freelance designer or small design company might give you the independent edginess that makes you stand out. For most of you you'll have no option but to pursue this route. Another option is to ask local design colleges or students to submit entries, incentivising them with a prize or vouchers for the site once it's open. There are a number of websites for budding, freelance or small design companies where you can pitch such competitions or request enquiries, with www.logosauce.com probably being the best. Just post your brief (remember to be as detailed as possible), set a deadline then wait for 'bidders' to upload their best efforts and contact the ones you like.

TIP

Having a number of designs to choose from certainly helps you decide what works well, so even if you decide to give the project to one person or company ask them to give you at least a couple of options and colour schemes. You're likely to favour one and then ask to see several variations of that until you're happy.

Logos should work well in a number of sizes; whether it applies to you or not, think postage stamp and billboard. Forward plan to ensure what works for you as a start-up will work for you as a burgeoning online business. Even if this isn't your goal, it'll almost certainly be how many of your customers will want to see you.

Don't make the mistake, however, of thinking everyone shares your idea of good taste and smart design. They won't. This isn't your house you're choosing a theme for; it's your online business. While it might be 'yours' its success will be dependent on others wanting to go there, so unless you're selling the type of product that lends itself to the weird and wonderful, remember that niches are niches for a reason. Instead, apply the property development mantra: design for the broadest range of people you're looking to sell to as possible.

Do your research, go online and look at how your competition style their identity and check out popular brands to see what they have got right. Also force yourself to study a successful website whose identity doesn't particularly appeal to you and consider what it is that makes it work for its customers.

> ### 🎯 TIP
> As a rule create a detailed brief, get a number of designs to choose from and go with what works best for your customer, not you.

Branding for you as a start-up online business owner shouldn't be a massive preoccupation but as it's closely aligned to what your identity and overall sales story is, it is a very worthwhile exercise trying to draw up a list of words you'd like others to describe you with. This will make a useful reference document to look back at when making buying decisions and help form marketing decisions and, eventually, a fuller branding strategy.

Style and design

Think of your website as a virtual shop window – in order to attract customers, you'll need to work on the style and design. It's one of the most important aspects of any web business, as it's the first thing your customers see so it's easy to understand why so many entrepreneurs invest time, effort and money into the look and feel of their site.

IN MY EXPERIENCE:
Jamie Murray Wells, Glasses Direct

The style and image of a website is very important. Have a look around at different sites and see what you like, make a hit list of different types of different sites for your designer and take some screen grabs.

Good design isn't just about making the site look good or attractive – it's about making it functional, reliable and easy to navigate round. There's little point in having an attractive, attention grabbing, iconic website if it's not user-friendly – your website has to be both appealing and functional. Sport clothes retailer Boo.com famously went bust in 2000, a victim of style over substance. Its website could not be seen by people who used Macintosh computers and the heavy use of graphics and 3-D images meant that only those people who had a high bandwidth internet connection could access the site.

Online customers also tend to be rather impatient and choosy – with the amount of sites available on the world wide web, there's little reason for them to persevere with your site if it fails to deliver to their expectations. So it's crucial you get the style and design right from the start. Of course, the benefit of an online business is that tweaks and changes can be made if necessary as your site develops, but you want to get the look and feel right from the start and ready for launch.

> ### ✦ TIP
> Good design isn't just about making the website look good or attractive. It's also about ensuring that it is functional, reliable and easy to navigate round. You want your customers to keep on coming back – if they have a good experience on your site, they are more likely to return.

With the myriad of sites available online, it can seem that the more research you do into competitive and non-competitive sites, the more varying types of styles and design you uncover. Don't get put off by the vastness of style choice available – there are some basic rules of website style and design you can follow. These include ensuring that there is enough white space between text so your pages do not look too cluttered, keeping fonts consistent across pages, and ensuring a navigation bar is visible across all pages so your customers can get round the site with ease. It's also about using the same colours and logos across all parts of the site and making sure that graphics and texts are well-placed on the page.

> ### ✦ TIP
> A cluttered website will turn customers off. You need to strike a balance between a website that is both aesthetically pleasing and functional – ensure that there is enough white space between the text so that pages can be easily read.

Things to remember:

- Identity must go hand-in-hand with every aspect of your planning.

- Don't agonise over your business's name but do give it careful consideration.

- Spend some time on your logo, but not necessarily lots of money.

- Keep your branding as consistent as possible.

Technical issues

T he technology you choose will play a vital role in the success of your online business. With the amount of choices available today, it can seem quite daunting choosing the right software packages and deciding which equipment to invest in. With the speed at which technology changes today, another worry is that whatever you choose to invest in will date quite quickly. The bottom line is that you should invest in what your budget dictates – it's easy to be seduced by the latest deals, gadgets and computers with a sleek design, but you need to maintain a practical head and buy what you need for your business and what will most benefit your customers.

In the first instance, carry out a technology audit, making a list of your technology requirements. It's a good idea to write out two lists – one looking at what you can't do without and one looking at your potential needs as the business grows (such as data storage capacity), so you can tailor your budget accordingly.

In this chapter, we'll look at:

- What equipment you need
- How to select a web host
- Creating your website
- Security issues
- Content
- Accessibility
- Payment systems
- Shipping options
- Returns policy

➡ WHAT EQUIPMENT YOU NEED

Hardware

The price of IT equipment has reduced substantially in recent years, which is good news for anyone thinking of starting an online business. There's a huge selection available in the market however, so it's important to be realistic about your needs as well as keeping a sensible budget in mind. Don't be tempted to buy more than you need, in terms of both hardware and software. Many businesses, for example, make the mistake of investing in more server capacity than they need from the start, when the reality is that you can save money by buying only what you need and adding more server capacity at a later stage, as your business grows.

 FROM THE EXPERTS:
Nick Robertston, ASOS

We used to buy our IT kit and servers off eBay – it wasn't the prettiest option but it did the job.

Essentially, you'll need a computer, modem, printer, monitor, scanner and image-capturing devices. When it comes to purchasing a computer, you may be tempted to buy one of the most up-to-date models but a basic computer will probably suffice just as well, as long as it can support the latest software. You'll need equipment you can rely upon as you will be using it to perform a range of tasks, such as handling customer queries, checking emails, writing correspondence and checking and maintaining your site. Shop around to see if you can get a deal on hardware that also includes some free or reduced-price software. Aim to get at least three quotes on the equipment you intend to buy. You could also try to negotiate a deal on software packages when you purchase hardware. As a rule of thumb, expect to spend no less than £500 and anywhere up to a few thousand. Second-hand equipment is also an option but ensure you check all the devices thoroughly before committing.

 TIP

Set out your budget before you go in search of your IT need. It's easy to become carried away with the array of equipment available and to buy more than you actually need.

Hard drive

Hard drive storage is an important consideration. The hard drive stores information such as text and audio files and most hard drives on the market can now store many gigabytes (GB) of information, at the very least 60GB, which should be more than adequate for the needs of your

TIP

Data loss can cripple your business so think long and hard about what storage capability you might need – not just now but in the future as your business grows.

business. You can also buy portable hard drives on which to back-up information and this is one area you shouldn't skimp on. It's essential you back up as much information as possible, in the event of any data loss caused by power outages, theft or damage.

Monitor

It's also worth spending some time choosing the right type and size of monitor. Bear in mind that most websites are optimised for monitors of between 17 and 21 inches in size, although obviously, you won't be able to have any control over what size monitors your customers have, and how much of the website they can see. Flat panel LCD monitors are all the rage now, they take up less room than more traditional ones and prices are very competitive.

Image devices

The other essential piece of equipment you will need is a device for capturing and transferring images, particularly if you are launching an online retail business. Pictures of your products are one of the main ways you are likely to attract customers to your site, so it's essential that any pictures you use look professional, attractive and represent the product in its best light. To do this, you'll need to use either a digital camera or a scanner. Digital cameras have dropped in price in recent years, and you can pick up a fairly decent one now for as little as £200. Check out the following criteria before you buy: can you download images from the camera to your computer using a USB device? Can you download images to a memory card? (This will enable you to transport the images and download them to different computers if necessary.) Scanners cost from around £50 – you place an image on the scanner and it reproduces it on screen for you.

Software

The good news for anyone starting an online business is that there is plenty of free software to download from the internet, particularly for security and firewall purposes (see p.146 later on in this chapter for more on software options in this area). Make the most of free tools provided by the likes of Google, many of which are useful for marketing purposes, such as Google Analytics, Site Maps and Product Search (we cover this in more detail in Part 5, p.237). The benefits of free tools are that they are readily available and can be more cost effective, depending on your needs. More often than not though, there won't be a free or low cost tool that will serve all your requirements, so assess what value such tools will bring to your business.

IN MY EXPERIENCE:

Jamie Murray Wells, Glasses Direct

In the early days when money was limited, we used free tools from Google, so make the most of these if you can.

Web browsers

In terms of other software needs, web browsers will be your first port of call – this is the interface through which content on the web is displayed. There are four main options to choose from. By far the most popular is Microsoft's Internet Explorer, which recently launched in version 8. Other choices include Firefox 3 from Mozilla and Safari, from Apple. Search engine giant Google is the latest to launch a product in the browser space, with its offering Chrome. It only works on Windows at present, but Google is working on a version for Linux and Mac. Deciding which browser to go for is mainly down to personal choice, so test the browsers out and see which one best fulfils your needs. It's also a good idea to test whether your site is optimised across all browsers, as you can never be sure which browsers your customers will be using.

TIP

There is an array of free software that can be downloaded from the internet. Much of it can be useful for marketing or web design purposes, but assess what value each tool will bring to your business before downloading.

Browsers – what to bear in mind

- Always focus on the user experience
- Test, test and test again. Ensure that your website is optimised across all browsers without the need for user intervention
- Compare the relative percentage of browsers that hit your website to statistics on overall browser share
- Users have a wide choice of browsers so you need to make sure they get the best experience possible, regardless of the browser they choose to use.
- Think about both the context of your offer and your customer when approaching browsers

Other useful software

You should also invest in tools such as web page editor and graphics software. Web page editor is a software application for creating web pages, formatting text and adding images and you don't need to know HTML or any other code to use it. Graphics software such as Adobe Dreamweaver will be useful if you intend to create your website yourself, as you can use the application to create and edit images. Count on paying about £450 for the software.

You can quickly and easily set up an online shop if you invest in shop-front software. It will automatically build a professional-looking store through a series of templates, even if you have no design skills. Many of the shop-front software options available enable you to start off by using just the basic features at first so it's ideal for someone who is new to the concept. Features include shop design and layout, shopping cart options (see p.139 for advice on this) and sales and marketing support. On the downside, these can be expensive to invest in so weigh up whether this software is something you truly need. As they use templates, they can also be quite restrictive.

One other type of software that is essential for any business is accounting software – it will help you to keep on top of your finances and enable you to manage your costs more efficiently (see Part 7, p.290 for more on this).

FROM THE EXPERTS:
Sergey Brin, Google

It makes sense to make sure you put core effort into technologies that work across the board. If you expand abroad, don't forget that you have to put some specialised technologies into each market and budget for some of them.

Connectivity

Bandwidth, the amount of data that can be transferred from one point to another over a given period of time, is also an important consideration for any online business. Broadband describes the bandwidth of your internet connection and there are some very attractive deals available, where you can have a cost-effective connection on a monthly basis. You'd need to have a very good reason to use a dial-up connection instead – it may be cheaper than broadband, but the amount of time you waste waiting for pages to load up will more than cancel out any savings you make on costs. Your bandwidth requirements will normally be handled by your web host provider (see our section below on web hosting for more information).

ALL ABOUT WEB HOSTING

Web hosting involves housing, serving and maintaining files for a website – essentially you rent space online in order to make your website visible to your customers. It basically means you can run an online business without having to incur the expense or carry out the legwork of maintaining your own server, as web hosts provide you with access to servers. As well as housing your website, your web host will also be providing you with email accounts, bandwidth and technical support.

IN MY EXPERIENCE:
Glenys Berd, LoveThoseShoes.com

If a web host is any good then they will be in one of the review lists that are published by several sites. Make sure they have out-of-hours support and remote reboot capabilities.

Choosing the right web hosting service can seem quite a daunting task, given the number of providers vying for your business. There are many deals that look too good to be true and the reality is they often are. There are a few factors you need to take into consideration when selecting a web host, such as exactly what capabilities you want your website to have. Price can vary from free to several thousand pounds so be clear from the outset what your needs are as it's all too easy to get talked into paying for a web hosting service that offers much more than you require at present.

TIP

There are hundreds of web hosting companies offering their services so shop around to find the best deal and don't be afraid to negotiate if some of the deals don't quite offer you all the services you want.

Assess your needs

If all you need is a simple brochure site with basic information about your business, hosting your site will be relatively easy and won't cost you anything.

So how do you get it on the internet? As is often the case in the virtual world of the internet, you don't need to have the server in your office. In fact, it's very unlikely that you will. The cheapest and easiest option, and the one which most small businesses choose at the start, is to have a virtual host.

Types of host

Having a virtual host basically means getting a third party to host your site. The files for your website are stored on the hosting company's computer along with the files for other websites and their server deals with requests for your website and others. This is called **shared environment hosting**. Currently in the UK there are hundreds of companies that will host your site in a shared environment. If you already have a website and domain name you may have already come across offers of free web hosting.

Your **internet service provider (ISP)** (the company through which you access the internet such as BT or Virgin Media) will often give you a small amount of space on which to host a website. Alternatively, the company that registered your domain name will often provide access to a free or low-cost hosting service. It may be a natural step to use one of these companies to host your website since you already have a business relationship with them. However, you need to be aware of the restrictions that they may place on you in terms of space, features and support.

You should bear in mind that the main activity of an ISP is connectivity – that is, getting and keeping businesses and individuals connected to the internet. The resources of these companies may not be prioritised on keeping your website up and running.

There are, however, companies that have been set up solely for the purpose of hosting websites. Some of these have invested a lot of money in technology and support services to ensure the sites that they host are secure and always accessible from the internet and that their customers are given all the necessary support.

If you just have a simple brochure site that needs little maintenance or technical support, using your current ISP or a free package is likely to be sufficient. For this type of website, your main concerns will be how quickly the page appears on the screen and whether there are any occasions when it doesn't appear.

One of the best ways to find out how good a service is is through trial and error. You won't be paying a great deal if anything at all for the service, so experimenting won't be expensive. You can always move on if you're not satisfied. If however, you are serious about running an online business and one with e-commerce capabilities, you're likely to need a web hosting service that stretches beyond what your current ISP can offer, as you'll require features such as additional webspace, email addresses, adequate bandwidth and most importantly, support, in the event of anything going wrong.

Email addresses and webspace

Check out how many email accounts you are allowed to set up. In the early days of your business, you may require one, but as your business grows and you employ staff, you'll need email addresses for them as well. You might also want to set up some generic email addresses, such as 'sales@. . .', 'customerservice@. . .' and 'info@. . .' The amount of webspace you can get will vary, but is generally from 5 megabytes (MB) to unlimited. You'll find that 5 MB will cater for a site that has about 8-10 pages, so you'll probably need more than this if your site is particularly complex or is likely to have a lot of graphics. Ensure that your web host will allow you to increase the amount of space you need as your business grows.

Bandwidth

Working out how much bandwidth you need can be tricky, as you're never sure how many people are likely to visit your site in the early days and numbers can fluctuate as your business grows and you are fine tuning your marketing strategy. You might be incredibly lucky in the early days and have more traffic than you anticipated – if this is the case, check with your web host to find out what penalties you might have to pay if you exceed your bandwidth allowance, and whether you can upgrade this easily and quickly if necessary. Some web host providers offer unlimited bandwidth allowance, but check the small print carefully, as this may be conditional on the type of data you are transferring.

The bigger and more expensive your web hosting service, the more likely it is to have a better connection to the internet, enabling pages from your site to be downloaded faster by your customers' browsers. Consider how many of your customers are likely to be using a broadband connection as opposed to a 56k modem for example, as they won't really notice any difference in speed if they are using the latter. Nowadays, it's quite likely that most people have a broadband connection, as prices have reduced in recent years and broadband is now often bundled in packages with television and telephone deals.

 TIP
There are plenty of web hosting services available so assess your business needs now and in the future and get a quote from at least three different providers before making a decision.

Reliability and technical support

Reliability and technical support goes without saying. You need a web host who can guarantee that their servers are well maintained – just think of the amount of business you could lose or trust that can be eroded if your site was down for any period of time. It will obviously cost you more to invest in a reliable web hosting service, but it's a small price to pay for peace of mind and to ensure your website is online at all times.

The effects of downtime

The effects of downtime can be extremely negative, as auction site eBay found out to its cost in the early days of its trading history. In June 1999, following a site redesign, eBay suffered a number of breakdowns in its service, with one lasting 22 hours. This had a severe impact on consumer interaction with the site and knocked more than $8 off the price of its shares. Further outages occurred and company revenues took a severe hit – according to reports at the time, the service interruptions cost eBay $3.9m of its second-quarter revenues, as it refunded listing fees and granted extensions on auctions.

At the time, the 22-hour outage was one of the worst internet crashes in history and a backlash quickly ensued as users wasted no time registering their complaints on an internet newsgroup dedicated to the site. Others raised questions about the robustness of the technology.

➡ CHOOSING A WEB HOST

You've worked out your web hosting needs and made a list of all the requirements you're after. So what is the best way to go about selecting one? Barry Mills, founder of digital marketing agency Netstep says that unless you are developing the site yourself and really know what you are doing, you shouldn't select one. Instead, leave the selection to whoever is helping you to develop and support your site (see Creating your website below). That way, there's no doubt about whose responsibility it is when the site stops working. If your developer doesn't have their own hosting service, then contract with the hosting company that they chose direct, so you aren't unnecessarily locked in to the developer. But make the same party responsible for maintenance, support and hosting.

You should oversee the selection though. Take up references, and in particular find out if any of the web host's existing clients have experienced downtime and how it was handled. The reality is that it's only really when something goes wrong that you find out how good your support is. Don't sign any long contracts unless you are dealing with one of the market leaders, and don't make a selection based on price. Remember that if your website host's business folds, your site will go down too, so do a thorough background check looking at how long the web host has been established, its client list and the nature of support offered.

IN MY EXPERIENCE:

Glenys Berd, LoveThoseShoes.com

Don't host your domains with your web host, pick a third party such as 123-reg.
co.uk to host them through. That way, if you have to move to another host you
won't have any problems with moving your site. Some hosts have been known to
hold domains hostage.

It can be awkward thinking about changing suppliers before you've even
got the relationship started but it's worth learning to recognise when it
might be time to switch web host providers. Poor performance or a change of
developers or technology are one of the signs that it might be time to change.
The main thing to do is to plan ahead. Always retain control of your domain
name. Make sure it's registered to you, and unless you have a very strong
relationship with the developer it is safer not to let them manage it for you.
Also, make sure you have current backups of your site files and any live
database content.

CREATING YOUR WEBSITE

As a virtual shop window, your website will make or break your business, so it's
essential to get the design and functionality right from the start otherwise it can
be a costly and frustrating exercise if you have to continually tweak the site. The
first decision you'll need to make is whether you will be designing the website
yourself or hiring a web designer to do the job for you.

IN MY EXPERIENCE:

Jamie Murray Wells, Glasses Direct

In recent years, technology has got cheaper and cheaper. When we started out,
good e-commerce products weren't as readily available as now, it was mostly
more expensive merchandising software. But if it's more economical, consider
building it yourself. I put a notice on the board at my university for a web
developer and he worked side by side with me.

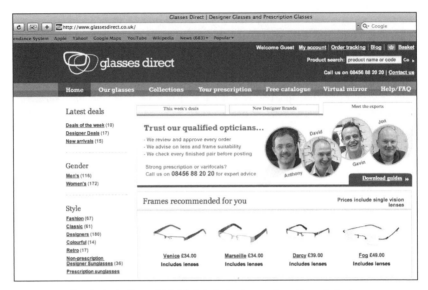

Glasses Direct: Founder Jamie Murray Wells initally built the site together with a web developer

Tailor-made or off-the-shelf?

You don't need to have design or technology skills to work on your site. Improvements in technology mean that there are plenty of cost-effective web build tools at your disposal, most of which lend themselves to being used by complete novices. In fact, you could find yourself creating a professional looking website in a matter of hours. But should you opt for a tailor-made solution or invest in an off-the-shelf one?

There are many factors to take into account when deciding between a tailor made e-commerce site and an off-the-shelf solution. Advocates of bespoke systems point to the advantages of a tailor-made website, while boxed e-commerce providers argue that the usability and speed of their products make them superior. Your decision will probably be influenced by finding a balance between cost, functionality and ease-of-use of both options.

Off-the-shelf

An off-the-shelf e-commerce package is easy to install and often easy to use. It is almost certainly likely to be cheaper and quicker than having a bespoke e-commerce site designed for you. However, updates can be expensive and sometimes unavailable. Another downside is that off-the-shelf packages only have so many templates and functions, so you could find that your options are somewhat restricted. The other disadvantage is that your site could be similar to that of your competitors and you will have no control over how and when functionality is updated, and so it will be difficult to differentiate your offering.

Tailor-made

A bespoke system will allow you to present your products in the most appropriate and effective way for your business. This is especially important if you have complex products, or product ranges with multiple components. A bespoke system can often be more easily integrated with existing IT systems and web services as it is developed from the ground up to meet your specific needs. This kind of system can help set you apart from competitors and you will be able to add additional features quickly and easily.

You will have to consider what you need from an online shop very carefully before you commit to either package. Another option, if you cannot afford the time or cost of your own online shop, is to run your online shop within a wider e-commerce community such as eBay or an online shopping mall (see p.155 for more information on this).

 # COMMISSIONING A SITE

If you are serious about building an online business that includes features such as a shopping cart and integrated payment systems, then you are probably better off commissioning a web designer. Costs can be substantial, but you will be able to have the site built to your exact specifications. The good ones are expensive, but they will be worth it. On top of the costs of site build, you may also have to pay an annual maintenance fee, but again, this means you can get problems fixed if necessary, and by someone you are familiar with and who knows the site well.

Have a look around the web to get a feel for the kind of sites available and bookmark a few that you like the look of and that you feel could be effective for your site. Check they have the kind of features you're after – such as an e-commerce facility, good navigation and clear signposting, for instance. Then, find out who's behind them: usually they will be credited on the site. If not, you could get in contact with the business itself and ask them who's behind their build.

This approach is a good option and quite safe, because you have already seen the web designer's work and like it. You could also ask around business associates and colleagues to see if there is anyone they can recommend. Alternatively, you could browse through directories of web designers and there are plenty of resources on the web where you can start looking.

Web design – where to look

- The UK Web Design Assciation: www.ukwda.org
- Web Design Directory: www.web-design-directory-uk.co.uk
- FreeIndex: www.freeindex.co.uk
- The Chartered Society of Designers: www.csd.org.uk

TIP

Commissioning a web designer does not come cheap, but it does mean you will have control over the look, feel and functionality of the site. You'll also be able to exercise more flexibility when it comes to testing the site and make any changes that are necessary.

Good web design, however, isn't just dependent on getting a professional web designer on board. It's as much about functionality and reliability but it's also important to establish a rapport with your web developer. It's likely that the run-up to the site launch will incur long nights, stressful times and continual testing so it's important to have someone on the technical side who is supportive and committed to helping you launch your business in the best way possible. You will also need to keep your customers' needs foremost at all times. Revisit your market research from your business plan and make sure that before you start thinking about your website you are really clear about what you are selling, who you are targeting, and what your unique value propositions are. Then you should brainstorm what you think customers want.

IN MY EXPERIENCE:
Mark Leather, Country Products

Use a small local firm, build up a relationship with your designer – someone who doesn't talk too much jargon, someone you can meet and speak with face to face.

FEATURES FOR YOUR WEBSITE

Shopping carts

A shopping cart is a page on the site where visitors can store one or more items before they actually commit to buying them. It lets consumers purchase more than one item from your website in one transaction. Shopping carts can be relatively inexpensive or even free depending on what kind of e-commerce software package you go with.

An online shopping cart gathers up items in the same way that an actual shopping basket or trolley would. The difference is an online cart will calculate the total value and added delivery costs.

Shopping carts can clearly improve the user-experience of an e-commerce site and they add an element of functionality, meaning you would be foolish not to consider one for your site.

Carts can be added to your site relatively easily, even if you don't have a boxed e-commerce package. Many carts can be incorporated into your site by adding some simple code to the links on your site that passes the product information straight into the basket.

Online catalogues

If your site has a large quantity of different products then you'll probably need to display them in an online catalogue form.

Online catalogues work in much the same way as a department store does. Shoppers can browse hundreds or thousands of products according to categories. This makes it easier for shoppers to find exactly what they're looking for, minimising the chances of them missing a product on your site.

There are four main types of online catalogue which vary in price and functionality:

ASP: Application Server Provider
With this type of catalogue you are given a user account and password that give you access to the site through your web browser. With this option you don't need a separate hosting site and you can make changes and updates from any computer connected to the internet.

Shopping carts allow customers to purchase several items in a single transaction.

Online carts calculate the total value and added delivery costs for your customers.

Software:

With this option you load the software onto your own machine, and then load it onto your shop from there.

Open source:

This is a kind of cooperative service where you use software which has been developed and given away free by developers. However, there may be some hosting costs associated with this type of system.

Free products:

There are free catalogues out there but with these you often only get the software itself for no charge, and are liable to pay fees on the transactions you make when using the software. Be careful with these catalogues as they may restrict your site development in the long run.

IN MY EXPERIENCE:

Mark Leather, Country Products

Don't penny pinch – go for value. Just because it's the cheapest certainly doesn't mean it's the best – but at the same time don't get talked into things you don't need.

Style matters

In terms of style, such as images, typeface and logo, the key is to keep things simple. Don't make it too fancy, don't use gratuitous animation or graphics, and don't let designers show off. Think about search engines, or make sure your designer does (see p.225 for more information on search engines). Keep all your key information and navigation above the fold (this means ensuring it is visible on the page without the need to scroll down or sideways). Generally navigation menus should be top and left – that's where users expect to find them. Use visual navigation aids within the central window of your homepage to guide users into your site.

ASOS: For a fashion website the style is important

Treat your website as a continuous project. Barry Mills from Netstep believes that the mindset of building a site and then thinking it's finished until it looks tired and ready for a redesign after a few years is completely wrong. You should be continually analysing your website traffic using analytics, developing ideas for improving the site, and testing, testing, testing. It's also important to listen to customer feedback.

IN MY EXPERIENCE:
Glenys Berd, LoveThoseShoes.com

The style and image of a website is essential, it's all the customer has to go on. The right style for your customer base will let them feel confident that you are a proper company they can trust. Even simple things like misspelling can lose you sales. Remember, your competition is only a click away.

Love ThoseShoes: Style and image have attracted customers.

➡ SECURITY ISSUES

Online security issues continue to make the headlines and it's vital that you are aware of the various security threats that can harm your business. These relate to the site itself and to how you deal with information such as customer details and payments. Your site could be susceptible to fraud and hacking and your customer details could be compromised. Online fraud is a growing business – it's often said that those who carry out fraudulent activities are always one step ahead of the technology being used to combat levels of fraud, so it's important to keep up to date with the latest solutions available.

Your website isn't necessarily a one-way street. It can also open the window to the heart of your company – the network, including the storage facilities that hold its data files, its most priceless asset. Lax security that enables hackers to break in can lead to embarrassment, and waste your time and money. And in extreme cases it could mean the collapse of your business.

What can go wrong?

A security breach can paralyse an entire network in a matter of minutes and/ or result in privacy controls being becoming ineffective, as several high profile brands have discovered to their cost. In 2008, for example, a lapse in security at social networking site Facebook resulted in strangers being able to access the personal photos of site subscribers. The incident was all the more embarrassing for the company as it came only days after Facebook had beefed up its privacy options. The financial cost of putting matters right can be very high. In addition, the impact on customer confidence can result in a severely damaged business reputation, taking months or years to reverse.

Security breaches

Online clothing retailer Cotton Traders, meanwhile, suffered a security breach during which its customers' credit and debit card details were stolen. It is estimated that up to 40,000 individual sets of card details were stolen when its website was hacked into.

You might not know immediately that this has happened though, but the repercussions from security breaches could last some time.

As well as spreading abusive graffiti, hackers can alter catalogue details and prices, or steal all the customer details, including their home addresses and sensitive information such as medical treatments. Apart from the embarrassment to your brand, this would be in direct contravention of the data protection regulations, and could lead to prosecution and fines.

Hackers often seek connection bandwidth, because this can be used to damage other businesses in so-called 'distributed denial of service attacks'. These involve numerous computers bombarding an internet server with data, overloading it and causing it to stall or crash, resulting in your website being unavailable for a certain period of time, all of which could mean lost orders and frustrated customers.

In the worst case hackers can get hold of customers' credit card details (as in the case of Cotton Traders and numerous other brands that have been the victim or hackers) in which case the bank that handles transactions could withdraw and the site owner could be liable for the debts. A fraudulent credit card charge leaves the holder only liable for £50 or so while an improper business-to-business transaction could bankrupt a company.

Credit card criminals are increasingly turning their attention to smaller e-commerce sites, using stolen credit cards to buy goods online, so it's imperative to have the right level of security in place. If your business accepts online payments, you need to ensure your site operates a secure online payment system and if you are taking note of customers' details, you need to keep their details safe. As a rule of thumb, no card holder data should be stored unless absolutely necessary.

Virus protection

One big worry for traders and customers alike on the internet is the threat of viruses. Headline-grabbing monster viruses such as Melissa and the Love Bug brought mighty corporations grinding to a halt, generating spurious emails in such numbers that the networks collapsed. Other varieties can corrupt data files or stop computers working altogether.

Ensure you install anti-virus software; virus experts such as Symantec and MessageLabs analyse viruses the moment that they appear and can quite often have a fix ready within a matter of minutes, that can be downloaded over the internet in time to provide protection. Your internet service provider should also have anti-virus software for your use. Ensure you keep up to date with viruses as versions are updated on a regular basis.

If your business is affected, it could mean several hours of downtime that could result in loss of trust and trade. There's no guarantee you'll escape a virus attack, but there are measures you can put in place to help lessen the risks. Viruses can be spread in a number of ways such as via email, instant messenger programs or infected files. Be especially wary of emails with attachments from people you don't know. Often, a virus infects people's email address books and the email appears to be sent by someone you know. If in doubt, don't click on the attachment – delete the email.

> ### TIP
> If your site is valuable, you should consider running a pen (penetration) test via a reputable firm. This is a friendly 'hacker service' that will test your website to see if there's any way they can break in, and tell you what you need to fix.

Firewalls

Installing firewall software will also help to protect your systems and your customer data. This can come either as a hardware device fitted as part of the system or as software, or a combination of both.

It's an application that filters the information coming through the internet connection into your network or computer system, so that if the filters flag a packet of data, it is not allowed through. A firewall is effectively a policing system which stands between a computer and the internet. It blocks unauthorised programs and viruses trying to hack into the computer.

Firewalls are also increasingly found as a default standard in products such as Microsoft's Office XP and e-commerce program and any decent hosting service should include firewall protection for your site – hosted web services often market themselves on their claims to offer tough security. As with anti-virus software, ensure any firewall protection you have is up to date.

Standalone units suitable for small businesses are provided by companies such as Sonicwall, ComputerLinks (formerly known as Unipalm) and Watchguard Technologies. These typically cost a few hundred pounds and are relatively easy to install.

Public key encryption

Many users will only give out personal details if the website they are using provides encryption technology; this is represented by a padlock sign on the internet browser. You may have come across the term SSL encryption and wondered what it stands for. SSL stands for **Secure Sockets Layer** and is a type of technology that protects your website, making it easier to build trust between yourself and your customers. Essentially, an SSL certificate enables the encryption of sensitive information (such as a customer's credit card details) during online transactions. It establishes a private communication channel enabling encryption of the data during transmission. Encryption scrambles the data, essentially creating a private message. You'll need to use SSL if your online business accepts credit card payments, you have a login or sign in facility on your site and you are dealing with sensitive data such as credit card details or addresses. Verisign (www. verisign.com) is one of the leading providers of SSL certificates and secures more than one million servers.

E-commerce sites will also be protected by the encryption used by payment clearance providers such as PayPal, which process credit card payments. This ensures that customer details remain secure and also mitigates liability if the worst happens.

Making sure your site is secure is vital if you want to instil confidence in your customers. If they are in any doubt that their personal information is not secure, it's unlikely they will enter details such as credit card information on your site.

CONTENT

The way in which people react to online shops differs from how they approach shops on the high street – those who browse the web tend to be more impatient and don't waste time looking at sites that download slowly. The way in which users approach web content also differs from how they would look at printed matter. Typically, people tend to scan content on the web rather than reading it word for word and there are certain guidelines you can follow when presenting your content. Here are a few suggestions:

- Make sure any text you use is broken up into easily digestible chunks, with enough white space so that the page and text do not feel too cluttered.
- Break up text with headings and images.
- Bullet points are also useful for listing characteristics of products or for drawing attention to a piece of content.

What you are aiming for is content that is easy to read and that is easy on the eye, so avoid creating pages where your potential customers will need to scroll either downwards or sideways in order to read them, as this will distract them and potentially put them off your site.

Consider carefully what colours you will use on your site and research other websites to see what colours might work best. You'll notice that there aren't many websites with yellow text on a white background for example. This is because together, these colours are not easy to read and can put a strain on the eyes. The same goes for choice of font – choose one that is clear, simple and easy to read.

TIP

Content isn't just about the words you use on the page, it's just as much about how the words are presented. Test a variety of fonts, backgrounds and colours and ask your friends and family for their opinions.

When it comes to supplying the copy for your website, the easiest and cheapest way is to write it yourself and as it's original, you will own the copyright. It's a good idea, however, to get a friend or two to proofread the content before you go live. Content that is misspelt and which does not read well is not going to appeal to your customers. Depending on the type of website you are operating, and the amount of content you might need, you could consider using a freelance writer to supply the copy for you.

➡ ACCESSIBILITY

Making your website accessible involves tweaking your site to make it as easy as possible for everyone to get the information they want.

According to Netstep's Barry Mills, the law relating to website accessibility is rather unclear. Generally, if your customers can use the site, you should be okay. But you may have disabled or partially sighted customers, so think about their needs. Accessibility isn't just about catering to the vision-impaired either; some users may have movement and coordination problems, which means they have to navigate sites using only the keyboard.

Designing websites for those with disabilities shouldn't be seen as a restriction of your creative development plans – if anything it should ensure your web development team comes up with more creative ways to address accessibility.

As well as evidence of compliance, accessibility is often very sound business practice and generally sites that are good for accessibility are also good for search engines, so it's in your interest to make your website as accessible as possible. In addition, making your website more accessible means it can be viewed by those users with older browsers who won't have technologies such as Flash installed. Making a website accessible, however, isn't an overnight job, it takes time as you'll need to test the site and review accessibility when the site has an update.

The WC3 guidelines are widely regarded as best practice for accessibility and you can find out more by logging on to: www.w3.org.

➡ PAYMENT SYSTEMS

With online shopping set to grow further in the next few years, more and more people are shopping online and they'll expect the majority of websites to have online payment systems in place. If you want to be one of the businesses to benefit from the increasing popularity of online shopping, online payment systems are an absolute must. In the 1990s, when the internet was emerging as a retail platform, online payments were dogged by instances of fraud and systems that were less than secure – but today, the technology and security options have come a long way. To accept online payments, you'll need to work with a payment service provider (PSP – see below for more information on this).

IN MY EXPERIENCE:
Simon Wadsworth, The Retail Factory

As an e-commerce provider, offer as many payment systems as possible – why deter someone from buying?

There are a number of ways to accept payments online and it's a good idea to consider these as you build your website, choose your e-commerce platform and shopping cart. Thinking about all of these elements at the same time will help you to make the right business decision. For example, you'll need to make sure that your shopping cart is compatible with your chosen PSP and that you have the option to provide a range of payment types and services. According to online payment processor Sage Pay (the UK's largest independent PSP), the following are the most common ways of collecting payments.

- **Regular payments:** this is instant and is the fastest way to get to your customers' money.
- **Deferred payments:** this is a method whereby you can capture payment and authorisation for a specific amount without immediately taking the funds. For example, this payment method works well for those who have longer lead times to dispatch goods, or those who are building bespoke goods. It's also important to note that there is a finite timeframe for settling a deferred payment; this is usually within 3–6 days.
- **Repeat payments:** these work in exactly the same way as regular payment, but stored card details (either by the vendor or the payment gateway) can be used to trigger a second, third and fourth payment
- **Refunds:** a payment has been taken, but needs to be allocated back to the customer. This is usually used in the case of returns or faulty goods.

IN MY EXPERIENCE:

Mark Leather, Country Products

We were recommended our payment system, Sage Pay, by our web designers. I would consider it one of our best business moves ever. The biggest benefit is the costs and charges, which are far more realistic and reasonable than our former supplier, the settlement times are far speedier, but I always look to far more than the old pounds and pence – the system is simpler; the reporting is far better, easier and clearer which benefits our customers.

Advice from Sage Pay. . .
Payment systems: What is settlement?

All payments are split into authorisation and settlement. Getting **authorisation** means that the card is valid, hopefully not reported stolen, has funds available and is a genuine card number. However, funds are not actually removed from the customer's account until the payment service provider (PSP) has sent the payment data to the relevant acquiring bank (your merchant bank) – this is what is known as **settlement**. This usually happens at a specific time each day. It is important to note that with the regular payment option, although authorisation is immediate, the money will not leave the customer's account until the transaction has been 'settled'.

www.sagepay.com

Types of service payment providers

Independent payment gateways

These have no affiliation with any bank and will work with a whole range of acquirers (a high street bank or other financial institution that offers credit and debit card accepting/processing services). The benefits of choosing an independent payment gateway are:

- If you want to change banks, you don't have to change your payment service provider, so there is less disruption and the PSP will just fit in with your new requirements.

- Pricing is very competitive.
- Funds are usually released quickly.
- You can integrate other payment types (eg PayPal) into the same system, making reconciliation much easier.
- Most can help you to get an internet merchant bank account – which you need to accept payments online – and could save you money.

Bank associated gateways

These are associated with a specific bank and therefore must be used in conjunction with a merchant account/number from that specific bank. Here, your business bank account, merchant number and gateway are all under one roof so it can be easier to manage, but if you change banks you may be forced to change your gateway too.

eWallet services

eWallet systems, such as PayPal (see below for more information), allow a merchant to accept payment from a customer who has an account with the particular eWallet provider. A number of eWallet solutions are integrated with independent PSPs, so that you can take advantage of a variety of payment methods. The benefits of choosing an eWallet service are:

- They don't use actual card details, instead they use funds placed into the eWallet account by the customer. These funds can be added or 'topped up' by the customer at any point through the eWallet interface, meaning card details are neither collected nor divulged at any point.
- Research shows that many shoppers regard eWallets as an extra pot of money that they willingly use to spend on online shopping. For example, if they've sold something on eBay themselves and the money is in a PayPal account, they are more likely to spend that online. For this reason many merchants choose to accept eWallets as well as credit/debit card payments.

> ## TIP
> eWallet services, including the likes of PayPal, Google Checkout and moneybookers.com, are suited to those businesses that don't anticipate a large number of online transactions and which don't have internet merchant accounts. You also have to rely on your customers having an eWallet account.

Setting up a payment system

Once you have registered your domain name and chosen how you are going to create your website, try to consider your shopping cart and payment options at the same time. That way you can make sure you get exactly what you want.

Advice from Sage Pay. . .
What you need to accept online payments:

- **A shopping cart:** these can be tailor made by web developers or simply purchased 'off the shelf' – they allow customers to select items and proceed to purchase as well as allowing the vendor to monitor stock and inventory and track orders.

- **An internet merchant account:** getting one of these is crucial if you want to accept a variety of cards and payment types. You won't be able to trade online without one. Merchant accounts are available from a range of acquirers (banks). The internet merchant account gives you, the merchant, the facility to get authorisations on customers' cards and have funds transferred into your business bank account. Some payment service providers can also help you to set up your merchant account. As they buy in bulk, they will usually have negotiated good transaction rates with the bank.

- **Payment service provider (PSP):** the PSP will facilitate the process of capturing credit card details and will securely transmit those details to your chosen acquirer for authorisation. The PSP will often also be able to offer fraud screening facilities as part of the payment gateway package.

- **A business bank account:** this is where the funds taken online will be deposited, pending agreement with the chosen acquirer (your merchant bank account).

www.sagepay.com

When choosing the right online payment system for your business, you should first think about the product you are offering to your customers and the manner of payment you would like to allow your customers to use. For example, purchasing a shopping cart that does not facilitate deferred payments when your business is based around deferred payments wouldn't make sense. Equally, signing up to a payment service provider that does not allow American Express, when you have a particular necessity or interest in accepting this card type, will cause problems and cost you money.

Costs of payment systems

Think also about the price. The cost of processing a transaction soon adds up so look at what options are available to you and make sure you account for these when pricing your goods. These are a list of potential charges you may have to pay:

Merchant bank

The bank/acquirer will charge you each time you process a payment. The fee varies, so check whether it is a percentage of the total transaction or a flat fee. Different acquiring banks will have different rates and if a payment service provider can negotiate a better deal for you, then it's worth investigating.

Payment service providers (PSPs)

There will be a small fee for the authorisation process, however there are considerable pricing and service differences between providers, so shop around for the deal that best suits your business. Some will quote you an all inclusive monthly fixed rate for a set number of transactions, while others may quote for the transaction only, but add charges like set-up fees or fraud screening. The good thing is that there are choices, but make sure you choose what is right for your business.

Fraud

Most PSPs will be able to provide you with fraud protection, however there are different levels of protection, so again look at what is available and don't pay for more than you need. Some PSPs will include basic fraud screening as part of their offering and this can work out to be more cost effective.

PCI compliance

The Payment Card Industry Data Security Standard (PCI DSS) is a set of requirements designed to ensure that all companies that process, store or transmit credit card information maintain a secure environment. It's not yet a legal requirement in the UK and the cost of compliance depends on the number of transactions that you process and whether you decide to capture your customers' credit card details or let your PSP do this. If your PSP is collecting the data and they are PCI compliant, it shouldn't be too expensive. Your PSP and companies like

Trustwave (www.trustwave.com) will be able to advise you further. Again, some PSPs may be able to negotiate rates so it's worth checking with your PSP too.

Advice from Sage Pay. . .
Why compliance is important

Compliance is important to prevent hackers and security breaches and lessen the risk of fraud. Any potential weaknesses in a network can be used by hackers to gain unauthorised access, and in the worst case, capture sensitive card information. Any breaches of this nature would not only compromise your technology systems, but also have a severe effect on your reputation in the eyes of your customers. In the online world, it's not a situation customers forget very easily, and with the high level of competition on the net, they'll simply go elsewhere.

There is also a moral perspective to think about. Companies that capture and store sensitive card and cardholder information must be aware that in the event that this information is accessed by an unauthorised source, their actions could cause untold damage to their customers.

There are 4 levels of PCI Compliance; information on these levels is as follows:

1. Any merchant – regardless of acceptance channel – processing over 6 million Visa transactions per year. Also includes any merchant that Visa, at its sole discretion, determines should meet the Level 1 merchant requirements in order to minimise risk to the Visa system.
2. Any merchant – regardless of acceptance channel – processing 1 million to 6 million Visa transactions per year.
3. Any merchant processing 20,000 to 1 million Visa e-commerce transactions per year.
4. Any merchant processing fewer than 20,000 Visa e-commerce transactions per year, and all other merchants, regardless of acceptance channel, processing up to 1 million Visa transactions per year.

PCI compliance can be an expensive ongoing cost, so you should seek out the alternatives. For example, choosing a PSP that is level 1 compliant and getting them to host your payment pages will mean that you only have to be compliant to the most basic level. This approach will often save you money and a lot of hassle.

www.sagepay.com

Online shopping malls

An online shopping mall collates a number of smaller e-retailers together on one site. The mall will host your shop as well as process the payments for you. Although they are relatively quick and easy to set up, there are some drawbacks.

They are generally the most expensive way of selling online, and may ask for both a joining fee and a monthly or annual fee. You are also less likely to have any control over the way your shop looks, as it will go through the mall's own templates.

All about PayPal

This is one of the most popular payment processing companies as it's owned by eBay but your customers aren't obliged to have an account with eBay to use this payment method. As with most PSPs, this system enables you to receive or make payments anywhere in the world. There are various ways to add a PayPal facility to your website. You could add a button, a shopping cart (one of the most widely-used options), use a PayPal-approved partner solution (which you can do if you have used an e-commerce partner to help build your site), or choose the customer integration route, which requires some technical knowledge. PSPs like Sage Pay include PayPal integration too.

IN MY EXPERIENCE:

Glenys Berd, LoveThoseShoes.com

Payment systems are something that is dictated by what your customers expect. We allow our customers to pay by PayPal, credit card, debit card and cheques. PayPal was a recent addition and we have been pleasantly surprised by how many customers prefer to use it.

Micropayments

These are means of transferring very small units of currency in situations where collecting such small amounts of money with the usual payment systems is impractical, or very expensive, in terms of the amount of money being collected. They've never really been that popular with consumers, but if you want to find out more about how to use micropayments, log onto www.mppglobal.com, a payment technology provider, for more information.

> **TIP**
>
> There are a host of payment options available, so do shop around for the best deal for you. Find a payment company that offers your customers an efficient service, and that provides you support and an easy to use system.

➡ PROTECTING AGAINST FRAUD

Online fraud can destroy a business. Recent research shows card-holder not present (e-commerce) payments represent the sector of fastest growing fraud in the UK, accounting for 15% of all fraud. Fraudsters are ever-more inventive and although systems are developed and employed to tackle online fraud, fraudsters will always work to find a loophole. They'll also find new areas to attack and new inventive methods of fraud.

Online fraud can take place through stolen cards and identify theft, but can also be as a direct result of poor security on the part of the vendor: you. A website without proper security measures could allow a fraudster to obtain details from a genuine customer. Even poor security within an office environment could up-scale a minor office break-in to a full data breach, resulting in card numbers used by genuine customers being compromised and used by fraudsters for their own ends.

Sage Pay gives the following example of how online fraud can affect a business: a vendor who has no level of vigilance or awareness towards online fraud and accepts a payment from a card which is

> **TIP**
>
> Online fraud should be a constant and ongoing consideration – vigilance is essential at all times.

later reported as stolen, will not only lose the value of the goods he has shipped, but will also be held responsible for refunding the monies to the real credit card owner. He'll also have to pay an additional fee to the bank which retrieves the funds, forcefully, from their business account. Go to www.sagepay.com for more information from the experts.

By signing up to initiatives such as 3D secure (which good PSPs will offer for free), you can ensure that your online payments will be protected against charge-backs – this will reduce your own risk and subsequently the risk of jeopardising your business.

> ## What is 3D Secure?
>
> 3D Secure is similar to an online version of Chip and PIN, where instead of a PIN number a user generated password is required. It aims to reduce the possibility of fraudulent card use by authenticating the cardholder at the actual time of the transaction and subsequently reducing your exposure to disputed transactions and charge-backs of this type.

Fraud screening tools may vary in complexity and effectiveness and it is worth noting that any results you get are only ever as good as the information you provided in the first place. If a transaction containing no details about a customer is run through a fraud screening system then the transaction may be marked as 'safe' or 'low risk' even if this is not an accurate representation of that customer. The more detail you gather about a customer or a purchase and provide to your PSP or fraud screening company, the higher the effectiveness of the fraud screening results.

Cardholder information is validated against huge databases, including card address, number of cards used at the address, card issue numbers and card security value.

Training your staff

Online fraud and fraud screening should be at the forefront of your payment policy and vigilance by yourself and other members of staff goes without saying.

Fraudsters may even strike by calling members of your staff to gather information about real life customers, a process known as 'social engineering'. Social engineers attempt to garner information gradually, one phone call at a time. By slowly making notes and building up a database of titbits of information provided by the company over the phone, they can eventually contact the company and provide detailed information relating to a particular individual/ company with the aim of passing all security checks and having unrestricted access. This demonstrates the importance of staff awareness and training and also management awareness around how fraud can be an internal problem.

Infrastructure is also very important; it is wise to always ensure that you are getting the best out of the security you have at your disposal. If you have a security feature on one of your networks, ensure that it's being used.

➡ SHIPPING OPTIONS

So you've got as far as persuading customers to actually buy from your site. Unless you're selling certain digital products that can be downloaded online, you now have the important task of getting the sold product into the hands of the consumer.

The key with shipping options is to make it fair and sensible for your market. Rates will depend on where you are located as well as where you are sending the goods. Experiment with different policies, such as absorbing shipping costs into prices and offering free shipping, or free shipping on certain order sizes to encourage larger baskets.

If your business is relatively small, you may want to send items individually using a standard service such as that provided by Royal Mail. The most important thing about shipping costs is to make sure that they are transparent throughout the buying process. Few things kill more sales than a hefty carriage charge that only appears unannounced at the very end of the checkout process.

IN MY EXPERIENCE:
Glenys Berd, LoveThoseShoes.com

Give your customers options, such as next day delivery and a slow but cheap solution. We use Royal Mail and Business Post but are always looking at how we can improve shipping options and provide a better deal to our customers.

The speed and service you offer in the delivery of products can make or break your business. If a customer isn't happy with how long it took to have the item they bought reach their hands, or it didn't arrive in good condition, it's very unlikely they'll order from you again.

You have to perfect your delivery strategy and work out a system that is both cost effective for your business, and of a satisfactory standard for your customers.

There are several options to look at when planning your strategy for delivery. The first is to deliver items yourself, or hire someone to do it. This is probably only a cost effective option if you sell locally, or sell a limited number of big ticket items.

Outsourcing

The most viable options are probably going to be using a postal service such as Royal Mail, or courier/ distribution services. If you choose to outsource your delivery you must ensure you choose a partner that can meet the standards your customers expect, and fits in well with the way you operate your own business. With the e-commerce industry increasing at such a dramatic rate, there are many different delivery outsourcing companies to choose from, so make sure you shop around for the right partner for your company.

Tracking

Keeping your customers informed about when to expect their purchases is one way of elevating the level of customer service you offer. Nearly all couriers offer online tracking of parcels. This works by allocating an ID number to the order which can then be used by the consumer to track the location of their order online.

The use of order tracking will probably only be really valued by consumers if the item they have ordered is urgent or expensive. For most small or low priced purchases an email from you telling the customer their item has been dispatched, and a delivery estimate, will suffice.

IN MY EXPERIENCE:

Simon Wadsworth, The Retail Factory

My advice on shipping options is to keep them simple and clear and easy to understand.

 # RETURNS POLICY

In the UK you are obliged to offer a no quibble seven-day refund on any hard goods, and clearly state that on your website. If you don't, the customer will have an automatic right to return the goods and be refunded any time up to three months after purchase, under the Distance Selling Regulations (see p.95 for more information).

Things to remember:

- Determine a budget for your technology needs before you source the equipment.

- Make the most of free software available to download from the internet.

- Research different web hosting options – get at least three quotes.

- Check out the best practice guidelines for website accessibility.

- Online fraud could cripple your business so ensure you take the necessary precautions.

- Shop around to find the best payment options available for both you and your customers.

- Offer a variety of shipping options if possible and gauge customer demand.

aunching an online business is what you set out to do and without doubt that's where your energies are best served. However, as a small business owner, you'll no doubt find yourself involved in many different aspects of your business and there's a substantial amount of administrative duties to be aware of. Many online businesses are started from home, but as your business grows, you may need to consider investing in premises. If you are selling goods over the internet, you'll also need to think about issues such as posting and packaging, as well as your after-service model, including managing returns. It is often the new financial aspects of running a business which people find the hardest to get used to.

You'll always need to put time aside for the financial aspect of running a business. After all, that's what allows you to launch and grow your business. You'll already have familiarised yourself with projections, forecasts and basic costings during the planning stage, but the reality of running any business is that you need a firm grip on the numbers at all times.

In this chapter we'll cover:

- Property needs
- Store rooms
- Packaging and sending
- Managing returns
- Accounting systems
- Profit and loss
- VAT

PROPERTY NEEDS

Many an online entrepreneur has set up shop in their spare room, bedroom, kitchen or garage. It's likely that your business will also be launched this way and you may find that you can run the business from home indefinitely. You might, however, require more space, particularly if you are in online retail, as you'll need space to store goods. You'll also have to consider premises if you are looking to hire employees.

> **IN MY EXPERIENCE:**
> ## Simon Wadsworth, The Retail Factory
>
> Start in an office even if it's tiny – the days of garage dot coms are rare and you need to have a work ethic.

Finding commercial premises, however, incurs considerable expense, so it's not a decision to be made lightly. Revisit your business plan and consider your cash flow and future forecasts. You'll need to consider exactly what you'll need from your premises. How much floor space will you need, for instance? And how much space and what special requirements will you need for stock and storage?

You can always create the necessary number of rooms and install special requirements but first and foremost you'll need to ensure you've got enough space overall – and, just as important, you're not paying for more than you need.

 TIP

You can tweak your website, change suppliers and introduce new product lines. Property, however, is likely to be where you have least flexibility and at the most cost, so you'll want to get it right.

Lease or buy

You've two options when searching for premises: to lease or to buy. For many of you there won't actually be a choice because you won't be able to afford to buy. Even if you can, especially in the current climate of declining property prices, it could be smarter to keep your money in your pocket and not saddle your business with a sizeable mortgage.

One major consideration should be the current state of the property market. While commercial property tends to withstand fluctuation better than the residential market, retail and office lets are at their lowest levels for 10 years, while many landlords have seen 10% sliced off the value of their portfolios over 2008. Basically, it's a far better time to be renting than owning.

Buying

Even given the current state of the property market buying does have its advantages. You'll have an asset to play with and the freedom to not have to go seeking your landlord's approval every time you make a change. Ask yourself the following questions before you decide to buy a property. If you can't answer yes to all of them, buying isn't for you:

- Is the space in the best location you think you can ever afford?
- Do you plan to keep to the same size indefinitely? Does it meet your needs now and in the future?
- Do you have both a sufficient deposit and the budget for a mortgage, or enough cash to purchase the property outright?

If you're in a comfortable enough position to buy premises, then there are several advantages associated with buying a property. The first and most obvious is that you'll own it, have the freedom do with it as you please, and not have to answer to a landlord. Another major advantage with owning your own premises is you'll have a major asset, either to secure loans against or think of as an investment.

As with any property purchase, domestic or commercial, you'll need to carry out the appropriate checks before you agree to buy. Bring in a reputable surveyor, get the place checked with the environmental health officer and find out what your business rates will be.

> ### ✎ TIP
> Do as much research on the building and area as physically possible because if something's not right with it once you've got the keys, it won't be easy to just pack up and move on.

Leasing

Leasing is far more common than buying, for the simple reason that it gives you more flexibility in both a physical and a financial sense. If you expand more quickly than anticipated and need more space, you can move at relatively short notice, provided you negotiated the right kind of contract when you took out the lease. Also, there are a limited number of properties on the market to buy and you'll find your options are far more open when looking for leased property.

A lease can be negotiated for any length of time that you and the landlord agree on but typically will last anywhere between three and 25 years. The landlord will be looking for a reliable tenant that will run a successful business and consequently be able to pay the rent on time. You may be asked to present a business plan and have your own financial history checked up on. If you don't have any trading history then it's not unheard of for the landlord to ask for anything up to a year's rent in advance, so bear this in mind when budgeting.

However, you have just as much right to do your own checks on the landlord. If possible talk to the current or previous tenants. Find out why they're moving on. If their business failed, was it because of something wrong with the property, or even as a result of a difficult landlord? These are the kind of things you'll want to know before signing a lease.

That said the one advantage to the current economic climate is that the power could be swinging back to you as a tenant. It's not uncommon for a landlord, especially if they're struggling to fill a space, to give you an incentive to move in. It's all about supply and demand and don't be afraid to fight your corner just because you're a start-up business. See if you can negotiate a period of free rent to help your business establish itself and use the argument that it's in both your interests for that to happen.

Here are a few tips and things to consider before signing a lease:

- What kind of rent rates are similar businesses in the area being charged, and is yours a fair rate in comparison? The simplest way to find out is to ask: you'll find most businesses will be just as interested to know if they're overpaying the current asking rate so will be happy to play ball.
- Is the length of lease suitable? If it's too short your online business will lack security but if it's too long and you don't have a break clause, you may find yourself stuck.
- Is the building sound and in a state of good repair? It's advisable to bring in expert help to check there are no serious faults.
- Will the landlord offer a rent-free period if there are repairs to be carried out?

- Do you need planning permission before you can build or alter the space according to your designs?
- Who is responsible for insurance? What's included in the rent, and what cover will the landlord expect you to take out yourself in addition?

This is by no means an extensive list of everything you should check before signing a contract. It's always advisable to have a solicitor or property expert to check over the small print for you.

Storerooms

Web shoppers are impatient and expect instant gratification – if you display items that you don't have in stock, it's likely you'll lose that customer pretty quickly and they will move on to another site. So maintaining inventory – and having space to stock it – is an important consideration. As a start-up, it's not easy to gauge what potential demand may be, but instead of ordering the bare minimum, order a bit more so you have enough left over. Having too much inventory is better than running out, but don't order in huge quantities unless you are absolutely sure the product is likely to fly off your virtual shelves, otherwise you may find you are left with stock that is impossible to shift and which you are paying rent on.

Keeping track of how much inventory you have and what is pending can help you decide whether you need to rent storage space or whether, as many entrepreneurs do to start with, you can stock the goods at your home initially. You could choose to do your stock control manually or use software. The manual option is likely to be the cheapest but you won't be able to access and retrieve records as quickly as if you were doing this through electronic methods. Most accountancy software packages include inventory management, so if you have invested in a package, it's worth seeing if it includes a function for stock control (see p.290 for more on accountancy package options). A computerised inventory control system is also worth investing in if you have many different types of stock. Before you invest in software, get two or three quotes from providers and assess your business needs now and in the future.

TIP

Efficient stock control allows you to have the right amount of stock in the right place at the right time.

If you are looking to rent storage space, bear in mind many of the guidelines that apply to leasing property also apply to renting storage space – check out whether the rates are suitable and see if you can negotiate terms.

Guide to inventory control

- Netsuite (www.netsuite.co.uk) offers an inventory management software that is integrated with customer relationship management, enabling customers to view updated inventory information on your online store.
- Orderwise (www.orderwise.co.uk) provides stock control software that integrates with many accountancy software packages.
- InventoryOps (www.inventoryops.com) is a website with information on inventory management.

➡ PACKAGING AND SENDING

You've got your online shop up and running and built the transactional part of your website. The next area you need to turn your attention to is order fulfilment – the packaging and sending of items purchased. It can seem like one of the least exciting parts of running an online business, but the fulfilment of orders is often the most important aspect for your customers.

FROM THE EXPERTS:
Nick Robertson, ASOS.com

Logistics is never far from my mind, it's such an important part of running an internet business. You have to keep an open mind as to what needs to be done in this area.

Deciding how you fulfil orders will depend very much on the type of items you are selling and where you are sending them to, but there are basic rules to stick to regardless of what type of online business you run.

- Use strong packaging to ship items – there's nothing worse than sending something, only for it to be delivered damaged. This is one of the quickest ways of losing customers.

- Take advantage of the shipment and place a small token, thank you letter for ordering and your business card – it will remind people of your site when they open the packaging.
- Product packaging can add value to your product and boost brand awareness, so consider what design you can use on your packaging to increase its impact.

IN MY EXPERIENCE:

Glenys Berd, LoveThoseShoes.com

We have offices and warehousing and do all our own dispatch. We have tried outsourcing dispatch but in the end we could only guarantee the quality of delivery by doing it ourselves.

MANAGING RETURNS

It's important to set restrictions on when people can return goods and expect a refund or exchange. Many businesses, for example, say that goods need to be returned within 21 or 30 days and that they should be unopened or undamaged. Your returns policy should be stated clearly in your website's terms and conditions. See p.159 for more on your legal obligations concerning returns.

ACCOUNTING SYSTEMS

If you decide you're going to manage the books yourself you'll want to get yourself some accountancy software. Whoever's job it is, yours or an accountant's, the person balancing the books, chasing invoices, managing suppliers and paying staff doesn't need to be worrying about the latest technology and it's probably the last thing on their mind. It's perfectly possible to work with an Excel spreadsheet but buying an accountancy software package can slash the amount of time and effort you put into managing your finances. Expect to pay from £500 for a system that supports two to three users.

From reminders for chasing payment to generating invoices, a good package is like a virtual accounts department. It can tell you how much you are owed and by whom; how long it takes you to pay your bills; what you have in stock and what you have in the bank at any moment in time. More importantly, it could also give you those vital breakdowns of how much you are making on each service, day or month. Of course, there's nothing stopping you or your accountant working from a basic Excel spreadsheet, but bear in mind that a good accountancy software package can drastically reduce your accounting bill every year.

There are a multitude of different systems on the market. Choosing the right system at the right time is critical. What is the right system? There is no easy answer to that question. System selection will depend on a number of criteria. Professional services firm RSM Bentley Jennison recommends that you ask yourself the following questions:

- Budget – how much do you have to spend right now?
- Compatibility – will the system you choose 'talk' to the on-line software you have created for your business? The last thing you need is to re-key the electronic information already collected into the accounting system.
- User friendliness – who will use the software and how accounts literate is the user?
- What information do you need from the system and in what format?

Leaving aside the manual bookkeeping systems, there are two broad types of software:

- Software that is hosted on a stand alone PC
  or
- Web-based systems (often referred to as 'software as a service' or SaaS)

According to RSM Bentley Jennison, the latter are becoming more popular as they are anytime, anyplace so you don't have to be at the office to either process data or obtain reports. There are a number of different 'families' of accounting software systems; each offering different packages from basic to sophisticated. It is worth choosing the one you think will best fit your needs in the medium term, at least, because upgrading within a family is far easier than changing from one to another. Here are a few examples:

- Sage: www.sage.co.uk
- Access Accounts: www.access-accounts.com
- Netsuite (web-based system): www.netsuite.co.uk

Advice from Sage
What types of accounting systems are available?

There are many different types of software that can help you manage your accounts. Very basically, they break down into desktop, server and online systems to help you decide what's best for you, here's a brief description:

Desktop software

This is software that you load onto your computer from a disk or download from a website. You access the software locally on that computer and all your data is stored in the same place. Sage Instant Accounts and Sage 50 Accounts are examples of desktop software. How desktop software differs:

Data held locally: the user holds their own data on their own machines, servers or hard drives. This helps with accessibility, up time, backing up data. Some customers prefer desktop software because of security as they are not sharing their data with a third party. However, some customers like online software as they share it with a third party that is responsible for their data.

Ownership and licensing: you tend to pay a one-off fee for desktop software then you own the software outright, whereas with online software you would tend to pay an ongoing monthly subscription fee.

Integration with other desktop products: more developers build for desktop than online but that trend is shifting quickly. This means you can integrate your accounts software with Outlook, ebanking/payments, payroll etc.

Server-based software

With server-based software, you still use your computer to access the data, but everything is stored on a central server. It makes it easier for several people to share information and access the same data at the same time.

Online or hosted software

You access online or hosted software through the internet. Your data may actually be stored miles away, but you can work on it from anywhere with an internet connection.

www.sage.co.uk

➡ CASH FLOW

Many of you would have heard of the saying 'cash is king'. Of course, in the long run, you have to be profitable to have a successful business but the mistake many businesses make is that they do not know whether they will run out of cash. Their systems are not robust enough, or the information from them not timely enough, to project forward to see where the cash holes are.

Two crucial questions

From a cash flow perspective, there are two fundamental questions to consider:

- Do you know when you should expect cash to come in from customers?
- Do you know when you have to pay your suppliers?

It's still surprising how many businesses still don't know the answer to these. Once you have discovered these then, with the aid of a simple spreadsheet, you can forward forecast income less expenditure and discover where the holes are.

 TIP
Web-based accounting systems are becoming increasingly popular as they enable you to work on the accounts without being tied to the office.

➡ PROFIT AND LOSS

Understanding whether you make a profit or a loss is one of the most critical key performance indicators of any business. If you're not making a profit, there's little point in being in business. Understanding what your income drivers are, and the associated costs, will enable you to have a firm grounding to understand the profit and loss account. Many accounting systems will produce a profit and loss report but, without the understanding behind the numbers, they are just that: numbers on a page. See p.76 for example profit & loss sheets.

There are many online resources that can be found to explain how to interpret a profit and loss account. You may be able to find courses at your local Business Enterprise agency (such as the Chambers of Commerce). The best way to find out how your profit and loss account works is to ask your accountant! After all, they are there to help.

VAT

Supplies of goods and services via the internet have become common place, however, for a new business the VAT rules can be complicated. Businesses trading via the internet should also be aware of HM Revenue & Customs' (HMRC) ability to track the sale of goods from a particular address. One professional services firm, for example, says that several of its clients have recently received visits from the VAT man armed with lists of items sold on eBay. An appreciation of the rules is therefore essential if an unexpected bottom line cost to the business is to be avoided.

Goods sold via the internet tend to be treated like any 'normal' supply of goods and should not present a problem where the rules are understood. A supply of services made via the internet can, however, be more complicated.

As RSM Bentley Jennison outlines, four basic conditions need to be met for a supply of goods to be subject to VAT in the UK, namely:

- The supply must be a taxable supply (at the standard or reduced-rate) made by a 'taxable person' (a natural or legal person registered or required to be registered for VAT in the UK)
- The supply must be made for consideration (normally money but does include barter arrangements)
- The supply must be made in the furtherance of a 'business'
- The supply must be made in the UK

Whilst the first three conditions are normally self-evident the fourth can be more problematic; however, the basic premise is that the place of supply of goods is determined by where they are located when they are dispatched to the customer.

Sales made via the internet by UK suppliers (where the goods are located in the UK when they are dispatched) to a UK customer are subject to VAT under the normal rules (zero-rated supplies made in the UK by taxable persons do not attract VAT).

Supplies of goods made by a UK business (where the goods are located in the UK when they are dispatched to the customer) to business customers in the EC or abroad are zero-rated, subject to the normal rules and should not present a problem to a business trading via the internet.

Where a UK business supplies and delivers goods to a non-VAT registered person in another EC member state (typically private individuals), the supplies will attract UK VAT, subject to the normal rules, unless the volume of sales is in excess of the 'distance selling threshold' for that member state. In this case, a liability to register in the particular member state may arise with a resulting requirement to charge VAT at the local rate. A liability to register in several EC member states could therefore arise where trading spans the EC.

The place of supply of installed or assembled goods is in the country where the goods are installed or assembled and a liability to register and account for VAT at the local rate may arise in the EC, although a simplified procedure may be available to allow the VAT registered customer to account for VAT instead.

Things to remember:

- Make sure you analyse your property needs thoroughly, is buying or leasing better for your business?

- Carefully plan your packaging and sending processes, the fulfilment of orders is one of the most important aspects of your relationship with your customers.

- Be thorough in your record-keeping. The better organised your figures are, the better organised your shop will be.

- Don't try to manage it all yourself if you don't have the time or skills. Hire an accountant if you need one.

- Check out the different types of accounting software available, it could reduce the amount of time and effort put into record-keeping.

- Be cautious in your forecasting. It's better to underestimate trade than overestimate. Be aware of your cash flow and profit and loss figures at all times.

- Make sure you are aware of all the regulations surrounding VAT and goods sold over the internet.

G ood suppliers and good offers won't just turn up in your inbox. You'll need to do the research, negotiate and put considerable effort into finding the right suppliers and the right products at the right prices. If you're planning on launching an online retail business, the type you choose will largely decide how and where you source your products and goods, and the type of suppliers you need to speak to. Mostly though, you'll buy through one of the following ways:

- Wholesaler
- Direct from manufacturers or suppliers
- From abroad / importers

You can find details of suppliers from numerous sources including magazines, newspapers, the internet and directories and you'll then need to get in touch with them to strike the best deal for your business. Remember that price is not everything so don't get too distracted by seeking rock bottom prices otherwise you risk alienating your suppliers altogether.

In this chapter, we'll look at:

- Wholesalers
- Going direct
- Trade fairs
- Sourcing goods from abroad
- Maintaining relationships
- Building good credit

➡ WHOLESALERS

Wholesalers specialise in certain types of goods and tend to cluster together in industrial areas of cities. In London, for example, most are located to the west near Wembley and Park Royal, making them more accessible for the rest of the country. The centrality of the Midlands also makes it a logistical hub for distributors and wholesalers.

✦ TIP

Some wholesalers will require you to have a trade or membership card, but don't be put off by this. It's usually something you can fill in at the counter with proof of business status such as bank statement.

Wholesalers are fairly traditional in how they advertise themselves and you're just as likely to track them down in the *Yellow Pages* as online. Slowly but surely however, they are beginning to use the web to reveal their whereabouts and even advertise their goods.

Before you set off on a visit, phone ahead to check about the products they've got on offer and in stock and for their best prices. Get the person's name that you speak to so you can find them when you get there. It'll make you seem more experienced and they'll be more inclined to help you find what you're looking for – and maybe even give you a discount.

✦ TIP

www.thewholesaler.co.uk is the most established site for UK wholesalers.

FROM THE EXPERTS:
Nick Robertson, ASOS.com

At the beginning, no one wanted to deal with us and we walked around Great Portland Street in London with a plastic bag. Now people knock on our door.

Negotiation is the norm when it comes to buying in bulk and the wholesale warehouse floor is where the deals are made. The prospect of battling it out with a cockney 'Del Boy' might terrify some of you but it needn't be anywhere near so scary. Simply open negotiations by asking something such as, 'If I take three batches of this instead of two, are you going to give me x% discount?'

Remember, it's in a wholesaler's favour for you to make a healthy profit to ensure your business prospers and you keep coming back for more stock, so there's always room for negotiation on advertised prices. Obviously, the more you buy the more flexible wholesalers are likely to be. A £200 sale isn't a big deal to them so be realistic. That said discounts of up to 20% are common place when a deal's there to be struck.

It's also possible to get credit from many wholesalers. The process differs little from applying for any other form of credit and just involves filling out the relevant forms and undergoing a basic credit check. It's definitely an option many online retail businesses take advantage of but you should probably stick to using bank debt to begin with as it's a lot easier to keep control of your finances if they're all in one place. You'll also want to make sure you're happy with a wholesaler's service before you start taking credit from it.

✦ TIP

Most warehouses are open Monday to Friday and for part of Sunday. As inconvenient as it might be, they also tend to close from Christmas Eve through to 2 January, so check times before you set off.

➡ DIRECT FROM MANUFACTURERS OR SUPPLIERS

As opposed to physically visiting a wholesaler and bringing your newly acquired goods back to your home or premises, you can also buy directly from manufacturers or suppliers who'll deliver to you.

Your decision to buy directly from a manufacturer could be because you specifically want to stock a certain brand or product. If they don't sell through wholesale most large companies will have a department set up to deal with direct sales and distribution and you should look to contact them directly.

Most suppliers welcome any trade and while you might struggle to get credit with them as a start-up, they'll be happy to supply you. Others though, and most often in the case of branded products such as clothing, will want to see evidence that your business profile fits their brand. You'll be expected to go to their premises to pitch to become an official reseller and prove you understand the way they'd like their goods to be sold. Certain brands are deliberately picky and, silly as it might seem, you'll have to work hard to earn the right to sell their goods. If they don't already sell through an online channel, this could improve your chances of getting them on board. If they do already have a web sales channel, find out which other resellers they use and see if you can improve on this service or at the very least, match it.

In turn, you'll find it'll work the other way round as well and you'll be approached by sales people asking you to stock their products. As the shoe is on the other foot you should be able to negotiate free or heavily discounted products for your first order to see how well they'll sell, so use such opportunities to practise and refine your negotiation skills.

When buying direct from suppliers or manufacturers you may also be able to negotiate or even be offered a 'sale or return' deal. This means you'll be refunded for any items you don't sell within an agreed period of time. However, most 'sale or return' will see you earn a commission of 10%–20% per unit sold, instead of the larger mark-up you'd expect from buying wholesale. It is a sensible way of testing the market for goods though before risking a large outlay.

IN MY EXPERIENCE:
Glenys Berd, LoveThoseShoes.com

If you're starting to look for suppliers, researching on the net is the best way, but it's imperative you know what you want to sell. There are several e-commerce forums on the net that you can join and it's always useful to ask people who they would recommend.

➡ TRADE FAIRS

The other way you'll find direct suppliers and manufacturers is through trade fairs. Here companies showcase their products and the latest ranges and it can also be a good hunting ground for networking purposes. It's always worth attending the main trade fairs in your industry, even if it's only to keep an eye on emerging trends and new suppliers who might be able to cut you a better deal in order to secure your services. Trade fairs also present the opportunity to find smaller suppliers that otherwise weren't on your radar and to pick up something unique. Exhibitions.co.uk is a listings site for the main UK trade fairs but you should also make an effort to find out about industry specific events by reading trade magazines covering your business sector and asking your suppliers which ones they attend and recommend.

IN MY EXPERIENCE:
Simon Wadsworth, The Retail Factory
We went to every trade fair in Europe and made contacts.

When you visit a trade fair, study the website or guidebook beforehand to highlight companies that might be of interest to you and try to be quite strategic about visiting them as a priority. Trade fairs tend to be large maze-like villages of generic exhibition stands and smiling faces handing out plastic bags and sweets making it easy to switch off and miss what you originally went for. Take a Dictaphone instead of trying to make notes as it will be easier to get all the information down, and wear something smart but comfortable – you could be there for hours.

TIP
On the issue of time, make sure you allow plenty of it. You might only attend one trade fair a year but that's your one window to potentially find your five best-selling products so it really is worth booking out the whole day – or even two. If you are there overnight, amend your hit list for the second day.

➡ BUYING FROM ABROAD / IMPORTERS

Why is it attractive to buy from abroad?

There are quite simply huge savings to be had from buying produce from abroad. In fact, it's not just savings, you'll find items that you can't buy anywhere else and which will have a mark-up far in excess of anything you'll buy and sell from a UK manufacturer or wholesaler.

China and India are the booming economies of the world, however, their export trades are very much geared to supplying big business and they rarely ship items in quantities less than 40ft containers. Smaller amounts are easier to source from countries such as Thailand and Indonesia, specifically Bali, where there's a good variety of products that are very saleable in the UK market. Increasingly, online businesses in the UK are importing everything from jewellery to clothing and interior design products, at rock bottom prices that make it mouth-wateringly tempting.

However, while international trade is becoming far more commonplace among small business owners, it remains laden with risk for a start-up like you. There are also significant costs to consider that will counter-balance what initially seem like massive mark-ups. In addition to purchase price, factor in the cost of finding suppliers, packing and transportation, insurance and customs duty.

You'll also need to account for a degree of leeway in this, as when you're managing large imports even a slight fluctuation in transport charges or exchange rates can eat massively into your profits.

TIP

Relying completely on goods imported from abroad is a riskier strategy than buying from home simply because there are more factors beyond your direct control.

Finding a supplier abroad

You've got two options for finding overseas suppliers, either seek them yourself and buy directly or go indirectly through an importer. Buying directly offers you the greatest mark-up but you'll have to find them, arrange the deal, transportation and maintain all lines of communication on your own. Using an importer is far less risky and taxing but, predictably, the profit you can make is nowhere near as high, while the chance of you importing something truly unique is also reduced.

If you're thinking of importing directly, the first thing you need to do is find a supplier. You can fly out to the countries you know specialise in your goods on a fact finding trip and go seeking suppliers yourself, much as you might plan an exploratory trip to West London warehouse depots. If you do this, try and plan as much as you can in advance so you can make the most of your time. Research regions that specialise in export supply, look for clusters of suppliers, try and contact UK business networks in that country and ask all your contacts for advice. Has anyone else you know been through the same experience and what recommendations and advice can they give you? While expensive it could also be worth taking a translator with you.

A safer and easier way to begin is either by using a supplier recommended via word of mouth from someone who has already successfully imported with them or by consulting trade bodies in your sector that might have a list of recommended international suppliers. Likewise, each country's embassy should have a commercial department. See the Foreign and Commonwealth Office website (www.fco.gov.uk) for more details.

✦ TIP
To ensure you're buying from a legitimate supplier look for a proven track record of supplying goods to the UK, ask for the name of UK customers so you can check this, and ask to speak to the main sales agent you'll be dealing with to ensure there will be no insurmountable language barriers.

Striking a deal and protecting yourself

The key here is to be absolutely clear about what you're buying and for how much. Get it all in a legally binding, bilingual contract and leave nothing unaccounted for. If you can, try to be there or have a representative present when goods are packed or transported. Chances are you'll be fine but there are plenty of horror stories of business owners who sign off and pay for goods only to see something that bears little resemblance arrive in the UK a month later. If you're in any way suspicious, first question why you're doing the deal. Second, order a small amount as a test.

Don't scrimp on insurance. Get some good advice from an insurance broker on product liability insurance for the goods you're importing, marine insurance (which covers you for all transportation) and look to cover goods for the contract price plus an extra 10% to account for the extra costs you'll incur if something goes wrong.

Transporting goods

Aside from cultural obstacles and the dangers of being ripped-off, the main problem is the unreliability of affordable transportation. Shipping is the cheapest option but involves taking out a container (20ft is usually the smallest, with 40ft the standard size) that runs the risk of being delayed at both ends of departure and arrival. You simply can't afford delayed delivery times, particularly if you are selling online – people expect almost instant

 TIP

By far the best way is to carry items back with you as luggage, but of course, this will only apply for goods such as jewellery, where you carry substantial quantities with ease.

gratification from the internet as a sales channel. The same applies to posting items, sending them by airfreight or loose cargo can be massively expensive as you'll pay by weight.

Paying customs duty and legal responsibilities

There are various legal obligations you'll need to comply with, depending on what it is you're looking to import.

There are limitations, quotas and special controls governing the import of certain products such as foods, medicinal products, plants, animals, metals and textiles. In some cases you'll require an import licence, in others you'll need to provide proof of country of origin, while many items are subject to inspection.

You'll also have to pay any duty and VAT that applies to the goods you're importing under UK and EC law before they are released to you. Your freight transporter can sometimes pay this and re-invoice you for it; otherwise you'll need to seek advice from HM Revenue and Customs (HMRC) or an accountant on what you need to pay. Make sure you do this in advance so you're clear about the real cost of the goods you're buying.

Is it really worth it?

In brief, while it's massively tempting, for most of you buying from abroad is better put on hold until you've established your business and can survive if an order is massively delayed or, worse still, doesn't arrive at all.

If you do go ahead, be as thorough as you can possibly be. Without doubt you shouldn't buy without flying out and visiting the supplier to see the goods. Indeed, you'll usually only find the best deals by doing this and it can be far more reassuring to see the products in person.

→ MAINTAINING A RELATIONSHIP WITH SUPPLIERS

Once you've established a network of suppliers you're happy with and can rely on, it's important you maintain a good working relationship with them. It's not just about paying your bills on time.

- Try to deal with the same sales representative or agent whenever you order. Building a relationship with one person is more likely to inspire trust and the odd favour when you need it.
- Keep a check on prices and review your bills against what other suppliers are offering. Even if you don't want to change suppliers you may be able to negotiate more competitive prices. Don't be afraid to do this; suppliers will understand your need to get a good price and be grateful for giving them the chance to match it rather than lose your trade to a competitor.
- Remember not to judge a supplier solely on price. Ensure levels of customer service, flexibility and, crucially, quality of product, don't slip.

Advice from Sage
Managing suppliers

Make sure you have clear terms and conditions stated upfront that both parties have agreed and understood. Clear invoice and remittance documents can also ensure there's no confusion over payments.

Using software that enables you to log all your communications history with a customer or supplier means that you can see exactly when you made a phone call or sent a letter to them. And having a good stock control system can also help. If you know you're running low on items, you can let your suppliers know in plenty of time to reorder them.

Finally, using BACS (see below) can speed up the time it takes for you to make payments to your suppliers, something which will always help the relationship!

www.sage.co.uk

➡ BUILDING GOOD CREDIT

In an ideal world we'd all be paid the minute we invoice and be given as long as we want to pay, and some companies, often the big ones with lots of weight to throw around, take that attitude. It won't even be an option for you as a start-up as suppliers will look to be paid promptly, but view this as a positive opportunity to build trust and earn the right to greater flexibility going forward.

Advice from Sage Pay. . .
Using BACS

BACS (Bankers Automated Clearing Service) is an automated payment method. It is used for batches payment and runs by using a link within your accounts software connected to your bank account.

The benefits of BACS are that it:

- Automates regular payments
- Reduces the time and cost of administering bulk payments
- Helps manage cash flow and improve financial control
- Reduces risk of loss, late payment and theft for customers

It's an easy and inexpensive way to start improving procurement efficiency.

www.sagepay.com

If you do buy on credit, ensure that keeping payments up-to-date is prioritised. Falling behind with repayments is the best way to ruin an otherwise good business relationship and if a supplier suddenly withholds delivery or demands payment of what you owe in full, the future of your business could be in real jeopardy.

Things to remember:

- Have a clear idea of what you are looking for: especially price and quality.

- Try to buy in bulk, or ask for discounts.

- Build up a mutually beneficial relationship with your supplier.

- Make sure you consider both the benefits and risks associated with importing goods from abroad.

- When researching importing, don't forget to add up the costs of transport and customs duty.

- If you buy on credit, make sure you keep up to date with your payments or you risk jeopardising relationships with your suppliers.

Many an online business is operated by one person, with the occasional ad hoc help drafted in to support busier times of the year, for example. But at some point in your website's growth, you may need to consider whether you need to hire staff to help on a more permanent basis. Whether or not you recruit staff will depend on the type of online business you plan to operate. If you are focusing on a retail model, it's likely you'll need to hire people to help with customer sales, order processing, stock returns and after sales support. If you are running a service-based online business, you may find you need to employ staff to handle customer queries as your business grows.

There's also the ongoing development and design of your site to consider. If it requires added functionality, it may be worth investing in the services of a web developer. If your business is being run from home, rather than actual premises, you could consider employing the necessary people on a remote basis, but the same rules apply as if you were working with them in the same premises. The people you employ to help run your online business will have just as much influence over its success as the goods that you sell, so it's crucial you get the right team on board. Recruitment is a tricky area, and one that ends up being extremely costly if you make the wrong decisions.

In this chapter we'll look at:

- Identifying your staffing needs
- Writing job descriptions and adverts
- Interviewing
- Training up your new recruits
- Ways of attracting the best talent
- Pitfalls to watch out for
- The necessary paperwork

➡ WHAT ARE YOUR REQUIREMENTS?

Your business plan should have included an idea of how many members of staff you'll need to run your online business smoothly, but will also have taken into account what you can afford. Ask yourself the following questions:

- What level of technical expertise does your staff need?
- Does it make sense to employ them part-time to start with?
- Will you need more staff at certain times of the year?
- What will be your busiest or most staff intensive hours?
- How much can you increase sales by adding an extra member of staff?

Once you've established exactly how many members of staff your online venture needs you will have to make a decision on what you can afford to pay them. You'll need to strike a fine balance between being practical and not stretching your budget too far, but also being realistic about what you need to pay to attract the right kind of talent.

FROM THE EXPERTS:
Nick Robertson, ASOS.com

I wasn't tech-savvy when we launched the business but I was fortunate enough to employ people who were. This was back in the days when technology failed a lot. We spent a lot of money on our website and it would take a while for sales to catch up.

Growth in the online sector means that salaries are competitive and demand for skilled employees – particularly web developers – can be high. This means you may have to pay more than you bargained for to secure the right person and staff may also be hard to retain. To gain long-term loyalty you'll have to think of ways of incentivising and motivating staff. In the past, many online businesses offered their employees shares in the company, with the potential to realise these when

TIP
Many online retail businesses incentivise staff with bonuses or commission on sales and this can work well.

the business floated on the market or reached certain milestones. In the wake of the dot com bust, however, employees are less tempted by the lure of shares from online businesses, so you may want to focus on more traditional ways of rewarding and retaining staff.

DISTINGUISHING JOB ROLES

Website manager

For many people, the whole point of starting an online business is running it on a day to day basis. It might be a desire to exploit technology or work with family; it might be a professional motivation to have control of choosing and ordering stock or managing customer services. Whatever the reason, they want to be in control, involved, the epicentre of all activity. And there's absolutely nothing wrong with that. Many successful online businesses thrive on the passion and personality of their owners.

For others though, often those online business owners looking to expand quickly or with outside interests who don't intend to be involved with the site full-time, there's a need for someone else to fill the website manager's role.

It can be a tricky role to fill – after all the hard work you put into starting the business, this person will have a major say in its success. The key starting point for any successful recruitment is a clear job description. However, aside from experience and skills, you'll need to find someone who you get on with, can trust and someone who shares your vision for the business.

You'll need your site manager to be motivated to drive sales and the obvious way to do that is through commission and bonuses. Better than a straight percentage are staggered bonuses or commission incentives above certain target thresholds incentivising them to keep striving for the next level. You'll also find loyalty in making them feel valued through training and further management opportunities should the company grow.

 TIP
A website manager will take a hands-on role in the business so it's important you get on, share the same vision for the business and communicate with each other at all times.

Technical staff

While not sharing the same level of responsibility as a site manager, your technical staff will play a big role in your site's performance and the experience of your customers. Technical roles can cover everything from web developers, to coders to site maintenance staff. They could be responsible for both the front and back end of the site, the way the pages are displayed, the navigation of the site and the checkout function. Online shoppers are notoriously fussy when it comes to the number of 'clicks' needed to complete a purchase – make this process too lengthy and they will defect in their droves, resulting in many an abandoned online shopping basket. All of this will have a bearing on how your customers communicate that experience to other people and, consequently, whether they return or encourage others to visit on word of mouth recommendation.

Finding the right technical staff can be labour-intensive: web developers, particularly those skilled in Web 2.0 technologies, are one of the most sought-after IT professionals and they've enjoyed a surge in salaries in the last couple of years. The current economic downturn is prompting many companies to invest more heavily in online ventures so demand for good web developers is likely to continue increasing.

IN MY EXPERIENCE:
Jamie Murray Wells, Glasses Direct

Building a team from the start is tricky, especially when creating a web business. From the beginning, we had limited resources. If you employ a web developer, it's the difference between succeeding and failing, otherwise you could be making it up as you go along and it's critical you get it right.

In order to secure the right technical staff for your business, put time into explaining what you expect of them, train them and give them the knowledge you'd like them to impart, and pay and incentivise them to perform to these standards and stay loyal. For all employees, show them they're important to you and that you're willing to share your profits with them, no matter how modestly, because they're part of your vision and you've shared aims.

TIP
Look at what types of incentives and perks you can offer staff ranging from discounts, commission, drinks down the pub, flexi-time, fun days out or sponsoring sports and charity activities. Keep it varied and try and set new targets for individuals and teams to be aiming towards.

Lead by example

If you're not punctual, smartly turned out, positive, polite and motivated, then you've no right to expect your staff to be. If you're having a bad day, you've argued with your partner, the bailiffs are ringing non-stop and your suppliers are threatening to withhold your order it's your job to put a smile on your face and convince the team it is business as usual. While running an online business means that you won't have to deal with customers on a face-to-face basis, you and your staff must still convey a sense of professionalism and empathy when dealing with customers on the phone or via email.

Casual staff

Many online businesses rely on temporary staff, especially for peaks and troughs in trade such as weekends and holiday seasons. It's also a sensible way to start recruiting if you're not entirely sure you need anyone full-time.

An ideal situation is to try and establish a flexible team of reliable casual staff who you can call upon when needed and whom you could possibly employ full-time if the opportunity arises. Students can make great casual staff as well, both during term times and those returning home for the holidays. Try to keep a pool of both and keep an eye out for replacements when they graduate. If they happen to be your target audience, students can also be great advocates to have on your side – provided you treat them well, of course!

Be prepared to give the same flexibility you expect in return: it's perfectly reasonable that someone can't work for you at short notice if they're not on your payroll. It's best to be clear about when you expect them to work, especially over key seasonal dates such as Christmas and Easter.

➡ RECRUITING STAFF

The key to successful recruiting is to put the homework in up front. It's tempting to rush out and put a job ad out and get applications in, but for several reasons, that isn't the way to go about it.

Start by drawing up a detailed job description of the duties and responsibilities of the role and the attributes, skills and experience needed from candidates. The more closely you define the role, the more likely you will be to get applicants that meet your requirements.

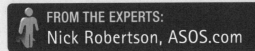

FROM THE EXPERTS:
Nick Robertson, ASOS.com

Looking back I would have recruited better staff earlier on. I might have struggled to get them but they would have been more experienced in areas I wasn't skilled in.

Recruitment has become embroiled in employment law in recent years with a number of high profile cases where business owners have been taken to tribunals on grounds of discrimination for not employing someone because of their race, gender, disability, sexuality or religious belief.

Being morally resolute that such a repugnant thought would never cross your mind sadly isn't enough to keep you covered from claims of discrimination. It's quite possible someone might see a fault in your recruitment process and look to take advantage, or you might inadvertently cause upset by your reason for rejecting a candidate.

Writing job descriptions

Therein lies the crux. Your job description (and advertisement) should lay out the criteria by which you will carry out your recruitment process. If you have specific requirements which you can legally justify, then providing you detail them in advance and expose every candidate to the same criteria you cannot be accused of discriminating against one candidate. That's why it's essential to spend time planning at the beginning of the recruitment process.

Once you've established firm criteria and requirements for the role prioritise them into primary and secondary requirements. This will give you a firm matrix to compare applications and interviews so that if any legal objection was ever raised you'd have clear written evidence that the process was fair and above board.

This might seem an onerous process for recruiting what might be a customer service role but as well as protecting you legally, it should also set you in good stead for finding the right person to make life easier. And once you've done it once, you can use the same process again.

Advertising for staff

Once you've made a detailed job description, making out an ad should be easy. List all the job requirements, criteria for applicants, information about your online business and also state the salary or wage you'll pay. Some people advise against this but by listing what you're prepared to pay you're ensuring you don't waste your time vetting applications from candidates expecting to earn more than you can afford to pay.

Just as important as what you detail about the job role, is the information on how you want people to reply. Be specific. Ideally you want everyone to reply in the same way so you're making a fair and direct comparison of applications. The best way to do this is to use application forms but you might not have the time to draw one up or deem them not personal enough. If you want CVs then ask for a personal letter as well. Try and tailor the response to the skills of the role. If you need someone to take orders over the phone it might be that you ask people to apply that way. If IT skills are important then applications by email only is another way of vetting.

> ## ✦ TIP
> Courtesy, people skills and technical experience are all likely to be important so perhaps ask applicants to explain why they have those attributes in their letters.

Where you advertise will depend on the role and type of online business you're running and it makes sense to advertise online, through online message boards such as Gumtree for example. For more senior positions such as site manager or web developer it might be that you target people already working in these positions through the technology press, recruitment websites or agencies that can prove they have candidates with the necessary experience on their books. Targeted advertising can make more sense than more general options, but be careful about what you're spending. It could be that networking contacts and job centres could be just as effective. Most likely, a combination will produce a decent response.

Short-listing candidates for interview

You'll already have done the hard work and this is where your matrix should pay dividends. Simply pass all your applications past your primary and secondary criteria ticking each attribute that they meet. If you've three candidates that meet all the primary boxes they're clearly the best suited for the job. If you have none then start consulting the secondary options and so on.

Be careful that you use these criteria and these criteria only. After all, you devised them. Bringing any other consideration into an isolated application could be discriminatory if you don't then apply the same to all the others.

It is likely confusion will occur when an applicant meets most of the criteria but either lets themselves down in some way such as poor spelling or incorrect information supplied, or you have a gut feeling the person could give you more in an interview than on paper. It's unrealistic to pretend gut feeling doesn't exist – it's very important because after all you're going to have to work closely with this person so it can't be a purely mathematical choice. Providing you're not discriminating against someone on gut feeling you should be fine and, remember, the interview process is just as important as the overall application.

Look to make a manageable shortlist but remember it's very risky to reject someone for an interview if they've met the same criteria as everyone else unless you've got a very good reason you'd be prepared to stand in front of a tribunal to defend.

➡ INTERVIEWING

Successful interviewing requires certain skills. If you've never employed people before you may find some training helpful. For more information on training contact the Chartered Institute of Personnel and Development at www.cipd.co.uk. There are various courses available to teach you effective interviewing techniques, but if you can't spare the time or finances for these, the basics are covered here.

Preparing to interview candidates

Interviews must be planned extremely carefully. You only have a short window of time to elicit all the information you need from a potential recruit. Not only do you have to ascertain their relevant levels of experience, you also need to gauge accurate impressions about whether they fit in with the kind of atmosphere and work environment you're trying to achieve.

After coming up with a shortlist for interview, you should contact prospective interviewees and give them clear instructions on where you're located, how to get there, what they should bring with them, who they should ask for and how long the process is likely to last.

Set aside some dedicated time to do the interviews – make sure there are no unnecessary interruptions such as ringing phones or other staff or even family members vying for your attention. To ensure you're not interrupted put a sign on the door along the lines of 'Interview taking place – do not disturb'. It might sound ridiculously basic, but it's amazing what a difference this simple measure makes.

TIP

If you are running your business from home, you could consider renting office space for a day to conduct your interviews, as this will help instil a more professional environment, as well as ensuring you will be free from distractions.

Remember, the interview stage is just as much about selling yourself and your business to them as the other way around. The best candidates are always going to be in high demand so you'll need to impress them too if you want to attract them to work for you. Think ahead about how to begin the interview by explaining a little bit about yourself, how you've got to the stage you're at, what your plans are for the business and what you're looking for in a candidate.

Conducting the interview

It's good practice to explain how you see the interview going, even if it's to say it's going to be an informal chat for 15 minutes. This should put the candidate at ease, help them relax and enable you to see their more natural personality. You learn far less from someone if they're nervous, uptight and adopting a false front. One of the main advantages of taking the time to refresh yourself on an interviewee's application before they arrive is that you can ask them a few light questions about their interests to help them relax.

Prepare your questions in advance by returning to your initial job specification. Include general questions regarding their personality, as well as questions that probe more deeply into how well suited they are to the job, but, again, make sure you ask all candidates the same questions that are likely to be decisive in your decision making and don't tackle issues of a sensitive nature that aren't relevant to the job. Ask open questions that encourage fuller responses.

Include any written or practical test you think might be relevant but it's usually fair to tell candidates about this beforehand. Give interviewees the opportunity to ask you questions, but don't feel you need to answer anything you aren't comfortable answering and never immediately reveal how an interviewee has got on.

If you think it's appropriate get the serious candidates in for a second interview and if you have someone else in the business at this stage, consider involving them for a second opinion.

TIP

Ask someone you trust, such as a business associate, friend or family member to help you with the interview process, so you can test interviewees' people skills with different groups. Another trick is to ask a friend to help out by showing interviewees in and out of the premises and to the interview room, as you'll find people tend to be far more relaxed in this situation and ask very different questions to other people than they'll ask to you, the boss.

Throughout the process keep clear notes that relate directly back to the primary and secondary requirements you first set out. It could be that you make out a tick box form in advance or mark a score next to each point, which is far easier than trying to scribble full notes and less intimidating.

The selection process

Once you've completed the interview process, if you've done as outlined, you should have one clear candidate and it's likely because you've been so clear in your thinking throughout that your gut feeling will be closely aligned to what's on paper. If there's not one clear choice then it's time to study your feedback and make a decision. Once you've done that and you're happy you've got the right person then contact them by phone, set a start date and confirm this in writing.

➡ THE PAPERWORK

Becoming an employer for the first time can seem a little daunting. There's a whole raft of administrative duties you'll now be responsible for, and neglecting them is not an option.

Your first port of call should be to contact HMRC on 0845 60 70 143 and request a New Employer Starter Pack. It contains everything you need to set yourself up to recruit staff.

Nearly everyone that will work for your online business will count as an employee, which means you need to be aware of your obligations for tax and National Insurance contributions. You must keep detailed records of every single member of staff right from the very beginning. All of the following types of staff count as employees in the eyes of the taxman:

- Directors
- Full and part-time workers
- Temporary or casual workers

Even if a worker claims to be self-employed and will pay their own tax and National Insurance, as an employer it is your responsibility to confirm that. HMRC will offer you guidance on how to do this in the Starter Pack.

Of course, making sure your employees' tax is in order isn't the only obligation you have. Make sure you also know your legal responsibilities regarding:

- Statutory sick and maternity pay
- Working time and pay regulations
- National Minimum Wage
- Redundancy pay
- Employing foreign nationals
- Part-time workers' regulations

TIP

You can find out more about legal responsibilities at the following websites:
http://direct.gov.uk
www.berr.gov.uk
www.businesslink.gov.uk

➡ INDUCTION AND TRAINING

Think ahead to your new recruit's first day. There's nothing worse than starting a new job and it being clear nobody's really ready for you. You're a start-up so it won't do your new person any harm to learn quickly that they'll have to take situations as they come, but it's important to set out clear expectations from day one.

On their first day, sit them down, detail what you expect from them, how you'll assess their performance, how they will be rewarded, who they will report to and all the other information you'll need to cover such as holidays and pay. Just as importantly, explain to them your vision for the company, what the USPs and identity of the business are and how you expect customers to be treated. It's your baby but the more people you can get sharing the vision the more chance you've got of seeing it blossom.

Be careful that you train people for any jobs they need to do or tasks that are likely to invoke health and safety legislation and make frequent and regular assessments to identify training needs. The more you make your people feel cared for and invested in, the more loyal they will be.

Starting out in business and recruiting for the first time will keep you busy enough without thinking of what to do when things go wrong. But the reality is that not every hire is the right one and not every recruit will fit well into your business or share your vision, despite what you thought at the interview stage.

FROM THE EXPERTS:
Nick Robertson, ASOS.com

The staff who you start with are not necessarily the staff you end up with, but at the end of the day, the business comes first. Some realise the business has outgrown them, others need a bit of push. It's essential to get the right people on board at the right time.

Things to remember:

- Try to keep a flexible approach to staffing numbers when you first start. You may need to keep some staff on stand-by while you get a feel for the average number of customers to expect.

- Work out exactly what you require in each role before you start recruiting for the job and come up with a clear job description.

- As well as agencies and job adverts, use online networks such as Gumtree to recruit staff.

- Be careful not to fall into any interview traps regarding questions about personal or family life. It could land you in hot water and contravene employment law.

- Make sure you fulfil all the legal responsibilities required of you as a new employer.

Establishing your presence

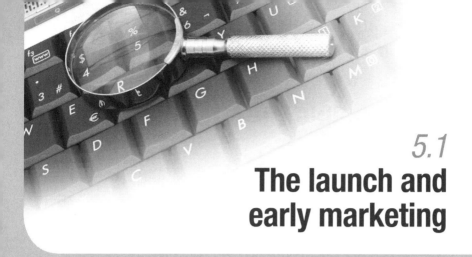

The launch and early marketing

M aking your site live is the day you've waited for and worked so hard to get to. From raw idea to writing a business plan, designing a site, testing it, sourcing suppliers and buying in stock, you're finally ready to start trading and, hopefully, make some money. Before you can do that however, you need to establish your presence and get customers to your site.

In this chapter we'll take you through the process of launching your site, including carrying out final checks, striking the right level of publicity to get interested customers logging onto your site and satisfied buyers coming back for more, and making the most of marketing techniques – both on and offline.

In this chapter, we'll look at:

- Preparing the site for launch
- PR, such as writing press releases
- Advertising, both online and offline
- Organising the launch

- Attracting customers
- Marketing techniques
- Measuring success
- Post-launch publicity
- Forming relationships with the media

PREPARING THE SITE FOR LAUNCH

While you've been designing your site, sorting out the copy and images, choosing payment systems and sourcing stock, you've no doubt been testing it at each of these various stages. Before your site officially goes live, however, you'll need to carry out a final risk assessment and test your website once more to ensure it is ready for launch. Once it's live, it will be visible to both your customers and your competitors, so it's important you get as much right as possible at the very beginning. It's true that in the online environment, mistakes can be rectified fairly quickly, but glitches can also occur fairly rapidly and escalate if unnoticed, which could damage your reputation as a business and result in fewer customers and sales.

Ensure that all the right content is in the right place and that the links work when you click through on them. Test and test again to catch and iron out any technical glitches, such as images not loading properly. It's also important to ensure that your website works across different browsers, as it's impossible to predict which ones your customers are using. If your site doesn't load properly in a browser, the customer is likely to see a page that loads slowly, with images missing – something that is likely to be unattractive and uninviting, so you risk alienating that customer if you don't test the site across different browsers.

 IN MY EXPERIENCE:

Jamie Murray Wells, Glasses Direct

We're always looking at ways to make the site more interactive – if you are looking to add new functionality to a site, it's vital to test, test and test again.

Final checks aren't just about the site. Depending on the type of online business you've established, you'll need to safeguard some other areas pre-launch. Ask yourself the following questions: do you have the right amount of stock in place, and can you get hold of more goods easily if necessary? Are your delivery systems in place and reliable? Are your contact details correct and do you have processes in place so that you or someone is available at the times stated, in the event of any customer queries?

 TIP

Get your friends and family to test the site pre-launch, by asking them to click on links, test the order facility and check the time it takes to download images.

Does your email address work and are you able to send and receive communications? You'll also need to ensure that you have web traffic monitoring systems in place so you can assess how many customers are visiting your site and where they are coming from (see p.236 for more information on this).

PR AND ADVERTISING

If you're reading this heading thinking, 'but I haven't got much (if any) money left for advertising', you're actually very sensible. Throwing money at advertising a new online venture isn't always the most sensible approach, especially until you've ironed out the creases that'll inevitably crop up in the first few months of trading.

When you're first starting out there's a lot of PR and self-promotion you can do for relatively little budget. If you're adamant you need to start paying for ads from day one, you'll need a clear strategy to ensure you're getting maximum return on your investment and are able to measure the effect your spend has had.

⇒ PR

PR is coverage of your business in magazines, newspapers, websites or TV, radio and in podcasts and webinars. For publications with any credibility, it is promotion you can't buy and so is hugely influential. Compared to advertising where you're simply paying to appear on a page billboard or web banner for example, it's assumed your business is being written about because someone thinks it's worthy of coverage. Providing the reason for that is positive and that the reader respects the publication, that's a very powerful endorsement.

 IN MY EXPERIENCE:
Glenys Berd, LoveThoseShoes.com

We have a highly successful in-house PR team that really helps increase brand recognition and drive traffic to the site.

Press releases

Journalists receive thousands of press releases from new companies looking for PR coverage. Many of them result in profile pieces, news stories and features offering months of free publicity to businesses that have literally just opened their doors. Admittedly, though, many press releases go straight in the bin.

The difference between those covered and binned though rarely has much to do with the actual business. Sure, if you're opening the world's first money tree shop you'd probably make a front page splash no matter how screwed up the press release, but most of the time, for ordinary businesses, it's about pointing out the one thing which makes you not so ordinary – and if you've followed the planning section you'll have plenty of USPs to plug and promote.

Pitching to journalists shouldn't be too different to pitching to the bank. You're looking to inspire them and tell them what they need to know to do business with you. They need to hear what's so great about your story and there's a story in every business somewhere, it's just a case of digging it out.

The key is finding the angle. It's not news that you're simply launching an online business selling designer clothes as that idea has been done many times over. It is news if you have secured some exclusive deals with well-known designers and the designs are available only in your online store. It is news if you have designed the clothes yourself and fashionistas such as Victoria Beckham and Paris Hilton say they like the site and your designs.

If you're blankly thinking, 'but I don't have anything interesting like that', then the answer is to engineer an angle. It is news if you're going to preview a new designer's collection or if some designs have become coveted by the stars and are selling out online. Think niches as well; if you're using eco packaging, this might be interesting to an eco title; if you're offering ethically sourced clothing target the appropriate magazines; if your online business has a celebrity following, point that out to the local papers. Every business has a PR story, it's just a case of sculpting it and pointing it out to the right people.

> **TIP**
>
> Consider writing some press releases yourself and ask your friends and family to critique them and offer you feedback. This will give you some idea of whether your content is newsworthy.

You should always start by doing this yourself. Try and get as many of these little unique stories saved in your head as possible because you'll find them invaluable when talking to a whole range of people, not just journalists, about why your business is so great. For actually getting coverage, you've two choices: go direct yourself or use a PR company.

Tips for writing a press release

- Make sure the wording is correct, the message is clear and direct and the correct information is provided so that a journalist will be able to use it even if they do not contact a member of your company or PR team.
- Your release should convey a sense of importance but not seem over-hyped. You want to provide information about your firm in a newsy format, not a marketing letter. Besides, if your announcement is worth sending a release out, it can probably stand on its own without marketing hype.
- All press releases should answer the journalist's five basic questions of: Who, What, Where, Why and How. This will require you to put yourself in the shoes of a journalist and chances are, answering those questions will give you a clearer idea of what you want to write.
- A punchy headline should be included that matches the release's first sentence, or lead, as those in the trade call them. The headline should be factual. It shouldn't try to make a joke or be smart.
- The first sentence should be direct, relate what is going on, convey a level of importance of the news and start off with the name of your shop.
- Include a quote from you about why you've decided to launch your online business. Quotes personalise stories and give journalists an idea of who to speak to. Most journalists will seek their own quotes by following up releases with interviews, but including a quote gives journalists the option to use it.
- Contact details for journalists who want to find out more can either go at the top of the release or the bottom.

Using a PR company

If you've got the budget, PR companies can be massively useful. The two key elements you'll be paying for are their wealth of contacts and their management of the whole process. Any PR company worth its salt will keep up-to-date on who occupies all the key editorial positions in all media organisations, has strong working relationships with them and can get a story to the right person. They should also look to apply their expertise to manage a full publicity campaign, staggering stories in different publications to achieve maximum exposure over a period of time. With all the other elements of running an online business to take care of, it's highly unlikely you'll have time to do this yourself and will end up snatching at publicity from any title that bites. PR companies should also be able to write a good press release – but for sanity's sake, you should ask to check everything before it goes out.

FROM THE EXPERTS:
Simon Nixon, moneysupermarket.com

PR can drive traffic to your site cost-effectively and help you with your brand. Find a good PR agency in your particular sector. We now have around 20 people in-house who manage our PR and liaise with our agency.

If you can't afford a PR company from day one, which is the case for many a start-up, have a go at doing it yourself. Target the titles you think should be most interested in your story, call them up to ask who the best person to send press releases to is, then put one together and send it off. Jamie Murray Wells of Glasses Direct wrote to lots of journalists he thought might be interested in the business, asking them to write about him. The media started to pick up his story and an article in *The Daily Telegraph* gave the company a much-needed boost.

IN MY EXPERIENCE:
Jamie Murray Wells, Glasses Direct

The article in *The Daily Telegraph* gave the business a massive boost. If you have a genuine hook or interesting story, persevere with getting some strong media coverage. It's one of the best ways to get a business going.

One thing to remember is journalists get inundated with hundreds of releases and sometimes even the best ones get overlooked, so don't get upset if you don't get a response. If you haven't heard anything within a couple of days, call the person you

TIP
If a publication calls you and say they'll feature you for a cost, don't do it. Paid for articles have zero credibility and regardless of what the person on the end of the phone tells you, aren't read. Politely refuse.

sent it to and ask them if they thought it was relevant. If it wasn't, ask them why
so you can tailor it closer to their needs next time.

➡ ADVERTISING

Online advertising

It goes without saying that you'll be using online advertising to promote your
website and in terms of measuring return on investment you won't get a
more accurate medium for advertising, as digital marketing is one of the most
accountable forms of marketing. There are a range of techniques you can use,
from banner advertising (a box containing graphics which a consumer can click
on to link to a site), to search engine marketing, to pay-per-click advertising such
as Google Adwords (the small advertisements you see down the right side of
Google). More than 90% of web traffic comes from search, and for search Google
is the main provider. While you should look to optimise your website to appear
in the central, natural Google search, one of the easiest way to advertise your
website online is using Google AdWords.

If you choose to invest in banner advertising, there are a number of different
styles and sizes to choose from – expect to pay more for more prominent
positions and length of time the advert is running. The most common size is
468x60 pixels and you can vary the content too, from using one static image to
using several animated images to rich media banner ads, which use audio and
video tools.

 IN MY EXPERIENCE:
Jamie Murray Wells, Glasses Direct

It has taken us a few years of work to get our heads around online marketing, site
optimisation and building above-the-line awareness of the business. In the days
when money was limited, we made the most of free online advertising tools.

Offline advertising

Many web businesses concentrate their marketing efforts solely online, which can be a missed opportunity – your customers could be just as likely to find you flicking through a local newspaper or directory as they would by performing a Google search. There are a host of opportunities for offline advertising and some will be more cost-effective than you might at first think.

Offline advertising such as print ads can give your customers something tangible to hold on to and to pick up, prompting brand recall. Print has been around for a lot longer than the web, and therefore customers are more likely to trust that medium. Many online businesses find that using some form of offline advertising helps to make their business less anonymous. The other advantage of using press ads to drive traffic to your site is if you are looking to tap into a local customer base rather than a global one.

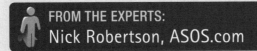

FROM THE EXPERTS:
Nick Robertson, ASOS.com

Press advertising has worked well for us as it reaches our core target market. We started off advertising in celebrity magazines such as *Heat* but we have moved to more fashion-based titles such as *Grazia*.

Print ads

The most common forms of print advertising that small businesses use are:

- Local/regional/national newspapers or magazines
- Trade journals
- Trade directories
- Telephone directories eg *Yellow Pages*
- Miscellaneous items such as calendars, local tourist information

Newspapers and magazines should provide an audited readership profile, which can be matched to your customer profile to identify if they'll attract the right kind of customers to your site. They should be able to provide you with information on their circulation, which is the number of copies that go out. Avoid advertising in publications without this kind of audited data.

⚓ TIP

While it's important to do your research on the circulation of the publications you advertise with, bear in mind that free newspapers and magazines may have a readership lower than the official circulation. In contrast, those with a cover price usually have a readership larger than circulation.

In terms of size, generally, the bigger the better if budget permits, although putting editorial onto the page either at the bottom or the left-hand side can actually help. You should also bear in mind that as print ads are repeated the impact lessens. It can, therefore, be better to spend the budget on a few high impact ads than a lot of small ones. But test the waters slowly. Don't blow your whole marketing budget on a massive ad campaign in the local newspaper only to find print ads aren't the right medium for you.

Publishers will quote you different rates for different positions and sizes. Prime spots such as near the front or in the news sections, right hand pages, or tops of pages cost about 20% more but, as a rule, are worth the extra investment because they're viewed by the most readers. If you're going to splash out on an advert to let people know you're open for business you could use the opportunity to run a special offer.

Sample prices

- A quarter page ad in a local paper can cost upwards of £250 depending on its circulation
- A full page ad in a national paper such as *The Daily Mail* can cost in the region of £30,000

Always negotiate. The first price is never the best price. Find out when the last possible deadline is before the publication goes to press then phone back. While you might not get your preferred slot, most sales people will give you heavy discounts on unsold slots just to get them filled.

Radio/TV advertising

As the web has ploughed ahead, the development of digital radio and TV has meant prices to advertise have tumbled, while the choice of audiences has widened. TV will possibly be outside your price range as a start-up, but if you'd like to explore this option then contact a small local production company experienced at producing broadcast advertisements on limited budgets.

You'll need to take a similar approach for radio, which can be effective at a local level. For radio particularly, it's worth speaking to the sales teams of stations to ask the optimum length and style of ads and any recommendations for production firms to work with.

Yellow Pages/directories

The days where if you were running a business then you simply had to be in the *Yellow Pages* are long gone. That said it can still be very effective if your firm provides a relatively unusual service people naturally need to search for. Directories work best for companies where people aren't automatically aware of their existence or don't use them frequently, so it may work well if you are planning to launch a niche online business, or one that is focusing on providing services to a particular area or location.

If you think you'd pick up business from the *Yellow Pages*, negotiate a trial period to see what success you have. If they don't agree to this, negotiate until they do as they'll almost always prefer to give you this than put the phone down without 'a sale'.

Listings and guides

Getting yourself listed in a local directory doesn't have to cost anything. Most directories such as *Thomson* or the *Yellow Pages* will allow you to have a basic entry with the name of the business, the web address and phone number for free. If you want a bigger advert with more prominence you will have to pay, however, you can expect to get a free trial for the paid-for premium services even if it means you pay for one month and get another free.

There are other smaller and more regularly updated local guides and directories which are often put through letterboxes or left in public buildings such as doctors' surgeries, information centres or local authority properties. These printed guides or directories will have details on how to get your business listed within them. There are also online versions which also have details of how to list for free or how to pay for greater prominence. Examples include, thebestof. co.uk, Welovelocal.com and Toplocallistings.co.uk.

➡ ORGANISING THE LAUNCH

Many online businesses can get it spectacularly wrong during their first few weeks so be wary about shouting your arrival from the rooftops too fervently. While you certainly want people to know your site is up and running, trading and more than happy to take customers' money, it might make sense to leave it a couple of weeks before you 'officially launch'.

Launch doesn't have to equal 'day one'. Far better to do a soft launch as they're called, to spot all the little problems and have time to put them right than risk problems you could have sorted out with a little more time.

Get your site up and running and start trading, get feedback from your friends and family and customers about how they find the site and what they'd like to see. If you have employed staff, use the first few weeks to make sure they are trained properly and are providing the right level of customer service.

Try and offer a few incentives during these first few weeks to get customers in and garner their feedback. Offer introductory discounts (be careful not to make this look too much like a desperate sale), free gifts if they spend a certain amount or even run a competition where you can collect customers' contact details in return for some gift vouchers.

TIP

Keep the first few weeks nice and relaxed (even if you're feeling the opposite inside) and keep your eyes and ears open for any way you can improve the service you're offering.

The launch party

Just because you've 'soft launched' it doesn't mean you shouldn't later have an official launch party. It's your first chance to let as many people as possible know about your new venture. See if you can negotiate hiring a venue for free in return for an ad on your website.

If you've hired a PR company, they should ensure local journalists are present, lured by the prospect of a great story and a glass of bubbly (wine if budgets are really tight) and hopefully a local celebrity or council member. If you're doing it yourself, make a list of targets, send out some invitations (email is sufficient and appropriate for a web venture) and follow-up with confirmation calls and a reminder email on the day.

If it's not feasible to hold a launch party, consider whether there are any local business events taking place near your planned launch – you could use the event as an opportunity to publicise your site and for networking purposes.

IN MY EXPERIENCE:
Glenys Berd, LoveThoseShoes.com

We have tried launch parties but find that in the frantic world that most journalists work in, it is becoming increasingly difficult to get them to attend. Launch parties are successful if you use them to establish relationships and have a PR team who will be relentless in building those relationships. So it would be a mistake to measure the success of a launch party based on the features that followed within a month of the launch – they'll mostly all fail on this principle. The focus should be on the relationships, it is an opportunity to get a foot in the door and then force it open.

Just as importantly, work hard to get your target customers to your site. Look at complementary associations or clubs where you can advertise your launch, while even a poster in the windows of local shops that complement your offering or where your target customer is likely to pass by can work well, as can giving out leaflets on the street.

IN MY EXPERIENCE:
Jamie Murray Wells, Glasses Direct

We decided to print some leaflets promoting the businesses and I roped in some friends to help me hand them out to potential customers. We gave them out on a train so people would have our fliers to read for the whole journey.

You'll need an incentive for shoppers so advertise a discount for a specified period of time for those who log onto your site within the first week of launch, for example. Print up some leaflets with a voucher code that people have to enter online, so you can track how effective these have been for future marketing purposes.

If you do have a launch party, on the night, make the evening as entertaining as possible. This is your one chance to make a first impression, so go all out. You should be on a complete charm offensive whether it comes to you naturally or not, and try to speak to every person, even if it's to simply introduce yourself and to thank them for coming.

➡ ATTRACTING CUSTOMERS

In order to attract customers, you need to look at several elements, such as any promotions you want to run, who your target audience is and how your creativity can help to convert sales. Hopefully, you will already have pinpointed your target audience through earlier research and created your website with them in mind – your task will now be to ensure they find your website and capture their interest.

To do this effectively, you'll need to define your target customer in more detail. Consider demographic characteristics such as age, income and location. You could carry out a survey of customers to find out more about their interests and what they might be prepared to pay for your product. You can then tailor your marketing accordingly.

➡ AFTER THE LAUNCH

Identify sources of traffic

It's important to have your marketing and promotion plans ready straight after the launch of the site – unlike a bricks and mortar environment, you can't physically drag your customers in off the street or account for how many pass through your door, so you'll need to have a strategy to both market to them and keep them coming back for more. Creating a professional looking website is only half the story when launching an online business – how good it looks or what functionality you have built in won't really count for very much at the end of the day unless you can attract customers to your website and build some solid sales. To do this effectively, you'll need to learn how to promote your site in order to build up traffic, increase your customer base and ultimately, your sales.

FROM THE EXPERTS:
Nick Robertson, ASOS.com

With the internet, there is no town centre – people don't walk past the web. To attract customers to your site, you'll either have to be a trusted retailer or do something different.

There are various ways for your customers to find you. This could be from simply typing in your domain name and arriving straight to your site, often prompted by advertising and marketing materials or by recommendations from friends and family. Or customers could use search engines, typing in words that are related to your company name or product. This is likely to be the most popular way for people to find your site and you will be reaching out to a broader audience base (see Chapter 5.2 for more on search engines).

It's all about you

Showcase what you sell, but make the website about you and your business as well. Have a page that talks about why you started-up, what you hope to achieve and how passionate and determined you are to provide a great service. Try and keep the site updated daily, perhaps carry relevant news and definitely write a blog where you talk about running a business in your sector and activity in your specialist area. It'll bring visitors to the site and place you as an expert in your field.

FROM THE EXPERTS:
Simon Nixon, moneysupermarket.com

Lead with insight – you can get a lot of this from your customers and you can prioritise changes to your site accordingly. We carry out an ongoing review of our site with many people in our IT department responsible for making changes.

This means investing time and money into marketing activities – if you don't undertake any form of marketing, it's unlikely that you will build substantial amounts of traffic. Marketing isn't just advertising. It's the means by which your online business identifies, attracts, and keeps its customers; and that's such a powerful proposition it touches on almost every other element of your business. If carried out effectively it will not only ensure that your online business is seen and heard but will give it the flexibility to adapt to changing customer demands in an ever-evolving business environment.

➡ LINK BUILDING

There are some ways of attracting customers to your site which shouldn't cost a penny, one of which is exchanging links with a website whose business is complementary to yours. Link building refers to the process of getting as many relevant websites linking into your site as possible. The world wide web was designed to make it easy to flit from site to site and more than 90% of website traffic comes from other websites.

The more links you manage to build up, the higher your chances are of getting your site ranked amongst search engines. Many of the main search engines now decide how far up the visibility scale your site should be, by the number of other sites linking into your site. This isn't the only distinguishing feature; metatag (a tag that is used to store information about a web page, but is not displayed in a browser) and good content are still just as important. But quite naturally, some search engines feel that if loads of sites are linking into yours, then yours must be a good site, and therefore worthy of being high up in the listings.

Do some research into sites that you can exchange links with and ensure that you check your links on a regular basis – broken links are guaranteed to turn customers away.

The link building process

Begin with your local links. Local businesses are often happy to reciprocate links if they are not in direct competition with you. Email them requesting reciprocal links and try to build up a local network.

Think about your suppliers and customers. Which ones would be happy to put a link in to your site? If you've done a good job for a customer, try to get a mention somewhere on their site. The same goes for your suppliers. Do they have a list of clients on their site? If so, get on it. If not, suggest they set one up.

Now look at industry links. Are there any professional bodies that you are a member of? If so, they should hold a member directory online. Make sure you're on it. Look at all the unofficial resources for your business sector and try to get links on those. Typing some relevant keywords into the main search engines will help you find suitable linking partners.

Whilst some websites make their money from advertising and only exist to be a bigger and better directory, most sites that you contact will not be prepared to add a link to your site for nothing. At the very least, it takes up their time to add you, so why should they? You have to be prepared to give something back. This doesn't mean paying for links, but you should have a link page already created on your site and be ready to offer a link in return.

A successful link building campaign will make a real difference to your website traffic, which in turn should make a real difference to your level of enquiries through the website, which ultimately should lead to more revenue.

➡ CREATING A BUZZ

Despite your best efforts, your site might not be getting anywhere near the customer numbers you want, so it could be worth creating a buzz around your product or business to get people talking. You'll need to emphasise the benefits of your product, service and website and really push any areas you think make you stand out from the competition. Revisit your USPs and consider if there are some areas you are not pushing as much as you could.

IN MY EXPERIENCE:
Jamie Murray Wells, Glasses Direct

You need to create some kind of buzz with your website, there's only so much you can do with paid search and affiliate marketing. We've given out gobstoppers shaped like eyeballs with our glasses.

Customer endorsements can help to get people talking about your site. Consider gathering testimonials from satisfied customers and creating space or a page on your website to showcase these.

MARKETING PLANS

Marketing will help you understand who your customers are, what they aspire to and how you can position your business as the destination they're looking for. It will influence your buying decisions, how you price items, what packaging you use, the level of customer service you provide and the area you look to next if you choose to expand, perhaps by diversifying your product range or going global. Successful marketing is about accumulating knowledge and is an art as well as a science. You should be collecting knowledge from every day's trade and every transaction and purchase made should influence the next one, as well as govern how you try and promote yourself.

Whichever marketing techniques you use, it's important that you keep what your customers need uppermost in your mind and direct your efforts towards this. While your online business started off as your baby, for it to grow and achieve its full potential you'll have to allow your customers to dictate which direction it takes. You won't be able to do that, or bring in more like them, if you're not fully knowledgeable about who they are and what they want.

IN MY EXPERIENCE:
Jamie Murray Wells, Glasses Direct

Try to set yourself apart from high street expectations, select a customer wish list to try at home. You need to come up with customers' problems and try to solve them.

But you shouldn't find the process daunting; keeping up with the changing demands of customers and finding new ways to get them to your site is to be embraced. If you've a great online shop offering what they want and know how to flaunt it, then marketing can be one of the most enjoyable elements of running an online business.

There are no hard and fast rules for creating a marketing strategy. It's up to you to set your own goals. However, as a general rule, you need to ask what you want your online business to achieve in a year, two years or even five years' time compared to where it would be without a marketing strategy.

Here are some tips to remember when devising your marketing plan:

- Start by setting clear objectives – where do you want your online business to go?
- Set clear financial targets for these objectives.
- Define your target market and identify your potential customers.
- Decide on the brand and the values you want to communicate.
- Plan your promotion strategy.
- Set a budget.
- Devise a schedule.
- Decide how the strategy will be measured, for example, increased sales, direct responses, coverage in local press etc.
- Implement the programme according to the schedule.
- Monitor and evaluate results as an aid for future marketing decisions.

IN MY EXPERIENCE:

Glenys Berd, LoveThoseShoes.com

We make sure we maximise the customer experience.

➡ MEASURING SUCCESS

You'll need to have effective monitoring processes in place, to measure how effective your marketing is and which areas to address. Check what the competition is doing and review this on a regular basis. This might mean you will need to tweak your prices or offers and although this can prove time-consuming, as a new venture, it's important for you to remain competitive and to be able to offer something over and above the competition.

Keeping track of trends is equally important, particularly if you are running a retail site. And don't make the assumption that just because you are operating an online business, you don't need to consider an offline marketing campaign. A multi-channel marketing campaign, one that is run across different media such as print, radio, and online can ensure maximum exposure and response, although it does require a substantial outlay. Test different mediums to see which ones return the best response (see p.207 for more information on this).

If you've got several marketing or PR strategies happening at once it can be difficult to measure which ones are actually bringing in the customers. You're not going to advertise in a newspaper and then ask each customer that purchases online if they've done so because they saw an advert in the local rag. If you're not sure which marketing technique is giving you the best return on investment then why not try them one by one, then calculate any increase in customers or turnover for that period.

Of course the success of certain promotions, such as vouchers or discounts using codes are easy enough to measure because you can count up how many customers make use of the offers. However it's important to remember that you need to bring in more custom as a result of the promotion than you spend on your marketing. It's no good offering discounts and doubling the number of visitors to the site if you end up making a loss on your products.

For each piece of marketing you do, set clear Key Performance Indicators (KPIs) that will help you assess if it's proved worthwhile.

✦ TIP

Online marketing is very accountable and there are plenty of tools available to measure your online marketing activity, so it can be all too easy to get lost in a wave of figures and numbers. Decide from the outset what you are measuring and why.

➡ PROMOTIONAL IDEAS

One way of attracting new customers is to run special offers or promotions. Online business, much like traditional shops, have end of season sales, but there are other ways to incentivise people to log onto your site.

Loss leaders

These are items you sell at cost price to tempt customers onto your site so they'll buy other items that are priced to give you the same overall profit.

Buy one get one free (BOGOF)

BOGOFs are now staple retail fodder. However beware that you could cheapen a product by offering it on such a deal or even set the wrong tone for your brand – and make sure you can afford to give away a whole unit for free. Chances are you won't find it as easy as the supermarkets do.

Limited special offers or introductory offers

Daily or weekly offers keep the homepage of your website looking fresh and feel like you're offering an incentive or weekly special more than trying to sell off stock that's out of season or end of line.

 IN MY EXPERIENCE:
Glenys Berd, LoveThoseShoes.com

Introductory offers are useful as a means of getting people to initially try our products and service. When you retail footwear over the internet there is sometimes a small hurdle to jump over in the customers' mind about sizing – 'will it fit, won't it?' So a small discount does work as a buffer not just for that specific concern but for any 'reason not to buy' whatever product you're retailing. It is all about establishing an initial 'sale' then building on your relationship with the customer from there.

Loyalty cards

While the Boots and Nectar cards are more about collecting customers buying habits, simple loyalty points can work as a way of attracting return customers. If your pricing allows you to, offer discounts or freebies after certain thresholds of expenditure or for a certain number of visits. You can then inform your customers about how many points they may have accrued through monthly email newsletters. Use this marketing tool sparingly though. Customers don't want to be inundated with junk mail (see the section on newsletters, p.248). Collect visitor information wherever possible.

Competitions

A great way to collect customer data is online competitions. Run competitions, ask people to sign up to receive special offers through and use that data to provide a weekly or monthly newsletter telling them what's new on your site and prompting them to visit.

Or you could offer an attractive prize and get customers to enter by filling in their details online. You can then email them all thanking them for entering and offering a call to action incentive – £5 off or 10% discount for example, to get them back.

More launches

Don't miss the chance to get your top customers and the press back for a drink (and shop, of course). If you start stocking a new range or brand of goods, contact your existing customer base to make them aware of the products and consider offering them an incentive to trial your new stock.

Partnerships

Seek out mutually beneficial partnerships with complementary online businesses or organisations. For instance, if you run a business selling pet accessories online, consider contacting kennels and dog-walking providers to promote each other's services. Look to local clubs, groups and companies used by your target customer and ask if you can put a poster up or distribute promotional material in exchange for providing them with a small discount. You'll find most will welcome this as a way of attracting members or employees.

Keep an eye on your diary and what's going on around you. If there's a bandwagon you can jump on, leap on it. If your town or local community is campaigning for an issue dear to your customers' hearts, you could flag this up on your website. If you can help local schools, help them. React to festivities and celebrations.

Post-launch publicity

We've covered the basics of advertising (see p.207), but it's important to consider the value of continuing to advertise. While initial advertising campaigns are good for attracting customers in the early days whilst you optimise your website for search, ongoing advertising can be great for flagging up promotions or new lines. However, this early on in an online business's life, you may not yet be breaking even, let alone have enough profits set aside to spend on advertising. That's where PR can prove the most effective route for promotion.

You may have had coverage in local papers or magazines when you launched but how do you keep the PR momentum going once you've been up and running a few months? Hopefully you've got more than one story to tell, so you can keep churning out the press releases. Remember, for everything that happens to your business and every new line your online business stocks, try and think of a newsworthy angle for it.

Another interesting way of getting your online business some free coverage in a local paper is to offer up your services to them. If you have a retail model, offer them a competition to win a £100 voucher to spend with you; even if you did it once a week chances are it'd still work out cheaper than buying an ad and £100 at sale value shouldn't be £100 at cost value.

⚓ TIP

See if you can help out a paper or magazine by writing a column or advisory piece as a local business owner or as an expert in your specialist area. Mock up an example and send it in. Don't make it too hard sell and, as many welcome free contributions, they might run it as a regular feature giving your business a nice plug in exchange. Remember to include your website address on any piece you write.

➡ FORMING MEDIA RELATIONSHIPS

There are plenty of ways to get free coverage but you have to make sure you're not a nuisance to the journalists who will potentially be writing about you. Here are some tips for getting the media on your side:

> ### FROM THE EXPERTS:
> ## Simon Nixon, moneysupermarket.com
>
> It's critical to have media coverage – you want to be seen as an authority in your area and you want the business to be talked about.

- Buy them lunch to find out how you can provide content they want. If you've met and spoken to them face-to-face they're far more likely to give you the time of day later on.
- Don't contact them too often. If you become a nuisance they may just start avoiding you.
- Don't contact them with irrelevant stories. It's important you tailor any press releases, stories or promotions to fit in with their publications and what their readers want to see.
- Find out when their deadline day is. If you contact a journalist when they're about to go to press they're unlikely to have time for you. Find out when their publication goes out and contact them straight afterwards as this will be the time they're most likely to listen to you.
- Write a good press release. Journalists receive endless quantities of them so you'll need to make yours stand out if you are to stand a chance of it being read, let alone covered. Have a look at the Marketing and PR channel of Startups.co.uk for more details on how to write a winning press release.
- Ask magazines and newspaper supplements for forward features lists so you can see if the journalists will be writing about an area that's particularly relevant to your business.

There are plenty of other online review and listings sites dedicated to the retail and services industry. It's a good idea to check out the ones specific to your area and make sure you're listed on all of those too.

> ## TIP
> Another site you may want to have your site featured on is TrustedPlaces. com, a social networking site where members of the public put up personal reviews of restaurants, bars and shops they've visited and recommend. The businesses featured then build up a ranking as voted for by the public.

Things to remember:

- Make sure you continually test your website to iron out any potential glitches before you officially launch.

- Have a clear and defined marketing strategy before you start spending your budget.

- Try sending out press releases or even having a launch party to promote the launch of your business.

- Also think about other forms of advertising such as print ads.

- Think carefully about what kind of promotions you offer and apply them to your slower days or times.

- Use PR sparingly but effectively. Don't become a nuisance to journalists.

- Look for strategic partnerships.

- Keep monitoring your sales to keep track of how successful your marketing is proving to be.

Y ou've done all the hard work in terms of setting out your business plan, getting suppliers on board, sorting out your stock, securing finance and getting your website ready for launch. However, if your site cannot be easily found by search engines, you could be alienating many of your customers and missing out on potential traffic.

This is where working with search engines comes into play. If you're looking for something on the internet, it's likely that the first place you'll visit is a search engine such as Google. Search engines are one of the main ways people access content on the web and search marketing – a range of techniques used to increase the visibility of a website and brand on search engine results pages – is big business in the UK. The industry was worth an estimated £1.6bn in 2007, according to research from the Interactive Advertising Bureau. Search traffic can make or break your business, particularly as the online world becomes more and more competitive.

In this chapter we'll look at the following:

- How search engines work
- Submitting your site to search engines
- Paid versus natural search
- Search engine optimisation
- Keywords and what they do
- Universal search
- Monitoring traffic/web analytics
- Affiliate marketing

HOW SEARCH ENGINES WORK

Your online presence can prosper from the strategic use of search engines. But to take advantage of this you will have to understand how they work. As a search engine is automatic, it uses unique software to read and index websites and links on web pages, placing them in order of relevancy and frequency. The tool they use is called a spider. This enables search engines to crawl through the world wide web (www) looking at metatags and eventually storing them in a vast database.

Within the metatags the spider looks at words that appear frequently throughout the page called keywords (see below for more information on this), the page title, a brief description of the page, and the author as well as emphasised text and other aspects. Metatags can be viewed on any website by clicking onto the 'view' icon on the menu bar in Windows and then scrolling down the list to source.

Each search engine's relevancy methods are different to the next. For example, while some look at the title of your document, some are case sensitive and will give varying results, and others score words higher in their relevancy rating if unique spellings or characteristics are included. So make sure you pay attention to what tags you eventually use.

But beware, it is ill advised to try and repeat a particular word as often as possible in the opening paragraph to obtain a high ranking as it is something most established search engines frown upon.

SUBMITTING YOUR SITE

There's a vast array of search tools available today and your site needs to be found by most of them if you are to establish your presence online. Once your website has launched and is live (which means it can be viewed on the internet) there's a good chance it will be picked up by search engines within the first few months. However, it is always worth submitting your website directly to the search engines so that they are aware of your website. The most important element to bear in mind is that site submission is something you need to be committed to for the long term – it can take several weeks or even months to get your site ranked by search engines and securing a top ranking can take longer still. It's not something that can be done overnight but building your content and improving your links will help to boost your page rankings.

There are literally hundreds of search engines out there and submitting your website to every one of them is a time-consuming process. There are really only a handful of search engines that are worth investing time in, as many others have a low usage rate and therefore are not likely to drive traffic to your website. On the plus side, you won't have to pay a penny to get into the major search engines.

IN MY EXPERIENCE:
Simon Wadsworth, The Retail Factory

The only long-term solution for search marketing is to rank high in natural search for your key terms in all the major search engines, but focusing on Google.

The biggest challenge you face when using search engines is the breadth of competition. Most people will only look at the very first few pages of search engine results and if they can't find the answers they want, they are likely to use different keywords (the words that people type when performing a search, see p.233 for more on this area) and perform an alternative search. This means that if your business does not rank in the first few pages, potential customers will not be able to find you.

TIP

The major search engines are the following: Google, Yahoo!, MSN and Lycos.

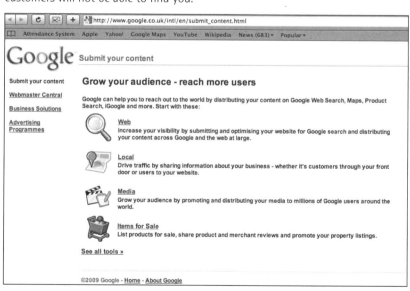

Google: How to submit your website

To submit your site, visit the homepage of a search engine and look for the 'submit link' or 'add url' link where you can simply enter or submit your domain name for free. Google, for example, has a very comprehensive guide detailing how to submit your website, which can be accessed at http://www.google.co.uk/intl/en/submit_content.html

Getting your site noticed

Be professional: Your website reflects your company, so keep the content clear, concise and accurate, and enforce your branding and messaging. A high-quality website implies a high-quality company.

Content is king: Visitors want information and something worthwhile to read. Give them a reason to come back to the website again; constantly updated content and independent industry information gives users a reason to bookmark your website.

Be consistent: Keep the layout, design, and navigation the same across the website. Different fonts and styles should be kept to a minimum, but remain consistent throughout.

Be readable: Yellow text on a black background is not easy to read, and neither are long pages of centred, capitalised text.

Don't re-invent the wheel: Visitors don't want to learn a new navigation style, or have to understand a complicated interface. Imagine you are a first-time visitor; usability is more important than showing off the latest flashy effects.

Speedy access: Not everybody will wait for large image files or animations to load; most visitors will leave a site within a minute if the page hasn't loaded properly.

Email your visitors: Have an opt-in mailing list and contact the people on it regularly. This gives you permission to email them with special offers, which builds your potential customer database, reinforces your brand, and updates them with the latest news.

Be visible: A website is useless unless people can find it! Get your site listed in directories and on search engines, either through search engine optimisation techniques or consider using a search engine marketing company.

Compatibility: Check how the website looks on different computers, screen resolutions, and browsers. Is your website accessible by everyone?

Track your visitors: Use your server logs or tracking software to identify your visitors' habits, how they find your website and what browser and screen resolutions they use. Then fine-tune your website to match your visitor profile.

TIP

Submitting your website to the major search engines is a great way to judge just how accessible your site really is. If a search engine can get to your website quickly and easily, then chances are your customers will be able to as well.

Some search engines such as Yahoo! offer paid directory submissions which can boost your visibility in its index. On the plus side, this means you can get your site submitted and registered quickly, but on the downside, your reputation could suffer among your customer base, as they may choose to trust the natural rankings rather than those that are paid for.

TIP

You could consider submitting your site to the Open Directory Project, a manually edited directory of the Web. It may take up to two weeks or more for your site to be reviewed, but it is used by many search engine crawlers as a source of sites, so your site will be indexed by the major search engines. Check out www.dmoz.org for more information.

➡ PAID VERSUS NATURAL SEARCH

There are two ways for a website to become listed within search engines – paid (also known as pay-per-click) or natural (also known as organic) search. Most businesses use a combination of the two and there are several pros and cons for each, which are outlined below.

Natural (organic) search

Natural search is free and works by algorithms determining the pages that are most relevant to queries entered on search engines. The biggest risk with natural search is that over the long term, your brand or business is at the mercy of search engine index changes, which can simply alter ranking systems. Natural search offers little in the way of guaranteed results compared to paid search, although developments in analytics software are striving to meet this challenge. The other downside is the time it takes – it can be up to six months before you notice if any benefits have been reaped and whether your site has achieved a high enough ranking.

Paid or Pay-per-click (PPC) search

Pay-per-click advertising focuses on specific keywords and enables you to list your site at the top of search engine results by advertising on keywords that best describe your product or service. These results appear above the natural listings or to the right of the page. The higher you bid, the higher your ad will be placed in the listings and you only pay if someone clicks on your ad and links to your site. This means you can control costs better and determine exactly how much of your budget you are prepared to spend in this area. Tools for tracking PPC campaigns are very effective so you can easily measure response rates.

As a rule of thumb paid search should be used as a tactical tool offering a responsive pricing or product-led call to action, with natural search listings more suited for a long-term strategy. Consider what your objectives are: are you using search marketing for a quick win to hit the market in a short space of time or is it more of a long-term branding exercise? PPC can ensure you get your message out quickly, making it suited to promotions and price-led creative, whereas natural search requires a longer time for changes to appear on the search results.

IN MY EXPERIENCE:

Glenys Berd, LoveThoseShoes.com

Something like 50% of our traffic comes from search engines, either organic search or through pay-per-click advertising such as Google Adwords.

Search experts also say that natural search offers access to a wider pool, citing figures such as 80% of search queries result in a click on a natural listing, as opposed to 20% on a paid one. Furthermore, with PPC, bidding on key words can be an expensive business so if your company is in a competitive area such as travel and finance, you might struggle to see a return.

How PPC works

- Choose a PPC provide according to your business model, such as a search engine or price comparison website
- Do some research into keywords that best suit your product or service
- Bid an amount per click on each keyword that you believe will put you ahead of the competition (this is the cost-per-click – CPC)
- You pay your PPC provider the bid price for keywords you have specified when someone who has searched for a keyword clicks through the ad and is directed to your website. This is known as the click-through rate (CTR).

 # SEARCH ENGINE OPTIMISATION

These days, most people access the web via search engines rather than typing in a specific website address and there are certain processes you can undertake to ensure your website appears in as high a position as possible in the natural search results. Increasing and improving the volume of traffic to your site via natural or organic search is known as search engine optimisation, or SEO. This basically involves building and maintaining your website through the use of design and keywords. Keywords are the terms that people type into a search engine when they are starting a search (see p.233 for more on keywords). The aim for any SEO campaign is to enhance your search engine listing and placement without having to spend any money towards it. Sites that are well optimised can expect to gain a higher page ranking, which means you can expect to gain more traffic to your website, build interest and ultimately sales.

 IN MY EXPERIENCE:

Simon Wadsworth, The Retail Factory

Search marketing is an important tactical marketing tool but is competitive and expensive and needs constant attention and monitoring.

SEO is more of an art than a science as different search engines have their own rules when it comes to indexing sites, however there are some general points you can take on board. In order to get the most from SEO, you'll need to bear in mind that you are not only designing and refining your site for the benefit of your customers, you are doing this for search engine spiders too. There are a few things you can do to optimise your site for search engines, such as submitting your site to the relevant directories, but bear in mind that it takes time to get results and you'll need to continually invest time and effort in SEO as your website develops, in order to maintain your ranking among the search engines.

Regularly updated content will improve your SEO ranking and give other websites a good reason to want to link to yours, not to mention ensuring that your website is maintained on a regular basis.

FROM THE EXPERTS:
Simon Nixon, moneysupermarket.com

We've perfected our search engine marketing over the last seven years – it doesn't come overnight. With search engine marketing, every penny of profit you get is critical, we have a team that is dedicated to getting us as high up as possible in the natural search rankings. In terms of our traffic on Google, around 60% is paid and 40% natural.

How to make your site design search-engine friendly

- Ensure your site navigation is as clear as possible, so consider adding tools such as a site map, particularly if your website has a number of pages
- Is your text easy to read? It might seem obvious to say that black is the most readable font colour, but you'll also need to ensure that the font is easy to read and that the font size is clear (most websites use a 12-point size)
- Images are great ways of attracting users, particularly if you are operating a retail site, but ensure that every image you use is relevant. If you have too many on the site, you risk users experiencing slower download times, which might encourage them to visit other sites
- Consider the kind of technologies you are using (such as Flash) and whether or not they add anything to the site

USING AN AGENCY

If you have the right skills, you can probably manage your search engine marketing needs in-house, but if not you might have to pay for someone to write the content or use the services of a search engine optimisation agency.

There are a lot of providers available but any agency you choose will need to work with you very closely to understand your needs and help you to manage your site in the best way possible. Effective SEO requires a good understanding of your site, your sector and what you are trying to achieve, as well as your target audience.

As with choosing any supplier, when it comes to selecting a SEO agency, shop around, get recommendations from friends and peers and draw up an agency shortlist, as SEO can be an expensive undertaking. Ask for references or testimonials from previous customers. Remember that SEO agencies should want to know as much as possible about your site in order to create an effective working relationship. You'll need to be comfortable with any provider you choose as working with an SEO agency is a long-term commitment – search engine rankings change all the time so you'll need to be in touch with your agency on a regular basis and discuss ways of improving or changing tactics if necessary.

 FROM THE EXPERTS:
Simon Nixon, moneysupermarket.com

We've always done our search engine marketing in-house, and have hired consultants to help us from time to time. If you outsource to an agency, you end up being just another client, so it can be difficult to keep intelligence in-house.

KEYWORDS AND WHAT THEY DO

If you've looked for something on the web, you've no doubt typed in a few words on Google describing what it is – these are known as **keywords** or **search terms**. If you've typed in one word, you've probably found that you get a whole host of answers, many of which are probably not relevant to your search. The more keywords you initially type into the search engine, the more refined your search is likely to be.

Keywords are crucial to the success of your website, as it's a free way of generating traffic to your website and is one of the main ways potential customers can find you. Imagine this scenario: you have built a site that is rich in content, with plenty of information and submitted it to a number of search engines. Week on week, though, you wonder where all your customers are, as traffic figures are disappointing. The answer is most likely that these customers cannot find your website as the keywords they are typing in are not on your website.

You'll need to aim for keywords that are often searched for and which therefore attract traffic to your site, but that are not so competitive that a top ranking becomes next to impossible. Research your competitors thoroughly and avoid choosing keywords that might end up directing traffic to their site, rather than yours. Ensure you use real sentences rather than just keywords in your content and don't use too many keywords in an attempt to improve your search rankings – search engines are likely to penalise you for doing this.

IN MY EXPERIENCE:
Glenys Berd, LoveThoseShoes.com

As with everything on the net you have to try whatever you can. So you need to make sure the main keywords for your site are not only organically listed through search engine optimisation techniques but also through pay-per-click.

To determine which keywords will work best for your site, put yourself in your customers' shoes and ask yourself the following: if they were looking for the products or services that your business provides, what words are they likely to type in? Review your website pages and note down all the words and phrases that might fit the bill. There's likely to be much more competition for the top ranking search engine results for single keywords, so think about phrases that appear on your website and which people are likely to type in. Consider words that are similar to each other too. For example, design and designer are similar terms but one or the other may rank higher when it comes to search and you may want to use both keywords if appropriate.

TIP

Don't be put off if traffic to your site appears to be slow once you've identified your keywords and optimised them – it can take weeks and even months to process keywords. But ensure you keep a detailed record of traffic information so you can assess how effective your keywords are.

Opt for concise keywords, rather than those that are long and which may be difficult to spell. Keywords can appear in a number of ways, in your domain name and the content on your website for example. You could focus on optimising words on your homepage and in the headings or images – the more places your keywords appear in, the more exposed your site will be. There are tools available to alert you to the most frequently searched keywords and many of them are free to use. Check out Google's Keyword Tool, which can be accessed at https://adwords.google.com/select/KeywordToolExternal. This service enables you to type in keywords to see how popular (or not) they are.

How many keywords should you include on your web pages? If you are using natural search, the ideal number of keywords really depends on what sector you are operating in – the more competitive the industry, the more selective you should be with the number of keywords used, although use too few and you risk search engines not picking up on these keywords. Above all, keep monitoring your keywords and how they perform so you can determine if your web content needs changing.

➡ UNIVERSAL SEARCH

Search isn't just about web pages anymore. Over the last two years, the likes of Google, Ask, Microsoft and Yahoo! have all developed their services to offer listings based not only on web pages with text, but also on different types of media such as blogs, videos, images and maps.

For example, if you're looking for a pair of Nike running shoes and you type in 'Nike', rather than just getting a link to a list of websites, a search engine results page is now more likely to provide images of the shoes, blogs, reviews and videos on YouTube. This technique is known as universal or blended search and can offer your business improved levels of indexing. If you were launching a new product or service, one of the first things you'd want an online searcher to see would be a link to some positive reviews of the product, for example.

Depending on the nature of your products or the content of your site you could make use of universal search to improve your place in the rankings. For example, if your site is based around music or entertainment, you may have several videos that you could look to optimise too.

➡ MONITORING TRAFFIC

Monitoring traffic to your website is much more than looking at the number of hits you get. You can track all the following elements:

- Information on the total number of visitors
- The different ways they navigate around your site
- What pages they view and for how long
- How any particular marketing initiatives have performed

There are various terms used to describe the science of recording and interpreting website statistics: web metrics, web analytics, web stats and site stats, to name a few. 'E-metrics' refers to analysis of electronic businesses. The 'metrics' of web metrics refers to measurement – the science of measuring websites, specifically, measuring website 'events', and extracting trends. In this case, those 'events' are human clicks. By measuring these events you can answer questions such as:

- Are there more or fewer people coming to your site this week than there were last week?
- Is your site doing better or worse this week?

What should your stats tell you?

Your stats will inform you about numerous aspects of your traffic, such as the number of (returning) visitors to your site, and how visitors surf through your pages. This information tells you about the content of your site and how visitors use it.

Your traffic statistics are an indicator of website performance. When applied in this sense, site stats can be used very effectively to make updates. They can tell you what aspects of your site are popular, and what aspects visitors don't like.

If your website generates its revenue from advertising, effective measurement of visitors to your site is crucial. The price you can realistically charge people to advertise on your site will be determined by how many visitors you get.

Web analytics

Web analytics, also known as page tagging or tracking, involves adding a tracking code to each page of your website, which collects user data. This can then be analysed to produce reports about how users are interacting with your site. There are basically two types of analytics tools you can use: free ones and more advanced web analytics.

Free ones such as Google Analytics (www.google.com/analytics) and Yahoo's Index Tools (http://web.analytics.yahoo.com/) offer analytics around statistics such as number of visits and sales your website has achieved over a set period of time. More advanced web analytics providers will tailor analytics to your site and can identify and analyse a greater number of metrics, such as the user journey (how a customer arrives at your site, what they do when they are there and where they go next) and how long it takes from the time they arrived to when they made a purchase. Companies such as Omniture (www.omniture.com) and WebTrends (www.webtrends.com) provide these services.

IN MY EXPERIENCE:
Jamie Murray Wells, Glasses Direct

In the early days when money was limited, we managed a Google account for a year, and used free tools from Google. Make the most of free tools.

The more bespoke and tailored your web analytics, the more you can understand about your site users. Using web analytics involves collecting and analysing data from a range of sources and the more sophisticated tools on the market offer increased insight into who is using a website and why. If you make use of free tools such as Google Analytics, it's likely you'll be doing web analytics in-house. If you outsource web analytics to an agency, ensure you get regular reports with updates on traffic.

IN MY EXPERIENCE:

Glenys Berd, LoveThoseShoes.com

We use analytics software and online chat programmes such as WhoseOn are very good because they show in real time what people are doing on your sites. It's amazing what you can learn by simply watching where people go and what they do.

 # AFFILIATE MARKETING

There's only so much you can do to promote your website and attract new customers, so you could consider affiliate marketing to boost your sales. Affiliate marketing involves you paying other sites (known as publishers) based on results for displaying your ads. You'll pay nothing to display an ad on another site but as soon as someone clicks through or it results in a sale, you'll pay. It can be a cost-effective way of attracting new customers and generating sales. The amount varies depending on how it is calculated. You can agree to pay a fixed amount per sale (known as cost per sale), a fixed amount per lead or enquiry, or a percentage of sale (this is common for those sites that sell a variety of products).

The amount of commission you choose for each type of payment will depend on how much you expect to make from a sale and how many leads you can expect to convert into sales – having a certain number of leads is all well and good but they will count for nothing unless you can get sales from them.

There are different ways to run an affiliate marketing campaign. You could choose to work directly with other sites or publishers, which means you'll be responsible for making payments and tracking the number of clicks and sales generated, or you could opt to join an affiliate network. These are companies that will manage your affiliate marketing campaign on your behalf. There are a number of affiliate marketing providers available.

TIP

Regardless of the network you choose, ensure that you communicate with them on a regular basis.

FROM THE EXPERTS:
Simon Nixon, moneysupermarket.com

Affiliate marketing can be a cost-effective way of sharing risk, and we used it effectively when we launched moneysupermarket.com. We worked with all the big portals – we had the content, they had the traffic. We still work with many different affiliates today.

How affiliate marketing works in practice

- A consumer visits an affiliate's website, which can be a shopping portal or other retail website, where an ad or link to your website, service or product is displayed.
- The customer clicks on this ad and is taken to your site to complete the purchase.
- The sale is completed online. Software records data such as what was purchased, when and for how much. You then pay a commission to the affiliate for the sale that has been generated.

Things to remember:

- Try submitting your website to the major search engines so they are aware of your site.

- Natural search is a long-term strategy so you will need to invest time and effort in this.

- The majority of businesses use a combination of natural and paid search.

- Use search engine optimisation to improve the volume of traffic to your site.

- Aim for keywords that are often searched for but which are not too competitive.

- If you can afford it try using an agency to manage your search engine marketing needs.

- Monitor the traffic to your website to allow you to make effective updates.

- Make the most of free tools such as Google Analytics or Yahoo's Index Tools.

- Affiliate marketing can be a cost-effective way of sharing risk.

Keeping customers

Keeping customers

T he saying goes that a customer who has a bad experience is likely to tell at least 10 people about it, whereas one that has a good experience will only tell one other person. No matter what kind of business you are running, you need to keep your customers and keep them happy or they will go elsewhere. This is especially true in times of economic uncertainty, where one of the biggest challenges facing businesses is how to increase customer retention. Customers defect for a number of reasons: they've had a recommendation from a friend, they've found a better product elsewhere at a better price or they are dissatisfied with the product or services received. While you can't predict why a customer might not revisit your site, there are many steps you can take to prevent this happening in the first place.

And when you consider that it costs six to 10 times more to acquire a customer than to retain one, it makes sense to invest in a retention programme. This is especially important for online businesses – your nearest competitor is only a click away and online customers are notoriously fickle at the best of times, with many being swayed by price alone.

Improving relationships with existing customers can help not only to generate repeat sales but will also give you the opportunity to up-sell and cross sell, which will be particularly useful if you choose to diversify your business at a later stage. Loyal customers not only generate repeat sales, but are likely to recommend you to others.

In this chapter we'll look at:

- Building customer confidence
- Implementing an online database
- Email newsletters
- Special offers
- Inviting feedback

➡ BUILDING CUSTOMER CONFIDENCE

Your business won't survive if your customers don't trust you, but building customer confidence online can be a challenging proposition. The anonymity of the web means that many customers will look to purchase goods or services from the big boys – brands they can trust and which perhaps also have a high-street operation. For a start-up business this can be a hard proposition to match.

IN MY EXPERIENCE:
Jamie Murray Wells, Glasses Direct

We had a customer-oriented approach right from the beginning, which was very important as the web can be quite anonymous. We needed to make it more transparent.

The reality is that online businesses come and go so building a reputation is the key to gaining customer trust and encouraging people to visit the site again. Besides ensuring your contact details, privacy statement and customer helplines are clearly displayed on your website, there are a number of other steps you can take to gain your customers' trust.

Don't promise what you can't deliver. The days of 28-day delivery are long gone – when shopping on the web, people expect instant gratification. If you say you can deliver next day, in three days or in seven days, ensure you stick to this. There's nothing worse than letting customers down when it comes to the fulfilment side of things – they will almost certainly go elsewhere. Of course, much as you can promise, you can't foresee any problems that may occur logistically or technically, so it's equally important to communicate with your customers as soon as you suspect there may be a problem with their order and see what solution you can come up with.

FROM THE EXPERTS:
Nick Robertson, ASOS.com

If you know an order is not going to go through, you need to let the customer know. We've had lorries breaking down on the M1, for instance. There's no point in driving traffic to your site if you are going to disappoint your customers. You can't fail in this area on the internet.

Keep your website content updated and refreshed – there's nothing worse than a customer logging back on weeks after a visit and seeing the same content on the same page or seeing news stories that are months old. It will make them think twice about whether you are still trading and they'll be reluctant to buy from you again. If you are struggling to provide updated content, get your customers to do this for you. Encourage them to post recommendations or reviews to your site (depending of course on what you are selling or what services you are offering) and you can then incorporate this into the copy on your website.

Make it easy for customers to contact you. They may be experiencing technical difficulties, have a query about stock or want to know about delivery times. Whatever the issue, it's imperative your contact details are correct, that your customers can reach you and that you respond accordingly.

TIP

If you want to build trust in your customers, try not to let them down and if any unforeseen circumstances threaten deliveries or stock levels, communicate this to them as soon as possible. Consider issues from their perspective and go the extra mile to exceed their expectations.

➡ IMPLEMENTING AN ONLINE DATABASE

In order to keep customers coming back, you'll want to stay in regular contact with them, which means creating and using an online database of customer details. In Part 4, we looked at your legal obligations when it comes to maintaining and using a database of customers. In order to do this, you have to persuade customers to part with their details in the first place.

There are many ways of collecting information from visitors to your website and many of them can be used regardless of the level of your technical skills. Remember that before you collect any data, ensure your site has robust security, by investing in an SSL certificate, for example (see Part 2, p.146 for more on SSL certificates and encryption).

Email alerts and newsletters

One of the easiest ways to stay in touch with your customers and to inform them of updates to your site content, new stock and services, and seasonal offers is to use email alerts or more detailed newsletters. You could also include links to vouchers and 'recommend a friend links' to boost retention rates and gain a few new customers at the same time. LoveThoseShoes.com, for example, sends its subscribers an email newsletter packed with news and tips while moneysupermarket.com sends email alerts which keep its users up to date on the latest best buys, with articles from a team of experts about the best and worst products on the market. In addition, when it identifies a money-saving deal, it notifies users by email.

IN MY EXPERIENCE:

Glenys Berd, LoveThoseShoes.com

It's absolutely essential to have a newsletter. We send one out every week and spend a good deal of time writing it. One trick is to add a joke to the end of each one so readers will forward it to each other and build your membership.

You might not have the time or the skills to devote to writing a regular newsletter, but consider sending smaller email alerts every few weeks with some information about your business that will not involve any extra work, such as drawing their attention to other parts of your site or reaffirming your product base. At the very least, it will remind customers that you are still in business and encourage them to click through the links to visit your site.

When it comes to the content of your newsletters, put yourself in your customers' shoes. Ask yourself what kind of information they would be interested in and what might encourage them to click through to your site. If you don't have the time or the ability to write newsletters, you could consider employing someone on a freelance basis to write them or depending on the type of industry you are in, you could seek permission to reproduce content from other (non-competitive) websites either by putting the content direct into the newsletter or embedding links.

Free shoes ?

Is that right ??

It sure is !!!

Today we're launching a
Special 3 for 2 Offer

 Buy 3 pairs and the lowest priced is **FREE!**

Select any 2 pairs and choose a third pair

...
ABSOLUTELY FREE!!

Don't miss this great opportunity to choose
ANY 3 pairs - and ONLY pay for TWO of
them. The lowest priced pair will be absolutely free.
The offer includes items in stock across the whole site, including The Clearance Store
(excludes pre-ordered items)
**You need do nothing complicated - simply put 3 products (or more if you want
!!) into your basket and the system will automatically deduct the lowest priced
item off your order**
And there's more !!!

FREE SHIPPING IN UK (by Royal Mail)
And even more !!!!!
FREE Mystery Gift with every order !
*Don't say we're not doing our best to help you through the credit
crunch - at least you can have shoes on your feet !*
Click here to start shopping !!

Email newsletters: keeping in touch with your customers

What to include

In terms of the structure, you'll need to keep copy short – no one likes to read
lengthy copy on the web or have to scroll down endless pages, so employ the same

style for your newsletters. The subject line will have to strike a balance between being concise and enticing enough for people to click on. Avoid using words such as 'hello', and 'free' or monetary signs as these are all likely to trigger spam filters. If you need inspiration have a look at your inbox and make a list of the emails you are tempted to open and those that you would delete without a second thought. It's also a good idea to test a small segment of your customer database before you send a mass email out; that way you can test just exactly what percentage of customers were enticed enough to open the email (known as open rates).

FROM THE EXPERTS:
Simon Nixon, moneysupermarket.com

We encourage people to sign up to personalised email alerts with news covering aspects of the industry the business is focused on, such as finance and travel. If you bombard people with crap, your open rates will reduce dramatically. You should aim for an open rate of 15%–20%, anything less than that and the quality and content of your emails are not good enough.

In terms of layout, you need to apply the same attention and creativity as you did to the design of the site. Your customers aren't likely to print the email out, they'll be reading it on the screen, so a clear layout that is easy to navigate goes without saying. Try and mirror the style or your website so you can maintain levels of consistency. Your privacy policy, where you detail how you will use any information that the recipient gives you in relation to the email, should be clearly stated and visible.

Adding a personal touch to the email, addressing recipients by their first names, for example, will attract more attention than a simple 'Dear Sir' or 'Dear Madam'. Text should be clear and easy to read and you should consider offering the newsletter in both text and HTML format depending on customer preferences, and because some software and web-based email accounts (such as Hotmail) block images by default. Use images wisely but sparingly – if you use too many, the newsletter may not display properly or may take too long to download. Include a link at the top of your email newsletter which says something along the lines of 'If you are having trouble viewing this newsletter, click here to see it on the web' or 'Show content' with a link to the email newsletter online.

Check that all the links used in the newsletter are correct and click through to the right page. Above all, an email alert or newsletter should not be used as a sales vehicle, but as a way of engaging with your customers and increasing their levels of loyalty.

Email etiquette

There are certain guidelines to follow when it comes to sending email news-letters – fall foul of these and you are likely to alienate customers rather than encourage repeat purchases.

Unsolicited email (spam) clogs up people's inboxes and is against the law. Regulations require that you get individuals to opt in before sending them marketing emails, unless they have already shown interest in products or services similar to the ones in your alert or newsletter. People may also have decided they don't want to receive communications via email from any business (known as opt-out), by signing up to the Email Preference Service. Check out the Privacy and electronic communications guide at the Information Commissioner's website (www.ico.gov.uk) and see our tips below.

Email newsletters

What you should be aware of

Electronic mail marketing messages should not be sent to individuals without their permission unless all these following criteria are met:

- The marketer has obtained your details through a sale or negotiations for a sale
- The messages are about similar products or services offered by the sender
- You were given an opportunity to refuse the marketing when your details were collected and, if you did not refuse, you were given a simple way to opt out in every future communication. The regulations do not cover electronic mail marketing messages sent to businesses.

⚓ TIP

Unsolicited marketing material by email (this includes texts, picture messages and emails) should only be sent if the person has chosen to receive them, unless the email address was obtained as a result of a commercial relationship. The individual should always be given the opportunity to stop receiving the emails.

Autoresponders

These are used to acknowledge receipt of customers' questions relating to technical support or stock query for example. You can either choose to install an autoresponder on your server or subscribe to an autoresponder service that is hosted on another server – your web host would normally offer you an autoresponder service too.

Special offers

One of the tried and tested ways of keeping customers is to offer them something more than they would normally expect. Exceed their expectations. Develop ways to reward your customers for repeat purchases. Ensure that any rewards or special offers are in line with what your business can afford – it makes little sense to come up with special offers that are not within your budget. Cost-effective rewards include vouchers offering a 10% discount for example, or money off dependent on spending a certain amount, gift certificates for recommending a friend, free shipping and money off future purchases. You can include special offers and discounts in email newsletters and on the site.

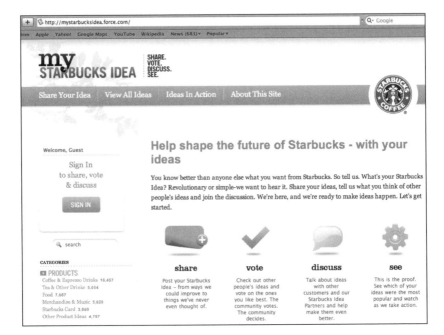

Startbukcs: inviting feedback via the web

For a longer-term approach, you could consider developing a customer loyalty programme, which will call for investment upfront. Price is not the primary reason most people stay loyal to brands, rather it is the experience they gain from interacting with your business and making a purchase. Before setting up a loyalty scheme, consider the resources you currently have available in-house. Are they able to support a loyalty scheme? You'll also need to assess how many customers you have on your database, how they behave and your budget.

Inviting feedback

One of the keys to customer retention is the ability to listen to your customer base, inviting comments and feedback and responding to these in a positive manner. Coffee giant Starbucks, for example, launched a website in 2008 to encourage customers to give feedback and suggest ideas on how it can improve its service. Customers shared their ideas and voted on the feedback of others. Computer manufacturer Dell, which has suffered its share of negative customer feedback in recent years, launched IdeaStorm, a website enabling customers to share their experiences and ideas directly with the company and their peers.

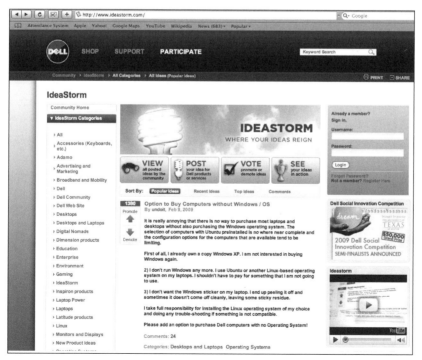

Dell: inviting feedback via the web

While gaining customer feedback is a simple enough process, many small businesses lack the time or the resources necessary to do this, by running questionnaires for example and then collating the answers, much less following up on anything learned from the process. Many view feedback as a cost of doing business rather than an opportunity.

FROM THE EXPERTS:
Simon Nixon, moneysupermarket.com

We invite comments from our user-base and encourage people to go to our forums online. It's a key way to engage with people and to keep them coming back. It's more cost-effective to retain existing customers than to acquire new ones.

Get feedback even when a customer is not happy with the service or goods they have received. The quickest way, however, to alienate any customer is to ask for input and then ignore it. Many small businesses make the mistake of ignoring such feedback or sweeping it under the carpet but the speed at which a complaint can be dealt with will signal to your customers that you care, regardless of whether their responses are positive or negative. Continued analysis of feedback can help you to identify any areas of weakness and to improve on them, upping your levels of customer service.

Make it as obvious and as easy as possible for people to get in touch with you – as your business exists in a virtual environment they can't physically pop in to return goods or voice a grievance. Put an 'About us' section indicating who to complain to. Collecting customer feedback and analysing it is even more valuable in a challenging economic environment as you are likely to be cutting back spending in other areas and looking to make more money from your existing assets. Set aside some space on your website for forums, where users can interact with each other and post advice and recommendations.

TIP

Set up a method for collecting and responding to customer feedback. This could be in the form of a general online questionnaire that you send out in the first six months of business for example, or you could encourage customers to give you feedback after a purchase, assessing areas such as ease of use of site and delivery. You could then use these on your website.

FAQS

FAQs or frequently asked questions are a resource that many customers will look at when browsing a particular site. Many websites devote more than one page to frequently asked questions that will provide information regarding your business operations. If you're tempted to do quite a few (and this really depends on the type of business you are running), consider grouping all the questions together at the top of the page, enabling consumers to scan and browse the answer, before clicking onto a link. No one wants to read pages and pages of FAQs and grouping the questions together means that customers can access the areas they need to quickly.

You'll also need to pay attention to what goes into FAQs – both in terms of content and style. Ask your friends and family to come up with potential scenarios based around your site that you can then answer. The latter need to be concise but informative and should be written in a clear and engaging style as FAQs can help to boost levels of interaction with customers further. In terms of presentation, have a look at other websites for inspiration and for ideas on how not to do it. As a rule of thumb, FAQs should be clearly presented and you should have information on how people can send questions clearly displayed on the site.

TIP

Check out your favourite sites and have a look at their FAQ sections for advice and inspiration. The key is to keep these concise and informative.

Things to remember:

- Complaints shouldn't be viewed as negative – encourage as much feedback as possible and if there are complaints, look at ways of solving them. This will encourage your customers to spread the word about your customer service so they become advocates.

- Deal with customer complaints and queries as quickly as possible – as the old saying goes, a customer who has a bad experience is likely to tell 10 other people.

- Email newsletters need to be concise as well as engaging. Ensure you measure open rates so you can decide whether you need to change tactics.

- Try giving customers special offers; its easier to retain loyal customers than find new ones.

- Check with your web host provider to see whether autoresponders are part of the package.

- FAQs need to be concise and to the point, otherwise you risk alienating customers. Check out other websites to see how these are displayed.

Keeping shipshape

Running and adapting the business

our site has gone live. The launch party is over. Your staff are trained and traffic is slowly but surely building up. You're the master of your own destiny sitting pretty, picking the hours you want to work.

This is the point where anyone who's already progressed beyond this point breaks into a knowing chuckle because, as you'll soon find out, going live is only half the battle. Maintaining the business and managing yourself, your staff and your time is the real challenge. This is the time when you should be monitoring your website and its content closely to make sure there are no glitches.

In this chapter we'll cover:

- Post-launch: what to consider
- Technology issues
- Adapting your website
- New trends
- Updating content
- How to manage yourself
- When to take advice
- Managing staff
- Work/life balance
- Staff costs/benefits

➡ POST-LAUNCH: WHAT TO CONSIDER

Don't panic. You should prepare for your first few weeks to be fairly slow so don't freak out when they are. It's always going to take a while for word to get out and it will take weeks, even months for your site to be well optimised to attract visitors. In turn, don't bury your head in the sand either, and use the time wisely. A slow start is not necessarily a bad thing, as it can give you a chance to hone your operation. A slower start allows you to perfect your model, test your ideas and assess what works.

As your reputation in the area builds, so too should your customer base. You should have accounted for a gradual increase in trade in your business plan anyway. The key to surviving the first few months is doing everything you can to keep the cash flowing in, while keeping overheads low. Too many online businesses actually get more than enough customers to their site and convert these into sales, but suffer because their overheads are disproportionately high.

If you are running an online retail business, from the first month's trading adjust your stock levels so you're not carrying more than you need to. Don't cut back your product range, just buy what you can best predict you're likely to sell and keep as much cash as you can in the pot. Similarly don't go employing staff until you absolutely need them and if you do, take people on a casual basis first explaining a permanent role will follow as soon as you can afford and justify it.

➡ TECHNOLOGY CONCERNS

You might have a fantastic range of products that literally fly off your homepage and dedicated customer service, but in the world of online business, your site is only as good as the company that hosts it. If there is a problem with your web hosting company, there'll be a problem with your site – which could range from pages that are slow to load, to those that don't load at all to a site that is unavailable most of the time. All of this will result in lost customers and sales, not to mention the damage it does to your reputation. In Part 4 (see p.111) we highlighted the importance of ensuring that your web host provider can accommodate your bandwidth needs. It's reassuring to see that traffic to your site reaches unexpected peaks, but it's a different story if your web host cannot support this growth. In the first six months of business, monitor traffic levels carefully and see if you can predict when further spikes will occur, so you can plan in advance if you need increased bandwidth.

➡ TAKING ADVANTAGE OF FREE TIME

While trade is slower this may be a good opportunity to bring in some of your marketing skills. Think about the different kinds of special offers you can introduce to try and boost trade. Avoid emblazoning your site with the word 'sale' as this can portray desperation more than invitation, but don't be scared to use calls to action on your homepage such as 'introductory offer', 'just launched', 'browse our great selection of . . .'.

The *Establishing your presence* chapter (p.199) gives you more detail on this but it's something to consider during your early stages of trading. You should also look to stagger PR throughout the first six months. If you've come up with five great PR stories, don't use them all for the launch and keep in regular contact with journalists. If you've had a great month, press release it, if you've had a celebrity visitor advertise it; keep thinking how you can make the news and stay fresh in people's minds. This could form the content for any email newsletters or email alerts, encouraging people to come back to the site.

If you've any budget for marketing, overcoming the lull that inevitably follows the highs of a launch month is the time to spend it. It's actually much better to spend money on advertising after a month or so because by then people might have heard of your business, logged on and be more influenced to browse – that's a far more likely scenario than reacting to an advert for an online shop you've never heard of before.

✦ TIP

Stagger potential publicity over the first few months post-launch. It will mean people keep on talking about your business and will give you time to develop some relevant news for your customer base.

More than anything, stay calm but focused. Measure everything. Record everything. You should know the unit sales of every product, the number of hits to your website, what you're making most mark-up on and not just how many sales each member of staff is making, but how cost-effective they are for you.

Resist outlandish, wholesale changes and stick to your identity and business plan, but carry out subtle experiments with website lay-out, and perhaps even products and measure the impact.

> **TIP**
>
> The first six months should teach you about your business and your customers – like any other relationship, you'll need to get to know one another and if you don't work at it, nothing will improve.

NEW IDEAS / TRENDS

One of the most common reasons any website either fails to take off or sees trade drop is because it takes its eye off the ball. The internet moves like the wind so all that work you did researching the products your customers want and expect can never stop. Indeed, if you researched it and then spent three months creating and designing the site, it was probably out-of-date the minute your website went live.

It's more of a concern for some sectors than others. If you're in the fashion or electrical market, anything longer than a three month cycle is archaic. You should always have a line of classic bestsellers but you need to stay in touch with the latest trends.

Buy the magazines your customers buy, know what and who they aspire to, visit the competition and work harder than them to find new suppliers and never miss a trade fair. You should be just as passionate and knowledgeable about the area or niche you're operating in as your customers are – in fact, you, your staff and your website should be the experts in that area that the customers turn to for advice and guidance.

IN MY EXPERIENCE:

Mark Leather, Country Products

Like fashion, a website soon looks dated. Who are you most likely to purchase from: a smartly dressed fashion conscious young lady or a long haired bearded hippy wearing loons and a tie-dyed t-shirt?

➡ ADAPTING YOUR BUSINESS

When you're getting your website set up and everything is brand new, it's easy to forget that all may not run smoothly. Being able to make changes and ongoing support are an important element of your website plans and something you should consider from the get-go.

While your first few months in business should be a constant learning process, there is a point where you need to stop, take stock and ask if the website is ever going to work without some wholesale changes.

If you've been tweaking, experimenting and measuring the impact of different approaches you'll be in a far better position to make the decision than if you've sat on your hands hoping that miraculously your site will soon receive thousands of hits. Just because you've pumped your life savings into a business, given up the safety of a salary and spent months developing your site, it can then be massively difficult to accept it's not going quite as well as you'd hoped.

Unfortunately, though, there are no assurances in business no matter how much planning and preparation you put in and the biggest celebrity entrepreneurs who sit on TV telling others how to do it have all had their flops – and will again.

The most important thing is to be open minded and prepare yourself in advance so if you do have to make some pretty drastic changes it won't come as a big shock – and if you don't want to lose face you can tell everyone that it was part of the plan all along!

Assessing what works

The key is to look at the business basics and get to the bottom of the problem. Go back to your business plan and hold it up to your website. Is it a true reflection of the plan? If it is, then you need to look for what's going wrong. Usually it'll either be that you're not getting enough hits to your site, that your customers are not buying your products or using your services, or, if they are, that your pricing or supply line is wrong.

If when you compare your site to the one in your business plan and you see something different then you could have found your answer. Is it true to the USPs and identity you outlined? Did you get lost or sidetracked from the original vision somewhere? Are you differentiating yourself enough and communicating the right messages as you'd originally intended? If you're not, then start reversing those problems and get back on track.

If you still can't work out where the problem lies, look at your finances because that's certainly where the problem will be hidden. Remember, it doesn't matter how many customers you have or how much you love your website if it's losing money. Money doesn't have to be your motivation for running an online business, but profit is your oxygen and you need to be striving for it in every buying and selling transaction.

Look at your suppliers. Can you source cheaper elsewhere? Can you buy better quality for the same price that would encourage more sales? Have you got any big overheads eating into your profit? If you have, be hard. Lose them. Yes, that includes people. Many, many entrepreneurs say that their biggest regret is trying to grow their business too quickly, getting in a mess and having to lay people off to save it. However, many of them did it, survived as a consequence and went on to employ multiples of the people they upset by letting them go.

> ## ✦ TIP
>
> Concentrate on the core business. If you're making big changes to your site and the business, update your business plan, then you'll have something to refer back to if you're still haemorrhaging money in a month's time.

➡ TWEAKING YOUR SITE

Wholesale changes to your website are not something to be taken lightly but making small changes to your website is something you should be prepared to do on a regular basis, as it's essential to both attract new customers and retain existing ones. Just as a shop changes its window display, you'll need to do the same with your homepage. Returning visitors will see new, fresh content that will encourage them to explore the site further, and you might want to appeal to new ones by adding testimonials to your site or replacing images to attract their attention.

Bear in mind the future development of your site and consider the kind of upgrades and new technologies you may require. If you want to add sub-sites at a later date for instance, you need to know whether this will be possible. Ask your provider what kind of costs you can expect in the future.

Revisit your website and make note of all the areas you think should be tweaked or which could benefit from a more substantial change; that is a list of changes which you 'need to have' and those changes which would be 'nice to have'. You should also do a thorough check to spot any errors or broken links. Of course, the bigger the change, the more time, effort and money it will cost, so only consider making a major change if you think it is strictly necessary, for example, the navigation could be made clearer or you need to insert a site map to help people find their way around the site. Carry out a thorough audit and organise any notes you have made into areas that can wait and those that need immediate attention.

What to check for

Check links on a regular basis – the more your site develops the greater the number of links you are likely to have, so it makes sense to check a certain amount at set intervals, otherwise you could find yourself overwhelmed. Make sure you remove 'dead links' (which click through to nothing) and links that are out of date, as these are areas that most frustrate consumers. Scan the content for any typos or formatting errors and to ensure that images are displaying properly. It's equally important to check that any ads you are hosting on your site are still live and that any affiliate deals you have in place are actually working. Load the site onto different browsers too to ensure that it displays properly.

Don't introduce changes just because you've noticed your competitors have added some features – you need to put your customers' needs first at all times. Having already built up a reputation, the last thing you want to do is to radically change your site – it will only result in confusing your customers and potentially sending them elsewhere. While new internet technologies are launched on a regular basis and it may seem tempting to try them out, remember that your customers may not be adopting these technologies at the same rate as they are being released and used.

> ## TIP
> Carry out a website review soon after launch. Check that all aspects of the site are working and use this opportunity to assess if any of the content or tools need tweaking.

Web content management system

If you commissioned a web designer, you may have factored in access to a web content management system (WCMS), which are basically maintenance tools for creating, editing, searching and publishing HTML content on your business website. This is particularly suited to those websites that have a substantial number of pages and where the contents needs to be changed on a regular basis. Even if you have no knowledge of programming or mark up languages, these web applications should allow you to create and manage online content – everything from images and audio files to video and electronic documents – with relative ease. A good CMS will allow you to edit content easily; manage your workflow; and extend your site's functionality to scale as you grow.

If you opted for a custom-built site, and don't have access to a WCMS, scalability depends on the people who built the site for you. You'll probably have to go back to that person or that company and have them upgrade it for you.

Updating content

New content on your website will not only encourage existing customers to come back but it will also stand you in good stead with search engines. They love new content and if you update your website regularly, you'll stand a better chance of achieving a higher ranking among search engines, not to mention increasing the number of visits to your site.

There are many ways to introduce updated content without incurring too much time, effort, resources or expense on your part. Consider writing a blog to promote your products or to give a view on your chosen sector. Sites such as http://wordpress.org offer free blogging software, enabling you to get a blog up and running in a matter of minutes (see Part 9, p.319, *Developing your site* for more information on blogging). Refresh your list of frequently answered questions (FAQs) as often as is possible and reasonable – new customers will often click on this section first to find out more about your business.

News and views

Creating a news section on your site will enable you to promote product launches, changes to your website, new staff hires – anything, in fact, that you feel would interest your customers and add value to your business. News stories don't have to be as detailed as press releases as they are not intended to be sent to the media but are being used more to promote your products and refresh website content, so you could try to write these yourself.

Archive your newslettters. In Part 6 (p.248) we discussed the importance of email newsletters and how to write them to create the maximum impact. Make sure you keep a record of all the newsletters you create and send out. These can then be uploaded to the site.

Statistics related to your business are also a quick and easy way of adding new content to the site. Depending on the type of business you are running, you could highlight the products that have sold the most for a particular month, or include general statistics related to your sector.

If you feel that your writing skills won't be up to scratch, then you could employ a freelance journalist or copywriter to help and draw up a schedule of when updates need to be done by, such as by a particular day once a month.

Is your website easy to use?

Have you ever been to a website because you know there is something you want, but even after numerous clicks, you simply can't find it? Most people's reaction would be to go elsewhere – if this happened to your business, you would potentially be losing out on sales. Website usability assesses how easy it is for users to find their way around the website, search for items and click on those pages and offers that you want them to click on.

With your website, you are aiming to build something that is easy to understand, navigate and use. If your customers can find what they need, then this results in sales, subscriptions, and everything else the website is intended to achieve. In theory, this seems like second nature, in reality, usability is an area many websites struggle with and lack of ease of use is one of the main reasons your customers will go elsewhere.

Usability includes areas such as links, content and navigation. When you carry out periodic reviews of the website, and each time you add any new content, ensure you click on the links to test that they take you to where you want to go. Carry out user testing among your friends and family and ask them to rate how easy it has been to find the content and features they want.

TIP
Aim to update your website content at least once every few weeks. You should ideally aim to refresh content once a week.

> **When updating content**
>
> - Check your spelling and grammar – the fewer mistakes the better
> - Keep your paragraphs brief – blocks of text are not search engine friendly
> - Lists (either bullet point or numbered) are quick ways to add new content and will stand out
> - Sentences should not be too long

➡ HOW TO MANAGE YOURSELF

The minute you employ another person you go from being a humble online business owner to a boss, a manager and the point from which authority and company culture flows. If you're not used to it, that can be quite a culture shock. Some people react by becoming too authoritarian, others try too hard not to change and end up losing respect. To run a motivated, disciplined workforce you'll need to strike a balance between the two and lead by example.

Taking advice

We covered the value of taking advice from others in Part 1 (p.29), but it's important to remember this is not something you should forget about once you're up and running. Mentors and established entrepreneurs can have something to offer your business even if it's a decade old. It's always good to have an outsider's perspective that may be able to tell you where your strengths lie, and which areas of the business or management you're neglecting.

Once you've established yourself as an online business owner you may find people more willing to confide and share with you as you can offer them advice in return. Networking should be an ongoing process. Try and mix with other shop owners at industry and local events, where you can share experiences and seek support. Also, don't rule out general free business networking events such as Startupslive, details of which can be found at www.startupslive. co.uk. These types of events bring together entrepreneurs from all kinds of industries, and you never know when a contact you make will come in useful.

As the owner of an online business, you mustn't think that only other online businesses can offer useful advice or guidance. Running a web venture shares the same principles of running any kind of business and you'll be surprised at how friendly and open to communication people can be when they share the same goals as you.

Identifying your strengths and weaknesses

As a business owner you develop and hone your skills everyday. However, if you want to maintain a successful business, you have to dedicate just as much time to your own self-development as to your business.

It can be hard to measure your own personal development when you're your own boss. Just because your online business turns over a tidy sum at the end of each month, doesn't mean you're as effective as you can be as a leader. That's where the focused and planned development of your knowledge and skills through training can benefit you.

Running an online business, much like running any other kind of small business, requires you to be multi-skilled. The role of an online business owner can involve everything from buying stock, dealing with customers, creative store design, business planning and taking care of the accounts. Regardless of whether you have a hands-on position in all of these roles you need to be at least familiar with what they entail.

IN MY EXPERIENCE:
Jamie Murray Wells, Glasses Direct

The challenge for the online entrepreneur is that you need to be quite rounded. When you have limited resources, you want it all in one.

If you employ someone with more online or technical experience than you and see them following certain processes, swallow your pride and ask them about it. They'll appreciate you showing an interest and you'll get valuable insight. Ask questions of your accountant. You may not be a whizz with numbers but you still need to understand the basics of a tax form or balance sheet. You might feel silly asking something a GCSE business studies students knows after term one, but you'll never know unless you ask.

IN MY EXPERIENCE:
Glenys Berd, LoveThoseShoes.com

You should hire technical staff as soon as you can afford them. They make all the difference to a business as they allow you to create something unique. Off the shelf solutions give you an off the shelf product, on the net you need to be different.

If you can't afford an army of experts to help man your online business then take advantage of the help available to you. Contact your local Regional Development Agency (www.englandsrdas.com), or visit a Business Link (www.businesslink.gov.uk) advisor. They can point you in the right direction as to what's on offer in terms of training. Many courses are free for small business owners, so you can't even use lack of funds as an excuse.

The industry moves fast. What's en vogue for an internet retail business one month may seem passé half a year down the line. You need to keep up to date with the latest online trends and fashions. Subscribe to trade magazines, other websites and visit trade shows. You'll be surprised at what you can get out of them – new ideas, inspiration and a wealth of new contacts, possible suppliers or even customers.

Motivating yourself

The fact that you've even chosen to start an online business suggests you're an incredibly motivated person, but once the site has launched and traffic increases, how can you make sure you maintain that level of enthusiasm? The start-up process is incredibly demanding both physically and psychologically. After all that hard work you clearly need to slow down the pace slightly, but you can't sit back and hope the business will run itself.

In the same way you might set targets for staff, and KPIs (key performance indicators) to measure performance and flag training and resource needs, you need to do the same for yourself.

If you see you're not performing as you'd like, take stock. Don't be too harsh on yourself though, it'll almost certainly be a case that you're doing too much and need to delegate more.

Again, sharing experiences and networking can keep you motivated. Running an online business, as with any company, can be a lonely experience where you're expected to shoulder all the responsibility. Having people to share that with you can really lift the load, reassure you you're not alone and replenish your determination.

More than anything though, make sure you appreciate what you have achieved as well as what's left to do.

IN MY EXPERIENCE:
Jamie Murray Wells, Glasses Direct

If you looked at any of the online businesses out there, such as Facebook, Yahoo! and YouTube, I don't think you need relevant online experience. You need a sense of pragmatism and determination – the online model lets you do things faster and has a wide reach and you have to put yourself in the minds of your customers.

Time management

With so many hats to wear in your role as online business owner, managing your time effectively is absolutely essential and is where many people fall down. It's absolutely critical that you grasp the principles of strong time management from a very early stage. This is particularly important for those running an online business, where there are no set working hours and your company is effectively operating every day of the year.

The most important aspect of time management is to list and prioritise everything you need to do. This will allow you to recognise the difference between what's **important** and what's **urgent**.

Running an online business will involve various 'to do' lists. This will include your long-term goals such as growing turnover and improving your margins, nurturing and expanding your customer base and developing your own skills as a business owner. Next come your monthly goals, which could be introducing a new product range, recruiting new sales assistants, finding a new supplier or getting your accounts in order. And of course there'll be daily and weekly objectives as well – stocktaking ahead of trips abroad to source supplies perhaps, changing the site layout or its design and sorting the payroll.

Whatever your role within your business' opening times, you need to set aside enough time to get on with these tasks as they are just as important as serving customers when it comes to running a successful establishment.

Here are a few tips for prioritising workloads and making sure you don't neglect important aspects of running your business:

- List all the tasks you need to do, and then prioritise them in order of what is most urgent and important.
- Don't underestimate the amount of time interruptions can steal from your schedule. When allocating time for a particular task, build in room for disruptions.
- Don't be afraid to turn off your phone or email and ask not to be disturbed when you really need to concentrate. If having no distractions helps you get a task done more quickly, you may end up with extra time to deal with clients, customers or staff.
- Break large tasks up into manageable chunks. It's tempting to run lots of little errands instead of getting stuck in to a big important job. However, completing it one stage at a time will make it seem less daunting.
- Build room into your schedule for unexpected problems or events. If nothing unforeseen crops up, you'll end up ahead of schedule.
- Make sure no more than half your time is allocated to top priority work. All those little jobs that aren't as time sensitive will start to mount up if you don't crack on with them.
- If possible, delegate. You may think the business will fall apart if you don't oversee everything, but perhaps your time can be more valuably spent.

Holidays and work/life balance

Deciding the right time to take a break is a tricky thing to master, particularly for an online business when all you need is a computer and an internet connection, and in theory, you can conduct business from a beach hideaway. The temptation to carry on working even while on holiday can prove too strong for some. It's understandable, as your online business will still be very much in its infancy at this stage. However, you will have worked incredibly hard to get the venture up and running and may feel in desperate need of a break by this point.

There's no specific right or wrong answer to when the best time to take a break or holiday is. At such an early stage in the company's life you may feel you simply can't afford to leave it in someone else's hands. The main thing to remember is that you need to achieve a balance between working hard to make sure the business thrives during its early days, and making sure you don't burn out yourself. Working too hard without a break can be counterproductive and bad for your health. It's always best to take a breather before you get to the point where you simply can't keep up the pace.

If you do decide to take a break then test the waters first. Don't book two weeks in the sun without knowing for sure you've got a solid team in place to run things in your absence, otherwise you might well end up doing business from the beach. Start by asking your second in command to deal with customer queries, then perhaps put them in charge of some site designs. Handing over the reins for a weekend while you're still close at hand, perhaps even just at home, is the next step.

By doing this you can test if things are capable of running smoothly in your absence while still being nearby if any real problems arise. It's actually a healthy situation to get into and the longer you leave it, the more you expose your business to real problems if something happens to you.

Once you're confident the whole operation won't collapse as soon as you've closed the door behind you, you'll find you have a far more rewarding break and can come back refreshed, raring to go, and hopefully full of new ideas.

➡ MANAGING STAFF

No matter who you're managing you need to clearly outline and put down in writing what their role is, make it clear what you expect from them and demonstrate how their performance will be measured. You then need to ensure you set clear lines of communications, both from you to them and them to you, to flag and deal with any problems.

There's nothing worse than a boss who doesn't communicate what they expect then reprimands staff for not delivering it. Yet it's equally galling how many people are motivated to start their own business having been on the receiving end of such poor practice then only succeed in doing the same.

The best bosses are fair. They're firm but they listen and they apply the same rules to themselves as they do on the shop floor. You should lead by example in every respect: dress smart, be punctual and have manners, be serious when it matters and have a sense of humour and fun when appropriate.

Despite this, there should always be a separation between you and the people that work for you. There's nothing stopping you getting on with your employees and even becoming friends, but keep a professional distance. It's far easier if things turn sour, stops resentment from other staff members and maintains a clearly defined structure where everyone knows their roles.

Staff training and courses

The online business environment moves at a fast pace, so it's vital that you provide staff with access to training and courses, particularly in areas such as online marketing and security. New techniques and technologies are being developed in these areas all the time and it's vital for you and your staff to have at least some knowledge of what is out there, even if you aren't likely to implement it for some time. Weigh up the cost of getting outside training. There are plenty of courses, most of which can be done in a day or less, which teach the fundamentals in any online skill.

Why not dedicate a day where all, or at least half, the business's staff can train together? This doesn't have to involve going off-site. Many courses involve a tutor or lecturer coming to you and doing on-site training.

Dealing with staffing problems

Most employers will experience difficulties with certain members of staff at various points in their career. Online businesses move at a rapid pace and some people who joined in the early days of the business may not have the appropriate skills as the business grows. Unless you're extremely lucky, or only hire friends and family to work in the shop, it's likely you'll have to confront some of the following problems.

Bad service and laziness

Every customer that visits your site should be important to you. That sounds like one of those annoying messages that you get on automated call systems that prove you don't matter quite enough to employ more staff to answer the phones. As such, it's no good just saying it, you have to provide a friendly and helpful service and provide a positive shopping experience every single minute over every single hour you're open, every single day of the year.

For an internet business, this can be a challenging problem as all of the contact you and your staff will have with customers will be on a remote basis, so you will have to work harder to create a professional and welcoming atmosphere. Good customer service is something you can't relent on and you should never tolerate a slip in standards, no matter how frustrating or downright awkward the customer. It doesn't matter if the customer is right or wrong if they go away and tell 20 people your online business is rubbish.

When recruiting look for natural enthusiasm and people skills, it's generally something you can't teach, unlike other skills. Encourage your staff to be enthusiastic but not too imposing. There's a fine line between being friendly and being annoying.

FROM THE EXPERTS:
Nick Robertson, ASOS.com

We're quite passionate here, there is enthusiasm from staff at every level. When it comes to dealing with staff, you have to have a cold heart sometimes – more often than not, it's better for the individual concerned.

Discrimination

We've already touched on the issue of discrimination during the *Hiring Staff* chapter (p.185) but it's important to note that this is something you must constantly bear in mind. There's plenty more detail on how to comply with discrimination laws on Startups.co.uk but to summarise, you must consider the following legislation in the day to day running of your shop or you could find yourself in serious hot water.

Legislation outlawing age discrimination came into force in 2006. It includes every member of staff that works for you, both young and old. Employers must have age positive practices. This means you can't recruit, train, promote or retire people on the basis of age unless it can be objectively justified. Many people over 50 want to work but are prevented from doing so by ageist practices. But remember, the recent legislation doesn't just concern older people; it covers young and old alike throughout their working lives.

Skills, experience and the ability to do the job are what's important, not someone's age. However, the legislation doesn't just have advantages for employees. As a business owner, stamping out age discrimination can have a positive effect on staff turnover, lead to higher morale, lower recruitment costs, better productivity and increased profits.

The same applies when it comes to discriminating on the grounds of race, sex or disability. It's your responsibility to make sure that not only do you treat all your staff equally, but that discrimination does not take place between other members of the team.

Discrimination can take many forms, and it's not just a case of refusing to hire someone for being a woman/gay/ 65 years old. There's also indirect discrimination, where certain members are denied opportunities within employment, experience harassment such as unwanted advances or comments of a sexual nature, or bullying.

If somebody working for you is a victim of any of these kinds of discrimination you could find yourself fighting in an employment tribunal, which is costly in terms of time, reputation and turnover.

Staff handbook

While you need to make sure every member of staff has the appropriate training in health and safety, some of the other expectations of employee policy can be detailed in a staff handbook. Here you can list your expectations of all staff and your policy on issues such as absence, use of email and general working attitude. That way if a problem ever arises you can refer back to the handbook as an explanation of why you may be taking disciplinary action.

However, you should also use the handbook as a way of flagging up staff benefits and the elements of your online business that you think are the advantages of working there.

What goes in a staff handbook?

Your staff handbook should cover your policy on:

- Company morals or ethos
- Dress code
- Dealing with customers
- Absence and lateness procedure
- What day of the week or month salaries are paid
- Holiday entitlement
- Any bonus or reward schemes
- Health and safety procedures

Staff benefits

Thinking about the extra perks which can make your online business stand out as a great place to work compared to the many other establishments your staff may have experienced can reduce your staff turnover.

Here are a few examples of the kind of things you can do for your staff to encourage loyalty and hard work:

- Offer exclusive online discounts
- Incentivise staff with individual and team commissions based on a percentage of sales for the website per day and on a monthly basis
- Encourage team spirit with after work drinks or activities
- Offer bonuses or gifts for staff as a reward for hard work and enthusiasm
- Celebrate birthdays or special occasions – this could be in the form of a toast or even something as simple as a card signed by all the other members of the team
- Offer extra benefits for long-term service. Offering an extra day's holiday per year of service can be far more cost effective then going through the same recruitment process every couple of months
- Offer regular appraisals and give staff the opportunity to discuss any issues they want to raise. There may not be time during normal shifts to talk about problems or ask questions. Make sure you're approachable when staff really need you to listen

Things to remember:

- Don't panic if things start slowly, use this time to hone your operation, such as ensuring your web hosting company is working properly.

- Stagger your PR efforts throughout your first six months, now is a good time to focus on your marketing campaign.

- Make sure you keep monitoring new ideas and trends, the internet is a fast moving market so you need to keep up.

- Carry out a thorough audit of your site and make a list of changes that are 'need to have' and those that are 'nice to have'.

- Introducing new content doesn't have to put a strain on your resources or time – look at your existing resources and see how you can best use them.

- Your site links should be checked on a regular basis or you could find yourself overwhelmed as your site grows.

- Ensure your content is easy to read at all times and make it as search engine friendly as possible.

- List and prioritise everything you need to do.

- Take advice as and when you need it, whatever stage in your online career.

- Set goals for effective time management, taking breaks when you need them.

- Learn to delegate. You can't do everything on your own.

- Be fair but authoritative, and make sure all your managers are the same.

- Reward good work wherever possible. An atmosphere where staff are only singled out when they do something wrong breeds low morale.

Finances when you're up and running

R unning an online business is what you set out to do and without doubt that's where your energies are best served. As you've had to do throughout this whole process, you'll also need to put time aside for the financial aspect of running a business. After all, that's what allows you to run the company.

You'll already have familiarised yourself with projections, forecasts and basic costings during the planning stage, but the reality of running any business is that you need a firm grip on the numbers at all times. In order to do this successfully you'll need to become familiar with the different types of financial records you should use, such as profit and loss sheets, and learn how to always be aware of your financial status by keeping on top of your cash flow and payments. It may be helpful to hire an accountant at this stage to help you through, or to invest in some accounting software.

In this chapter we'll cover:

- Accounts
- Balance sheets
- Profit and loss (P&L) sheets
- Cash flow forecasting
- VAT
- Day to day finances
- Managing payments
- Hiring an accountant
- Paying your staff

➡ ACCOUNTS

Running a business involves meticulous record-keeping, some of which you are obliged to do, and some of which simply helps you run your business more efficiently. Your accounts can be separated into two main categories – financial and management.

Financial

If your business is incorporated, ie a limited company, you are required by law to put together a set of financial records every year and file them with the Companies House. Unincorporated businesses are not required to do this; however they must still keep thorough accounting records to be used alongside their annual tax returns. You are obligated to keep a minimum of the last six years' worth of accounts for HMRC to call upon at any time.

There are detailed guidelines for how to prepare financial accounts on the Companies House website at www.companieshouse.gov.uk, but you will generally have to include the following:

- Balance sheet
- Profit and loss account
- Cash flow statement

Management

Your management accounts are the records you must keep in order to run your business well. This is where you'll cover everything, from how many units of stock are bought and sold, to the payroll data for your staff. You simply cannot run your online business efficiently without up-to-date and methodical records. You also need to take the necessary steps to ensure this information is stored safely and backed-up.

What records do you need to keep when running an online business? Your accounting records will be split into daily, weekly, monthly and annual figures, all of which are important. Efficient records will allow you to identify the strong and weak areas of your business and therefore take appropriate action in your day-to-day management and long-term planning.

Records you should keep to have an accurate reflection of your online business's financial health include:

- All sales transactions broken down by date and product
- Stock levels – daily, weekly and monthly
- Receipts for credit card transactions
- Invoices from suppliers and service providers
- Any licences you require
- Property and lease documentation
- Staff shifts and wages
- Employee tax details
- Cost of other overheads including site maintenance and development

It's important to note this is not a complete list, and you will need to add to it depending on the type of online business you run.

FINANCIAL RECORDS

Balance sheets

Essentially, reading a balance sheet is like checking your bank balance – it simply tells you what the business owes or owns at any particular time. But unlike your bank balance it doesn't just give you a number, it also tells you what makes up that number. In essence the first part is everything your business owns, its **assets**. The second part is everything you owe, the **liabilities**.

The balance sheet has a debit entry and a credit entry for everything, so the total value of the assets is always the same value as the total of the liabilities.

An example balance sheet is shown at the back of this book (see p.335) but here's a more detailed explanation of all of the sections of a balance sheet.

- **Fixed assets:**
  This is typically anything that you count as an asset of the business but not something that you are likely to sell as part of your daily business. They can be tangible and intangible, so include any premises, website domain names,

trademarks, equipment such as computers or furniture that you use for the business.

- **Current assets:**
  Anything that you sell.

- **Debtors:**
  Anyone that owes you money should be included in here. If you offer accounts or sell to clients who settle monthly, then include sums owed in this column.

- **Current liabilities:**
  Anything that you owe that is payable within one year. In our list we have included creditors – which might include your suppliers as you will typically pay them in around 30 days – and the overdraft as this is probably repayable on demand.

- **Net current assets:**
  This is simply the sum of your current assets and liabilities, both of which are likely to be under one year in lifespan. This is quite a useful figure to calculate as it will show whether you could pay all your debts if you collected all the sums due to you.

- **Total assets less current liabilities:**
  Unlike the last number you can include all the long-term assets like property in this number.

- **Equity:**
  Any money that is invested in the business, for example your savings if you used those to set up the business initially.

Profit and loss (P&L) sheet

Put simply, a profit and loss sheet details your business' transactions, subtracting the total outgoings from the total income to give you a reading of how much, if any, profit you have made.

> ## TIP
> A profit and loss sheet, unlike a balance sheet, displays the financial health of your company for a period of time – a month, a quarter or a year. A balance sheet only represents your finances at a particular moment in time.

If your business is incorporated, you are required by law to produce a P&L sheet for each financial year. If your business is not trading as a limited company you don't have to produce one, but the information you give to HMRC to work out your tax bill will amount to the same thing anyway. Even if you're not required to produce one, the P&L sheet is useful to show owners and investors not shareholders, as if you're not required to produce the P&L sheet it must mean that you're not a company — ie that there are no shareholders how the business is doing at a glance.

You can find an example shop P&L sheet on p.76.

Cash flow statement

A cash flow statement shows your online business's incoming and outgoing money, enabling you to assess how much money you have at your disposal at any one time. Poor cash flow is one of the main reasons that businesses fail. Some businesses can be profitable on paper, earning more than their outgoings, but if the cash isn't in the bank to buy stock and to pay staff you'll soon find yourself in trouble.

Your first few months are the time you're most likely to run into difficulties with cash flow. A lot more money will have been spent by you – on equipment, initial stock, web design, staff – than the first few customers will pay you for their purchases, so on paper you'll be cash flow negative. There are certain things businesses can do to increase their cash flow and the most obvious is to ask their customers to pay them quicker. Online businesses can't really do that but here's a few things you can do to improve cash flow:

- Lease rather than buy the really expensive equipment you need. You'll then pay a monthly or annual charge rather than having to splash out all at once upfront.
- Order less stock – don't order too many of the items that will sit in your stockroom for months before interest grows.
- Make sure you forecast your cash flow as accurately as you can. That way you can plan ahead for slower revenue periods and make sure you still have enough cash in the bank to cover your outgoings.

Good cash flow forecasting isn't just important for your own business management. You may be required to provide this kind of detail if you need a loan from the bank during your first few months of trading. The forecast will allow you to identify the amount and origin of cash coming into your business and the amount and destination of cash being paid out during any given period of time.

Sage Pay's tips on managing cash flow

Knowing how much money you have coming in and going out helps you make informed decisions about your business. Investing in software is a great way to ensure you have that information when you need it.

Keeping all your financial and business contact information in one place helps you keep things organised. And when you store that information electronically, it's easier to keep it up to date, and you run less risk of losing it.

Accounting software places key information at your fingertips. For example, instead of having to calculate how much money your business has made and how much you owe, software packages such as Sage Instant Accounts and Sage 50 Accounts can show you that information at a glance via an easy-to-read Dashboard.

Integrated systems

The same applies to understanding your customers, as the software helps you identify those who have paid and those who have not. Most good accounting software will also enable you to integrate with Microsoft Outlook so you'll be reminded to do things like follow up a sales call, quotation or chase payment.

Another way to encourage cash flow is to use electronic payments, by credit or debit card or BACS (see p.182), reducing the time you have to spend banking your cash. If you're accepting payments over the phone or online, the fastest and most effective way to reconcile payments is to use systems that are integrated. For speedy and accurate results, an accounts package that integrates in some way with your payment gateway and shopping cart for example is worthwhile. That way you can limit the risk of human error and spend more time developing your core business.

Finally, using accounting software can also make sure you calculate VAT and tax correctly when submitting returns to HMRC, and avoid potentially costly fines. With accounts packages like Sage Instant Accounts and Sage 50 Accounts, you have the added advantage of making these payments online, leaving you more time to do your tax returns.

www.sagepay.com

Generally you'll produce a forecast for a quarter or year in advance, but during the early stages of trading you might want to do this more frequently, such as a month in advance. When compiling a cash flow forecast it's really important that you don't overestimate your incoming cash.

> ### ✦ TIP
> It's much easier to get an accurate reflection of your outgoings as you will know what these are at this stage. However, you won't yet have a really accurate estimate of how many customers you'll have each month, so err on the side of caution to be safe and keep your incoming cash estimates low.

There is an example of a cash flow forecast sheet on p.336.

VAT

VAT or Value Added Tax applies to the majority of transactions involving the sale of goods or services. Once your business reaches a certain level of turnover, currently £67,000 per year, you are legally obliged to register for VAT. You will then have to apply VAT to what you sell and keep records of your incomings and outgoings in order to pay the correct amount of VAT to HMRC.

> ### ✦ TIP
> To register for VAT go to the VAT Online Registration Service on the HMRC website.

If your turnover is under £67,000, you can voluntarily register for VAT, which can result in a number of cash flow advantages.

- If you sell zero-rated items and buy standard-rated items you would receive a VAT refund from HMRC
- If you have not yet sold anything or don't sell anything during a VAT accounting period, you can still claim VAT back on your purchases
- You have the use of the VAT your customers pay you before you have to pay it to HMRC

There are three rates of VAT:

1. The standard rate – 17.5% (currently reduced to 15%)
2. The reduced rate – 5%
3. The zero rate – 0%

Note that the standard rate of VAT has been reduced to 15% from 1 December 2008 to 31 December 2009. The standard rate will change back to 17.5% on 1 January 2010.

It's really important you register for VAT in good time because otherwise you will liable for all VAT due from the time that you should have been registered. In other words you have to pay HMRC the right amount of VAT even if you didn't charge your customers for it. You could also be liable to pay a fine for delaying your registration. How much you'll be fined is dependent on how late you registered, but fines start at £50.

The average time for processing VAT applications is about one month, however, it can take up to six months if HMRC feels it needs to carry out extra checks on the application. You must account for and pay VAT between applying for your registration and receiving your actual VAT number, but you are also allowed to reclaim any VAT you have paid suppliers on your purchases during this period. To do this you need to keep accurate records of any invoices where your suppliers have charged you VAT.

TIP

If you find the prospect of dealing with VAT daunting don't worry. You can appoint an agent – accountant, bookkeeper or tax advisor – to deal with it on your behalf by registering them on HMRC's VAT Online Registration Service.

➡ PRICE CHANGES

The cost of your outgoings will change, sometimes on a weekly basis. The price of products and the cost of energy are variable and may go up and down frequently. While customers accept inflation as a fact of life, they'll start to cry foul play if your products have jumped in price every time they visit your site. Consequently you need to find a balance between covering your own costs and maintaining reasonable prices for your customer.

One way of doing this is to set yourself a variable acceptable mark-up. For example, calculate what the lowest possible mark-up for an acceptable return is (for example 60%) then the highest mark-up you can reasonably expect to charge (for example 70%). This gives you some leeway for price changes for your own costings without leaving you out of pocket for not passing the cost on to your customers. However, when your own costs go up so much that it's no longer possible to make at least the 60% mark-up, that's when you'll need to change your prices.

ACCOUNTANTS

Even some of the most mathematically-minded entrepreneurs will tell you a good accountant can be worth their weight in gold. You're running an online business first and foremost and as stated at the beginning of the chapter that's where your passion should remain, not getting bogged down with invoices, PAYE slips and credit notes. Handing that responsibility over to an accountant or someone who completely manages your books can free up your time to spend on planning, development and working on your grand designs for your business.

Choosing an accountant

When you're just starting out, your accountant can act as one of your most valued business advisors so you need to make sure you employ one that you trust. There are many ways to find a good accountant and one of the best methods is through a recommendation. Ask friends and contacts if they would recommend their accountant. Also ask businesses around you if they go to someone locally.

> **TIP**
> Your solicitor or bank manager may also be able to recommend an accountant, or if not a particular person they should be able to point you in the right direction for an accountancy firm that specialises in your chosen sector and has experience of working with small independent online businesses and start-ups.

When seeking recommendations, make sure you ask people what they used their accountant for as you might not need the same kind of service. Ask what in particular they recommend about them and what their weak points are if they have any. Most importantly it is advisable to choose someone who is a member of one of the main professional accounting bodies. There is no legislation to stop anyone setting up as an accountant so asking for member accountants in your area will ensure you are getting someone fully qualified.

These are the main accounting organisations in the UK:

Association of Chartered Certified Accountants
Tel: 020 7059 5000
www.acca.org.uk

Institute of Chartered Accountants, Scotland
Tel: 0131 347 0100
www.icas.org.uk

Institute of Chartered Accountants, England and Wales
Tel: 020 7920 8100
www.icaew.co.uk

Remember you're likely to be working closely with your accountant and if you don't get on at a basic level, your professional relationship may be more difficult than it needs to be. If you find someone you think you like ask if you can speak to their other clients. This is like asking for references and will be a real test of the calibre of the firm or individual accountant. If they are confident that their service has impressed, they shouldn't have a problem referring you to a few people.

Accounting software

If you decide you're going to manage the books yourself you'll want to get yourself some accountancy software. Whoever's job it is, yours or an accountant's, the person balancing the books, chasing invoices, managing suppliers and paying staff doesn't need to be worrying about the latest technology and it's probably the last thing on their mind. However, buying an accountancy software package can slash the amount of time and effort you put into managing your finances.

> **When choosing a package consider the following before you buy:**
>
> - Value for money: what services do you get for your buck?
> - Level of support: does the package include a free helpline you can call for technical or set-up support?
> - Is the software industry specific?
> - Does it integrate easily with HMRC's online filing system? This can save you a lot of time when it comes to filing your returns.

➡ PAYING YOUR STAFF

Online businesses often have a lot of casual and temporary staff to cope with seasonal demands at busy times such as Christmas and Easter, for example, and it can be tempting to just pay them cash at the end of each week or shift. However, it's your responsibility as an employer to make sure the payment of your staff is all above board and both they and your business are making the appropriate tax and National Insurance contributions.

PAYE

PAYE (Pay As You Earn) is HMRC's system for collecting income tax and National Insurance at the source of payment – ie before the employee receives it. It's your responsibility to make sure you know how much to deduct from your staff in terms of their personal tax requirements. You must send the deducted amounts to HMRC by the 19th of every month (or the 22nd if you make electronic payments). However, if monthly payments are under £1,500 you can do this on a quarterly basis.

You have three choices when it comes to organising PAYE. You can either keep written accounts and calculate tax and National Insurance deductions yourself, buy specialised software to help calculate it for you, or outsource the whole operation.

PAYE is applied to all payments your employees receive when working for you. This includes:

- Wages
- Overtime
- Tips
- Bonuses
- Statutory sick pay
- Statutory maternity/ paternity/ adoption pay
- Any lump sums including redundancy payments

Once again, a quick visit to the HMRC website will allow you to register your business for PAYE. You should have already done this before employing your first member of staff, but if you haven't done so already, give the New Employer Hotline a call on 0845 60 70 143 and order a New Employer Starter Pack. This will talk you through the basics of registering.

Staff records

There are three main types of documentation to give your staff so they have a record of what they've earned and how much income tax and National Insurance they've paid. These are:

- Wage slips: this shows how much they've earned and how it has been calculated
- P60 form: this shows the tax deducted during the whole tax year. You can order this from HMRC by calling the Employers Order line on 0845 7646 646
- P45: you only need to give your employees this when they stop working for you. It will contain their individual tax code which they need to pass on to their new employer

Outsourcing payroll

Many businesses decide to outsource their payroll duties so they don't have to calculate tax and National Insurance deductions themselves. This will obviously be an added expense for your business but can save you a lot of time and money in the long-run. By outsourcing your payroll you get rid of one of the biggest administrative headaches of running a small business.

If you have an accountant, they should be able to provide you with advice on outsourcing your payroll, and may even be able to do it for you. As with any service, shop around for the best deal as much as time permits.

Before you decide on an outsourced payroll provider, make sure you consider the following:

- Are they used to dealing with online businesses?
- Do they supply monthly or weekly pay slips? (You may find weekly slips are more suited for casual staff.)
- How much will they charge for setting up your payroll system?
- What are the ongoing fees?
- How easy is it to add extra members of staff to the account?
- Is the software they use approved by HMRC?

Things to remember:

- Keep accurate staff records and ensure these are as up to date as possible.

- You are likely to run into cash flow problems in your first few months, so ask for help if necessary.

- Keep an eye on your prices and adjust them according to your outgoings.

- Make sure you register for VAT in good time to avoid HMRC delay fines.

- Don't try to manage it all yourself if you don't have the time or skills. Hire an accountant if you need one.

- Consider outsourcing your payroll but carry out the appropriate checks before handing the process over to a third party.

eBay: What it's all about

eBay: What it's all about

I f you've bought or sold something online before, the chances are it was through eBay. The online auction site is something of a retail phenomenon and arguably one of the most successful companies of the dot com era. Set up in 1995 in the US by Pierre Omidyar, the site is now established in 39 markets and hosts upwards of four million auctions a day, with half a million new items being offered for sale every 24 hours. According to the site, a mobile phone is sold every minute and a car every four minutes. Its three biggest markets are the US, the UK and Germany. In the UK alone, the site has around four million customers, so it's easy to see why so many people choose to set up an eBay business.

Reputation is the key to surviving on eBay but once you become a 'Power Seller' the opportunities are endless. Setting up an eBay store is something which many sellers use as a way to have their own store front without having to set up their own website.

In this chapter we'll cover:

- Quick guide to eBay
- How to sell
- Getting stock
- Managing your reputation
- Payment options
- Opening an eBay shop

➡ QUICK GUIDE TO EBAY

Opportunities offered by eBay are far and wide – it's not just a place where you can get rid of clutter or sell unwanted Christmas gifts and bric-a-brac items – it gives you the chance to turn an interest or hobby into a business, incurring relatively low costs and using secure transactions. It has allowed millions of people to start their own online businesses when they previously would not have considered it and tap into an international customer base. For many others, an eBay business is generating healthy second incomes and for some, sourcing and selling items on eBay for a profit is a full-time job. Another advantage of an eBay business is that you shouldn't be too tangled up in red tape – the site is user-friendly and accessible and there are tools available such as a customised website and credit card merchant that can do all the hard work for you.

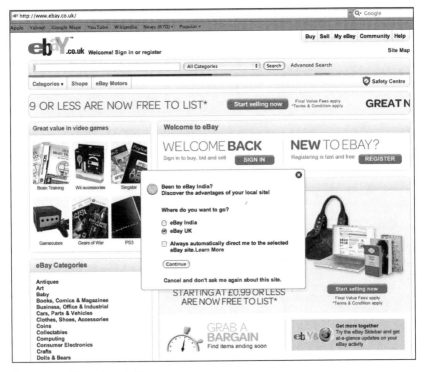

Ebay: Opportunities are far and wide

You can sell just about anything on eBay – if you've ever wondered whether someone would have a use for an item that you no longer need, then you've got a good chance of finding such a person on eBay. Of course, there are some items that are not allowed to be sold on the site (see below), so ensure you check out the list of restricted items before proceeding. eBay promises tough action against those breaking the rules and you could find yourself barred if you persistently flout the code of conduct. Admittedly, there are also some fairly wacky items for sale that constantly make the headlines, such as the housewife who put herself up for sale for £25,000, but there are also plenty of thriving businesses taking advantage of what eBay has to offer.

What eBay considers unacceptable items for auction:
Aeroplane tickets
Alcohol
Animals and wildlife products
Catalogue and URL sales
Counterfeit currency and stamps
Counterfeit and trademarked items
Credit cards
Drugs and drug paraphernalia
Embargoed items and prohibited countries
Firearms and ammunition
Fireworks
Football tickets
Franking machines
Government IDs, licences and uniforms
Human parts and remains
Lockpicking devices
Mailing lists and personal information
Offensive material
Prescription drugs and materials
Recalled items
Satellite, digital and cable TV decoders
Shares and securities

Obviously most UK small firms wouldn't consider selling human remains or grenade launchers, but it's worth going through this list as selling agreements on items such as football and aeroplane tickets are strictly controlled. Other items such as food and batteries are in a grey area for eBay, which describes them as 'questionable'.

While eBay may be a ready-made business model to tap into, you stand to make real money from the site so you'll need to comply with all the legal rules that apply to any other online business. You'll need to register with HM Revenue and Customs within three months of starting up and profit on your business will be subject to income tax. Those eBay sellers who are not paying their share are likely to be under increasing scrutiny from the taxman so ensure you keep records of all your transactions.

Whether you are looking to sell personal items on eBay or run a full eBay-based business, this guide provides the information you need to get started on eBay and become an eBay success story. In this chapter, we'll look at how to use eBay to your advantage, how to open an eBay shop and we offer information and advice on the most common problems encountered with eBay and how to overcome them.

➡ HOW TO USE EBAY TO YOUR ADVANTAGE

Researching how and what to sell

The first rule of thumb is to understand how eBay works – an eBay business should be approached like any other e-commerce venture you are considering. Do the necessary research first, as there are many different selling formats. You can sell auction-style, where you receive bids and sell to the highest bidder in a fixed length of time, sell at a fixed price so buyers can purchase items immediately without any bids, sell through a reserve auction, where you specify the minimum bid that needs to be reached or a multiple-item auction, where you can sell more than one identical item at the same time.

Once you've chosen a selling format, you need to decide what to sell. One of the most important things to consider is finding a niche that few other people are competing in. You might think this is easier said than done, given the number of businesses trading on eBay, so the trick is to spend some time checking out both eBay and other similar websites. eBay has a section which will tell you what are currently the most popular searches, what items are being watched the most and the largest shops. Here is an example of what to look for.

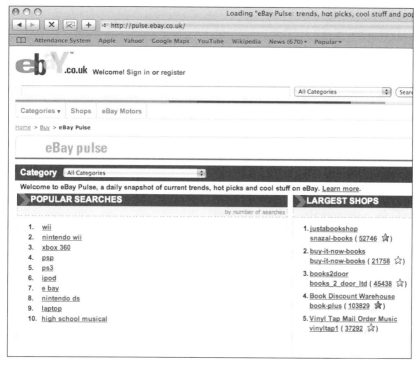

eBay: List of popular searches and the largest shops

Identify items that are niche, those that sell like hotcakes and those that everyone else is selling. While you'll be primarily interested in the selling side of the site, it's a good idea to consider the experience from the customer point of view. It's not uncommon to find that some of eBay's most successful sellers started off as buyers. If you haven't already bought from eBay then consider doing so – it will help to put you in your potential customers' shoes.

The process will give you an idea of how the system works, what buyers are looking for and any problems you may come up against. Make a note of your experience in the following areas, assessing any problems you may have encountered and what solutions you would come up with if you were the seller.

Successful eBay businesses

Rochford Tyres has been selling car wheels and alloys on eBay since 2003. It initially trialled the site in a bid to shift around £60,000 worth of stock and was surprised by the amount of interest and sales generated. It says that upping the stakes is easier if you have the ability to buy cheaply and that's where the wholesale leads that the business had worked hard to build over the years became so valuable.

Parkers of Bolton has been selling bicycles on eBay and says that sites such as eBay provide a market where smaller businesses can compete with the big boys. It says that eBay's level playing field is encouraging because it means that any seller can reach millions of buyers. It says that you just need to get under the skin of eBay to make it work.

eBay research: what to ask

- How was the customer service your experienced?
- Was the item well described – did it come across genuine?
- Were there any pictures of the product and what was the benefit of this?
- Were delivery costs reasonable?
- How easy was the final transaction?
- Was it easy to communicate with the buyer? What areas would you improve?
- Was the eBay shop well designed?

➡ ADVANTAGES OF USING EBAY

Making a profit on the items you buy and then sell is the very essence of starting an eBay business. There is no sure-fire way to make a profit, but by sourcing goods at a low price and selling them at the going rate, with prompt delivery, you should begin building up your takings. There is certainly no shortage of people out there looking to buy and in the current economic conditions, people are likely to be more price sensitive and will actively be seeking out models such as eBay.

As any financial risk to your eBay enterprise is small, you can experiment with the goods you are putting online. If you have, for example, amassed a collection of vintage clothes, designer shoes and handbags, you could consider making this an eBay business. Vary the prices to see what the market rate is and then stick to it. Check out what your competition is doing whenever possible, as they may be undercutting you. With so many eBay businesses in the UK, the chances are that someone else is doing what you are doing.

By their very nature, auctions are unpredictable, but they are the only way to 'test the water' and see what kind of demand there is for your stock. When you are posting your first few products, set a low price and see how many bids you get and how much the price rises. Remember, though, there is no guaranteed way of making a profit on the site.

There are plenty of online resources too that you can refer to for more tips and hints on selling through eBay.

---

eBay resources

- Federation of eBay Businesses: www.foeb.org
- Discussion boards on eBay, including feedback forums and blogs: hub.ebay. co.uk/community
- News and blogs: www.tamebay.com

➡ START SELLING

Simply choose a name and password and you're in. To begin selling on eBay, register and then create a seller's account (which is free), providing credit or debit card details and bank account information for verification purposes. All new sellers must offer PayPal as a payment option (see p.155 for more on this).

To start selling you follow the clear instructions giving details of the item you are selling and selecting the relevant subsection. You can also upload a picture from a digital camera, or one from the web, to illustrate your product. Buyers like to see what they may be spending their money on, so including a picture can enhance sale prospects.

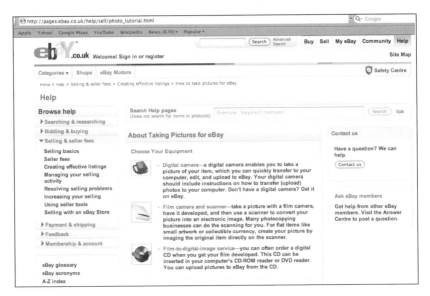

eBay: Guide to taking pictures of goods to be sold

The next steps are creating a business account, and setting up an online shop. To start trading under your business name, set up a business account when you register with eBay. All you need in order to do this is a UK address, to receive a confirmation letter through the post, and bank account details to set up a direct debit.

If you enter your VAT registration number when you create this account, then you won't pay any VAT on seller fees. (If you don't have a VAT registration number, register with HM Revenue & Customs. See p.288 on details on how to do this.)

➡ WHAT IT COSTS TO SELL ON EBAY

It costs between 10p and £2 to list an item on eBay, depending on the opening value or reserve price of the item, although fees are different for specific products, such as mobile phones with contracts. The site takes a slice of the selling fee once an item is sold, depending on how much the item is worth.

The fees you will be charged are directly related to the listing and sale of your item and the majority of fees are paid only when you sell the item. These include:

- **Insertion Fee:** a non-refundable fee charged to your account when you list your item on eBay – you pay it even if the item does not sell. The level of this fee depends on the starting price of your item and varies by category.

- **Optional Feature Fee:** these features, such as Bold and Buy It Now, can help enhance your listing, making it more attractive to buyers and increasing bids. The fee is dependent on the type of feature you use.
- **Final Value Fee:** depending on what you successfully sell your item for, eBay will charge a small percentage of the final value in fees. This is only charged if the item sells.

➡ GETTING STOCK

If there's one thing that sellers will never reveal, it's where they get their stock from. One of your biggest challenges when setting up an eBay business is likely to be finding plenty of low cost products you can sell at a profit. Many older items are sourced from markets and charity shops, whereas newer items tend to originate from wholesalers, manufacturers and liquidators.

The most obvious and efficient way to accumulate products is to buy them in bulk from wholesalers. Finding a wholesaler that will supply you with cut-price stock can be a challenge, but if you shop around you will be able to find bargains. Remember that you make money on eBay when you buy your stock, rather than when you sell it, so it pays to drive a hard bargain. If you strike an agreement with a wholesaler, you should be able to get a constant supply of warehouse stock for your new business but never rely on one supplier only – it's like putting all your eggs into one basket. If they let you down, you'll have to turn elsewhere to source products.

Above all, when sourcing stock, keep in mind the margins you expect to make – any effort you put into sourcing stock, such as time and money needs to be justified by the profit you expect to make. There's little point in selling many items if you are only able to make the smallest of profits or just about break even – it might be wiser to concentrate on selling a few items, but those which command higher prices and therefore better margins.

➡ REPUTATION IS KEY

The anonymous nature of online businesses is such that reputation and trust are key to building repeat business and encouraging customers to come back time and again. Having an eBay business is no different. As a seller, your reputation is the most valuable asset you have and it will depend on a number of factors, such as how long you have been a member of the site and more importantly, your feedback score. The system enables members to rate sellers by leaving positive, negative or neutral comments.

The more positive feedback you gain, the better the prospects will be for your business. The ratings you receive and leave for others reveals a lot about what you are like as a seller, and it's an area that any potential customers will focus on before parting with their money.

As with any business, issues likely to affect your reputation include effective customer communication, ensuring the buyer has had a positive experience, dealing with any problems swiftly, developing clear and concise terms of sale and knowing how to handle those awkward customers who never seem satisfied.

There are a number of precautions you can take to ensure your reputation is as enhanced as possible. It pays to do the research thoroughly and to be sure of your answers before you list any items for sale. There's nothing worse than withdrawing or changing your terms once a transaction has been completed as it will do little to instil confidence in your abilities to run an eBay business. The following areas are important when considering how to build and enhance your reputation.

'About me' page

This page, as eBay describes, enables you to tell the world about yourself and your interests. You can use it to display items you are selling and to describe your hobbies or profession. It's a simple enough process and it's free and easy to create so there's every reason to take advantage. To get started, enter your page content, add pictures if you want and select a page layout. You can preview before submitting the page to be published and can update information on this page as and when necessary.

Sales descriptions

Preparing items for sale on eBay is no different to any other e-commerce business – you'll need to come up with a concise description of the goods, take pictures where possible and combine these to create an online catalogue. Of course, as eBay is an auction site, you don't need to specify a fixed price, but can suggest one at which the bidding should start. For help with descriptions, have a look at how other people have described their items. Essentially, you should be looking to keep any descriptions you use concise and informative, with a heading that engages a buyer and attracts their attention.

> ### ✦ TIP
> When compiling sales descriptions, be honest, give concise details and
> include photographs of items you are selling wherever possible. People like to
> browse in bricks-and-mortar retail shops and the same is true online. Give as much
> detail as possible but without being over-wordy.

Terms of sale

There are no hard and fast rules when it comes to setting out your terms of sale,
but these should be clearly and concisely communicated and be visible to the
buyer. Ensure that you are comfortable with any terms of sale you have listed.
Ask yourself the following: how quickly are you expecting payment, what type of
payments are you willing to accept and are you prepared to send goods abroad?
How quickly can you expect to get the goods to the buyer – the faster you ship,
the happier the buyer will be and you are likely to generate repeat business. It's
important to promise what you commit to – if you have problems with shipping,
for example, inform your customer as soon as possible and offer them an
alternative arrangement.

Be clear with payment options

Everyone seems to know someone who has encountered problems with receiving
payments after selling an item on eBay. This could range from all contact with
the buyer coming to a sudden end, cheques bouncing, or the buyer insisting on
paying in ways that eBay strongly advises against, such as cash. eBay provides
protection to sellers but familiarise yourself with their guidelines. If problems
arise at time of payment, you are under no obligation to send the item to the
winning bidder but instead can relist it. To ease problems with payment, it's to
your advantage to accept different forms of payment.

Guide to payment options on eBay

- eBay requires all sellers to offer payments through PayPal, a system that
  allows people to pay with a debit or credit card, bank account or balance
  in an account, without sharing any financial details with the seller.
- Listings in some categories are exempt from PayPal, including cars,
  caravans, boats and property.

- You can also offer buyers the option of paying directly with a credit card online or by phone, if you have a merchant credit card processing account or use a third-party credit card processor.
- Don't be tempted to accept cash in the post, even if the buyer insists – cash should only be used for transactions carried out face-to-face.

Pay attention to packing and shipping

Your job is not done when an auction ends – you have to get the item safely and quickly to the highest bidder or buyer. Goods that arrive damaged or badly packed are hardly a good selling point. Ensuring that items are packed in such a way as to minimise damage will reassure buyers – you might even consider adding a note to tell them of any similar items you have recently listed or are going to list in the near future. This might encourage them to actively seek you out next time they want to buy.

 TIP

Any discrepancies between what you write in your sales descriptions and what gets delivered to your customer could cause your reputation permanent damage in the long-term.

eBay language

You'll come across many different sorts of terms when researching an eBay business, everything from an affiliate to a power seller. Check out our list of the key terms to be aware of and what they mean.

Affiliate: Driving traffic from your site to eBay's site that results in a sign up or purchase.

Power seller: those who sell an average of £750 per month or 100 items, for three consecutive months.

Turbo Lister: a free software programme that helps you create item listings in bulk on your computer and upload them to sell at eBay. It's suited to medium to high volume sellers.

Verified Rights Owner (VeRO) programme: enables rights owners to report listings that infringe on their rights (such as copyright, trademark, patent).

➡ OPENING AN EBAY SHOP

The simplicity of setting up an eBay business is a big attraction for many people. You don't really need anything other than a computer, an internet connection and storage space for your goods. You could take this one step further by opening an eBay shop, a feature from eBay offering you the opportunity to showcase your listings in a customisable, eBay shop front – it's basically just like having your own website, in return for a monthly subscription.

You post items for sale at fixed prices and can keep stock listed for 30, 60, 90 or an unlimited number of days at a time. There are three different types of eBay shop: basic, featured and anchor. According to eBay, 75% of sellers say that opening an eBay shop increased their sales. Impressive as this figure is, opening an eBay shop is not for everyone as there are certain criteria you need to fulfil.

To open a shop you must be a registered eBay user with a seller's account. You'll also need to meet the following requirements, depending on the type of shop you set up.

eBay: Example of eBay shop

Basic Shop:

- Minimum feedback score of 10
- Must be PayPal verified

Featured Shop:

- Must be a registered business seller on eBay
- Must be PayPal verified
- Must maintain a 12-month average detailed seller ratings score of 4.4 or above in each of the four areas

Anchor Shop:

- Must be a registered business seller on eBay
- Must be PayPal Verified
- Must maintain a 12-month average Detailed Seller Ratings score of 4.6 or above in each of the four areas

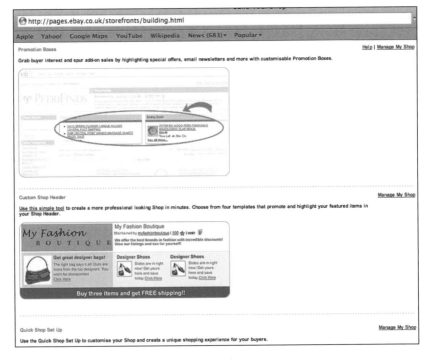

eBay Shops: There are a variety of tools to increase buyer interest.

According to eBay, the shop is most suited to those people who have already acquired considerable experience with the site, in terms of listing volume and sales generated. There are a variety of ways you can increase buyer interest and sales, using tools such as promotion boxes, where you can highlight special offers and post email newsletters. The Listing Frame tool enables you to add your shop categories, search box and category navigation to all of your item pages in one click, while with the Custom Shop Header you can choose from four templates to promote and highlight featured items.

➡ BECOMING A POWER SELLER

As mentioned previously, Power Sellers are those who sell an average of £750 per month or 100 items, for three consecutive months. They have also achieved and maintained a 98% positive feedback rating and a solid sales performance record. You'll also need to have been an active eBay member for at least 90 days and not have breached any severe policies in a 60-day period.

It doesn't cost anything to become a Power Seller, although the process is reviewed on a monthly basis to ensure that people qualify to maintain their status. There are numerous benefits to be gained. You are eligible to receive substantial discounts on final value fees in return for providing a good service to customers, measured through eBay's Detailed Seller Ratings. You can also use the Power Seller icon next to your user ID, so buyers are aware of your status. There are five levels to aspire to: Bronze, Silver, Gold, Platinum and Titanium (the lowest being bronze, the highest titanium). All offer personal phone support, fast priority email support and a range of final value discounts. A personal account manager is assigned to gold, platinum and titanium members only.

There are certain tools you can use to help improve your sales and your chances of being rated as a Power Seller. Software such as Turbo Lister and Selling Manager Pro can help you to create professional listings, automate your process and track sales, while eBay's Picture Services can enable you to present your items in the best possible way. Consider setting up an eBay shop as this will give your goods more exposure and will encourage repeat buyers to find your listings easily.

➡ FREQUENT EBAY PROBLEMS AND HOW TO OVERCOME THEM

Setting up an eBay business can be a relatively pain-free process but once you are up and running, there are a number of issues over which you need to exercise caution. Many of these can be applicable to any internet business and the more familiar you are with these problems, the better equipped you will be to deal with them.

Be aware of fraudulent emails

One of the biggest threats to the security of your eBay account and your identity is fraudulent email and websites, called 'spoof email' and 'spoof websites'. Like many other internet sites, eBay has been the subject of spoof emails so it's important to recognise any warning signs that someone is trying to access your personal and account information. Both spoof emails and websites are used to get personal and account information. A spoof email pretending to be from eBay typically contains a link that takes you to a fake website that requests that you sign in and submit personal and account information.

Dealing with fraudulent payments

Make sure that the payment has been received and confirmed before you despatch any items. eBay recommends that if the buyer uses a credit card, contact the card issuers and verify that the name on the card matches both the postage and contact information.

When a buyer does not pay

Try to communicate directly with the buyer to resolve the situation. eBay guidelines stipulate that if seven days have passed since a buyer won your item and you have not received payment, you should contact the buyer to assess the situation. If this fails to work, you can open a case at eBay's Resolution Centre, which helps create a dialogue between you and the buyer and tracks your case for you.

Top tips for selling on eBay

- To build up your experience of the site, start off by selling something you know about or are familiar with.

- Do some thorough research, both on eBay as well as on other sites to get an idea of what level to pitch your product.

- When researching the competition, try and identify any unique selling points related to your goods.

- Build up positive feedback. This is the bedrock of eBay and will set you apart as a reliable seller. Excellent customer service is key here, if you say you will do something, honour this.

- Monitor the competition – don't just do the occasional research at the beginning – it's something you need to do on a regular basis, as your competitors will be checking you out too.

- Start small and then look to build the business depending on demand for certain products, the experience you have had or what you notice the competition is doing.

- Don't spend huge amounts of money on stock until you have gauged levels of interest and demand.

- Be as upfront and open with potential buyers as possible – hidden costs and misleading product descriptions will alienate your customers. Trust is vital for building an eBay business.

Developing your site

9
Developing your site

As the internet is a market in continual development maintaining and developing your site is the real challenge you will face. It requires constant attention, careful planning and a willingness to adapt. This may include adding applications to your website or even branching out to include online forums or writing your own blog.

You'll need to keep up to date with the latest trends, continue to optimise your website and perhaps look at ways of diversifying the business. You'll also need to retain a flexible outlook, adapting your business plan if necessary, revisiting your marketing plans and assessing the quality and competitiveness of your product or service.

In this chapter we'll cover:

- Diversifying
- Adding applications to your site
- Monitoring the competition
- Blogging
- Online communities

➡ DIVERSIFYING

One way to expand and develop your business is to diversify into new areas. It might be that you decide to widen your offering by selling complementary items, or branch out into new areas altogether. Not only can this offer you multiple streams of income, but you might also be able to use it to overcome seasonal voids.

Any kind of diversification away from your core business is likely to carry some risk as you'll be directing funds and your energies elsewhere. As such you shouldn't look to diversify too early. Many businesses have damaged a profitable and thriving business model by investing in a new range of goods or expanding into other sectors that don't work.

FROM THE EXPERTS:
Simon Nixon, moneysupermarket.com

Our goal was to become the number one price comparison site, and not just for money matters. We looked at other areas to launch into. We established an insurance price comparison site as it was close to the original idea of finance, then we went into travel and home services and we have recently launched a shopping comparison site.

If you do diversify into selling other goods, be careful not to dilute your identity or the USPs that make your business unique. For instance, if your online business has established itself by selling premium, organic goods, don't try and cash in by selling cheaper, non-organic products as well. You might gain a few extra visitors to your site but you stand to lose your differentiation as a stand out destination for your original target customer.

Diversifying – you've basically got three options:

- Find new products or expand your range for existing customers
- Find new customers for existing products
- Find new products for new markets

Finding new products for new markets is the riskiest strategy as you will be venturing somewhat into the unknown and will have to carry out careful research and assess demand – much as when you were starting an online business in the first place. The thought of adding a new revenue stream to a business gives some entrepreneurs a boost and reminds them of the time when they were starting up. But as you have done it before, it's worth reminding yourself of what that entailed and where you made mistakes. It could also put a strain on your time and your resources, although you won't need to put all the administrative and back end operations in place. And remember too that the online environment is fast-paced and can change rapidly – what might be popular today might not be tomorrow – so it's important to keep an open mind when assessing the likely present and future success of your existing business model.

You'll also need to consider the effect diversification will have on your reputation. You've worked hard to build a brand and a name for yourself so you need to ensure that new business interests do not impact negatively on your established reputation – you may be keen to attract a new customer base but you could end up alienating your existing one.

> ### ✦ TIP
> It's not advisable to consider diversification until your core business is stable and profitable. If you're still struggling to win orders and build a sales time for the core product, there is a real danger that diversification will take your eye off the ball.

➡ ADDING APPLICATIONS

Running an online business involves carrying out periodic reviews of your website, checking that links are working and that the copy you have is still current. While carrying out a review, you might also decide that certain applications are worth adding, either to enhance your offering, to increase levels of interaction on your site or because you think it would benefit your customers. And with the high level of broadband penetration available today, the majority of people will be able to download and view multi-media content.

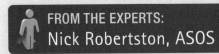

FROM THE EXPERTS:
Nick Robertston, ASOS

You need to present what you sell in the best possible way and if that means showing clothes on a catwalk, in motion, then that's what we do with our catwalk facility. There's a very fine line between what is the next best thing and what is a must have and we have continually innovated and pushed the boundaries.

It might be tempting to use the latest graphics and animations if this is what your competitors are doing, but ensure you put your customers' needs first. Technology changes fast – what is possible now wasn't just a few years ago and it can be tempting to invest in the latest web applications without much thought as to why you are doing this. Jamie Murray Wells of Glasses Direct for example, says that many of his site's current applications would not have been possible just a few years ago, but they have all been developed with a benefit to the end customer in mind. One of these is a virtual mirror with advanced facial technology to enable customers to upload photos of themselves or use examples of faces to try glasses on.

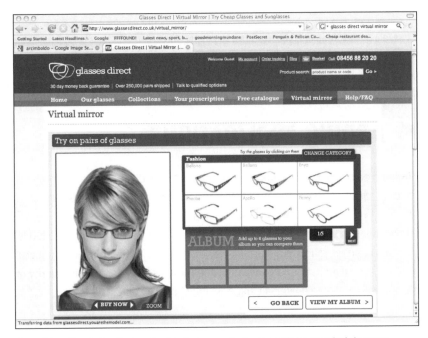

Glasses Direct: The site has developed a virtual mirror application to enable buyers to 'try' glasses on

The key is to choose technology that answers a customer's needs, rather than technology for technology's sake. Technology changes at a fast pace and people are certainly getting used to richer browsing experiences, but their needs won't be adapting at the same pace as technology is changing. Applications you can use include online videos, podcasts, RSS feeds and widgets.

Online video

You don't need to be a genius with a camera to use online videos, nor do you need to have first-class editing skills. What is important is to produce videos that are both engaging and entertaining for your target audience and which say something meaningful about your business. You could choose to host the videos on your site, or follow the lead of many other online businesses and post your videos on YouTube and direct people to the site. Chocolate retailer Hotel Chocolat, which has a presence on the web, high street and through mail order, posted videos on YouTube showing the company's co-founder, Angus Thirlwell, explaining why the business bought a cocoa plantation and showing the process of making chocolate from bean to bar.

Hotel Chocolat: Making use of online video

Posting a video on YouTube is free, but you will need to sign up to a YouTube membership to do this. Any videos you post will remain live until you choose to remove them, or they may be taken down by YouTube if you violate any of their terms of use (go to http://www.youtube.com/t/community_guidelines for more information).

IN MY EXPERIENCE:

Glenys Berd, LoveThoseShoes.com

As long as it is in context then applications such as video are very useful. You need to avoid the temptation to have a lot of 'eye candy' though, as it will distract from the main purpose of your site. It's about showing off the products, not how pretty your site is.

Using videos will help to make your site more interactive and will put a 'face' to it. Depending on the type of online business you are running, you can use videos to showcase your products, for interviews or to explain the background to your business in more detail. Using online video normally involves using Flash technology which the majority of browsers now support, so video files on your website should be visible to your customers. Video files, however, can take up a lot of bandwidth – every time a customer clicks on the video, they'll use up some of this bandwidth, so check with your web host to see how much bandwidth is allocated in your contract, or you may need to pay extra if you exceed your limits. You'll also need to ensure that any videos you use are of high quality otherwise it is likely to put people off as well as looking unprofessional.

IN MY EXPERIENCE:

Simon Wadsworth, The Retail Factory

Video, 3D and other techniques that make the shopping experience come to life will be essential differentiators in the long run as the online experience becomes more like the offline one.

Podcasts

An increasing number of people are downloading podcasts – audio files which are stored on a computer – and you can use these to both market your website and increase levels of interactivity with your customer base. You can create podcasts to promote new products or new content on your site and depending on the type of business you launch, you could demo a product or deliver a tutorial via podcast. Decide on a format and length – podcasts can range from 60 seconds to

30 minutes so work out exactly how much time you can devote to them and how many you are thinking of doing in, say, a six-month period. You may decide on a five minute podcast once a month, but to film, record and edit this could take you several hours and doing this once a month will soon add up.

Equipment-wise, you will need a computer, microphone and recording software. Don't skimp on the quality of the microphone as your podcast needs to come across clearly to your listeners and sound quality is key. One of the most popular voice recording software programs available is Audacity, and it's also free to use (http://audacity.sourceforge.net/). It enables you to record and edit sounds and can be used across most operating systems, including Mac OS X and Microsoft Windows. Once you're recorded your podcast, you'll need to convert it to an MP3 file and upload it to your website.

RSS feeds

RSS (Really Simple Syndication or Rich Site Summary, depending on who you talk to) feeds enable you to deliver newsletters and messages direct to your subscribers' desktops, instead of doing this by email, for example. It's a method of distributing links to content in your website that you would like others to use, as if you were syndicating content. You can alert customers who have opted in to receive messages from you about new content added to your site so it can be a powerful way to stay in touch with your customer base. It's basically a text-based headline with a link with a short summary attached; this is what a subscriber sees. If your customers/subscribers want to read more, they can click on the link and be taken to your site. If your content is interesting enough, other people may add it to their website, increasing your exposure.

Widgets

These are embeddable chunks of code that can be implemented into any HTML coded site, basically small boxes that you can place on websites. They can hold a variety of content, from games to audio files and you click on them to activate them, interacting with a website in the process. Websites are increasing their use of widgets to simplify and enhance the internet user's experience. Buttons, drop-down menus, and basically any other element located on a web page that is able to be manipulated by the user to perform a function is considered a widget.

> **TIP**
>
> There are a wealth of web applications available to use so think carefully about the ones that would bring the most benefit to you, your business and your customers before making your choice.

→ MONITORING THE COMPETITION

When you run an internet business, the world is your oyster as far as customers are concerned, with a global audience to tap into. Customer potential may be huge but so too is the competition. Online customers are very savvy when it comes to using the internet to find competitively priced products and services – after all, it only takes them a few clicks to browse, compare and buy. So it's important to keep a close eye on the competition and to monitor their sites carefully. Check out whether they have lowered or raised their prices, if they are running any sales or promotions or if they have expanded their product offering.

 FROM THE EXPERTS:
Simon Nixon, moneysupermarket.com

It's critical to monitor the competition and to see how their performance compares to yours but don't copy them. We build new products and services with customer insight – we ask our users what they think and design offerings on the back of this.

Take a look at your prices to see if this is an area where you can beat the competition. Ensure you're not just selling at a price people can afford, but a price that's high enough to make your profit. Anyone can trick themselves into thinking they're doing a rich trade if they're pulling in the crowds by simply undercutting the competition. It's a perfectly acceptable strategy, of course, but only if you can do it and still make a profit. It's what the 'experts' mean when they say 'turnover is vanity, profit is sanity'.

If you're keen to offer discounted prices to beat the competition and incentivise customers, you need to claw that profit back elsewhere. Most retailers have some items, often referred to as 'loss leaders', that they use to pull in trade. Don't take this too literally, loss leaders should be sold at cost price, never at a loss. Look to do it with core items or where there's little margin to be made anyway.

If you can't compete on price, consider what else you can offer to incentivise customers, such as a gift with every purchase or free delivery on items over a certain price. Assess your customer service and look at ways you can improve this – your customers are likely to appreciate excellent service over cheaper prices.

> ## TIP
> Keep a close eye on the competition and if you can't compete with them on price for example, look at other areas you can improve on. Customer service on the web can be just as important as price.

➡ BLOGGING

Blogs, an online diary or commentary that is regularly updated, can be a great way to develop your site, by promoting it in the eyes of your customers, your industry and the press. They are also useful for getting your content onto other people's sites and it's a great way to stay in touch with your customers. More importantly, though, blogs can help to attract more visitors to your website and help to get your site noticed by the search engines and attempt to achieve higher rankings.

There are millions of blogs in existence and they work because they have a following among a niche audience so it's essential to identify a target audience, decide what you want to say and write it in an engaging and concise way. Blogs, if done successfully, can engender trust as well as adding a personal touch to your business.

You'll need to invest time and effort in writing and updating them however, so consider if you can do this on a regular basis – blogging once a month is not likely to get customers coming back for more. On the plus side, blog software (available from the likes of www.blogger.com and www.typepad.com) is easy to use.

➡ ONLINE COMMUNITIES

It's not enough to get customers to visit your site once. You've got to get them to keep coming back and build a loyal community of users. But how do you remind them that you're there?

The rapid rise of social networking sites such as Facebooks, MySpace and Twitter making it easier for online businesses to gain publicity, which adds up to increased traffic and potentially bigger sales. Glasses Direct for example actively drives word of mouth referrals using a variety of marketing mechanisms from social web features to member-get-member incentives.

You could choose to create a branded page on sites such as Facebook and MySpace or you could opt to build an online community on your site, which will give you more control overall, using formats such as chat rooms, forums and blogs. By using tools such as bulletin boards or newsgroups and scheduled online chats, you can develop a community of users who return to your site even when they aren't ready to buy something. Each time they return, they are exposed to your new products or special offers and in turn give you increased traffic numbers to boast to your advertisers about.

TIP

Online communities will expose your site to customers time and time again, as well as increasing levels of interactivity and time spent on the site. All of this will boost your traffic figures.

➡ FORUMS AND DISCUSSION GROUPS

Another way to build up your site's online community is to take part in forums and discussion groups. This doesn't have to take up much of your time. By joining a forum or discussion group that is relevant to the type of visitors you attract to your site, you can direct more traffic back to your business. If there's a question in a forum you feel you have the expertise to answer, put your views forward and include a link to your site at the end.

However, avoid asking people directly to visit your site, as this will not only come across as spam, but may also get you banned from the forum or group.

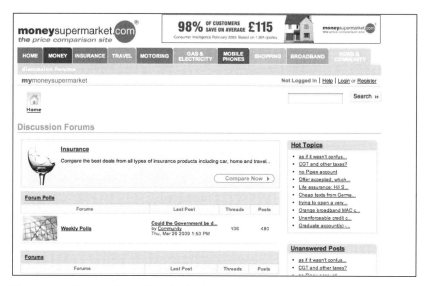

Moneysupermarket.com: offers a variety of online forums

Things to remember:

- Any kind of diversification away from your core business is likely to carry some risk.

- Add applications that will benefit your customers and your site – not because you've noticed a competitor does this.

- Consider if you can compete on areas other than price.

- Online communities can help to build loyalty among customers.

- When joining or participating in forums, avoid asking people directly to visit your site.

Appendices

SWOT analysis table

Strengths	Weaknesses
• Why should you succeed? • What do you do well? • Why do customers say they enjoy doing business with you? • What distinct advantages does your company offer? • What are your USPs?	• What could be improved about the business? • Is the market strong enough? • Do you have enough/good enough staff on board? • Are your management skills up to scratch? • Do you have enough finance to make it work? • What stumbling blocks do you continue to encounter? • What does your company do that can be improved? • What should be avoided? • What do your competitors do better than you?
S	**W**
O	**T**
Opportunities	**Threats**
• Where are the openings for your business? • Has the market significantly changed recently? • What customer needs are not being met by your competitors?	• What is your competition doing that could take business away from you or stunt your company's growth? • How might your competition react to any moves you make? • What trends in the market do you see that could wipe you out or make your business obsolete? • Might technology changes threaten your products or services? Or your job? • Do you have a stable relationship with suppliers or partners?

Market analysis example for an online lingerie business

Competitors	Number of years established	Price bracket (eg average cost of an underwear set)	Their strengths	Their weaknesses	Your USPs/What you offer the market
High street retailers/with or without internet presence	20	£15	Recognised brand, well established, opportunity to try on pieces	For those without internet presence, limited by choice and opening hours	Sizes that can't be found on the high street
Specialist mail order	15	£12	Wide choice of items	Impersonal service	Ability to look at different colours online and use a 'virtual model' to try on pieces
Other online lingerie business	3	£25	Unusual designs, not found on the high street, easy to find sizes	Prices are high	Aim to offer more unusual pieces but at a more favourable price

Financial budget plan

Startup costs	Estimated cost
Business registration fees	
Initial stock	
Down payments on equipment	
Website design fees	
Technology infrastructure	
Utility set-up fees	
Operating costs	
Your salary	
Rent or mortgage payments	
Telecommunications	
Utilities	
Stock	
Storage	
Shipping /Distribution	
Promotion	
Loan payments	
Office supplies	
Maintenance	
Professional services (such as accountancy fees)	
Website maintenance	

Balance sheet example

	£	
Fixed assets		
Intangible assets	1,500	
Tangible assets	25,000	
Investments	500	
		27,000
Current assets		
Cash in hand and at bank		5,500
Stock	7,000	
Debtors	8,000	
	20,500	
Creditors: Amounts falling due within one year		
Bank loans and overdrafts	1,500	
Trade creditors	3,000	
Other creditors including tax and social security	1,000	
		5,500
Net current assets	15,000	
Total assets less current liabilities	42,000	
Creditors: amounts falling due after more than one year		
Bank loan	2,000	
Net assets	40,000	
Capital and reserves		
Called up share capital	35,000	
Profit and loss account	5,000	
Shareholders' funds		

Cash flow forecast

	Month 1	Month 2	Month 3	Month 4	Month 5	Month 6	Month 7	Month 8	Month 9	Month 10	Month 11	Month 12	YTD
Receipts													
Debtors	8,297	8,572	6,798	7,569	7,719	8,071	7,765	7,175	6,179	7,637	5,978	7,173	88,933
Cash	276	421	1,403	1,386	874	835	1,142	1,607	1,946	818	2,036	918	13,662
TOTAL RECEIPTS	8,573	8,993	8,201	8,955	8,593	8,906	8,907	8,782	8,125	8,455	8,014	8,091	102,595
Payments													
Purchases	1,687	1,967	2,173	2,469	2,284	2,982	2,642	2,381	2,974	3,129	2,367	2,894	29,949
Rent	2,160	-	-	2,160	-	-	2,160	-	-	2,160	-	-	8,640
Rates & utilities	528	528	528	528	528	528	528	528	528	528	528	528	6,336
Telephone	-	-	509	-	-	521	-	-	539	-	-	517	2,086
Wages & Salaries	2,750	2,750	2,750	2,750	2,750	2,750	2,750	2,750	2,750	2,750	2,750	2,750	33,000
PAYE	1,018	1,018	1,018	1,018	1,018	1,018	1,018	1,018	1,018	1,018	1,018	1,018	12,216
VAT	102	-	-	47	-	-	156	-	-	174	-	-	479
TOTAL Payments	8,245	6,263	6,978	8,972	6,580	7,799	9,254	6,677	7,809	9,759	6,663	7,707	92,706
NET OPERATING CASH FLOW	328	2,730	1,223	(17)	2,013	1,107	(347)	2,105	316	(1,304)	1,351	384	9,889
Fixed Asset purchases	539				1,299				3,675				5,513
Loan repayments													-
Net cash inflow/(outflow)	(211)	2,730	1,223	(17)	714	1,107	(347)	2,105	(3,359)	(1,304)	1,351	384	4,376
OPENING BANK BALANCE	1,628	1,417	4,147	5,370	5,353	6,067	7,174	6,827	8,932	5,573	4,269	5,620	1,628
CLOSING BANK BALANCE	1,417	4,147	5,370	5,353	6,067	7,174	6,827	8,932	5,573	4,269	5,620	6,004	6,004

Web analytics report sample for online lingerie business

Visitor profile	Last visited	Average visit duration	Visits	Repeat rate
Viewed special offers	January 20, 2009 at 12.43pm	2 minutes and 40 seconds	7,890	23%
Registered for newsletter	January 20, 2009 at 5.15pm	1 minute and 10 seconds	550	25%
Clicked through promotion on home page	January 25, 2009 at 9.05am	50 seconds	6,789	37%
Purchased online	January 27, 2009 at 11.50pm	6 minutes and 10 seconds	290	35%

Index

www.crimsonpublishing.co.uk